LEGENDARY LOCALS OF PRAIRIE DU CHIEN WISCONSIN

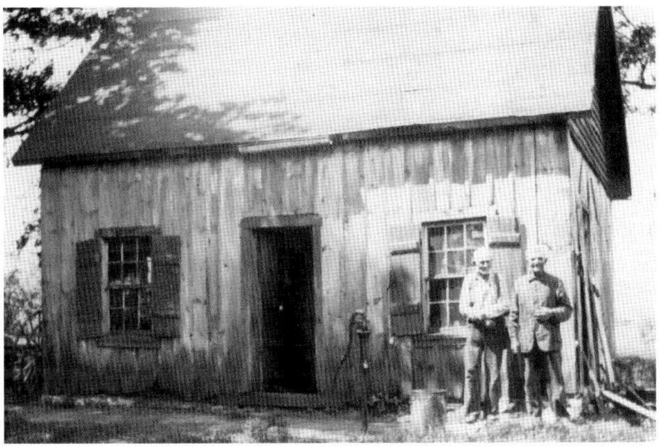

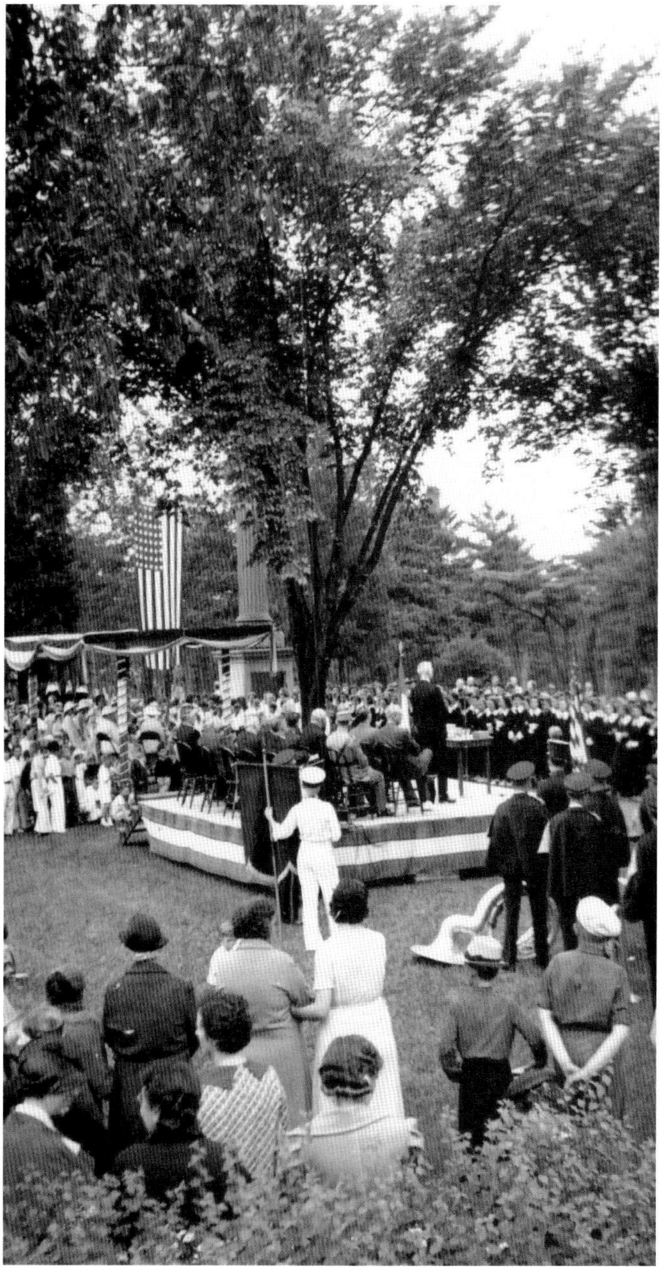

Tercentenary Celebration
On June 1, 1937, the residents of Prairie du Chien celebrated the 300th anniversary of the birth of Father Jacques Marquette with a pageant and speeches. (Courtesy Prairie du Chien Historical Society.)

Page 1: Theodore and Frederick Chenevert
Brothers Theodore (left) and Fred (right) were sons of Theodore, who had come to Prairie du Chien from Quebec to work in the fur trade. A house builder by trade, Theodore constructed homes in the French-Canadian tradition. (Author's collection.)

LEGENDARY LOCALS

OF

PRAIRIE DU CHIEN

WISCONSIN

MARY ELISE ANTOINE

LEGENDARY LOCALS

ISBN 978-1-4671-0193-6

Legendary Locals is an imprint of Arcadia Publishing
Charleston, South Carolina

Printed in the United States of America

Library of Congress Control Number: 2014914030

For all general information, please contact Arcadia Publishing:
Telephone 843-853-2070
Fax 843-853-0044
E-mail sales@arcadiapublishing.com
For customer service and orders:
Toll-Free 1-888-313-2665

Visit us on the Internet at www.arcadiapublishing.com

Dedication
To all the residents of Prairie du Chien who have made this a legendary community.

On the Front Cover: Clockwise from top left:
James R. Bittner, mayor (courtesy the Bittner family; see page 101), Lyman J. Howe, editor (courtesy the Howe family; see page 28), Lori Jane Knapp (courtesy the Knapp family; see page 40), Black Hawk, Sauk warrior chief (author's collection; see page 17), Roy L. and Geraldine George, benefactors (courtesy the George family; see page 123), Norb Aschom, broadcaster (courtesy *The Courier Press*; see page 117), Bette Valley Beneker, Fourth Ward historian (author's collection; see page 90), John Lawler, entrepreneur (courtesy Prairie du Chien Historical Society; see page 49), Matthew Antoine, Olympic athlete (author's collection; see page 73).

On the Back Cover: From left to right:
Dan Swingle, motorcycle racer (courtesy the Swingle family; see page 64), Pete Panka, merchant (courtesy Prairie du Chien Historical Society; see page 29).

CONTENTS

Acknowledgments		6
Introduction		7
CHAPTER ONE	A Lasting Impression	9
CHAPTER TWO	Generations of Business	25
CHAPTER THREE	Educators and Active Minds	47
CHAPTER FOUR	Coaches and Athletes	63
CHAPTER FIVE	Part of the River and Heritage	75
CHAPTER SIX	Promoters and Entrepreneurs	91
CHAPTER SEVEN	Neighbors	105
Index		126

ACKNOWLEDGMENTS

When I began the writing of this book, little did I realize what a difficult venture I had undertaken. I had written *Prairie du Chien*, part of the Images of America series, four years earlier. It had been a challenge to write the history of my community within the space allocated by the publishers and to select the prints and photographs to illustrate the history. But the result was worth the effort. So, when Arcadia Publishing asked me to write *Legendary Locals of Prairie du Chien*, I did not hesitate; I knew the people behind the history of Prairie du Chien.

The writing of this book has been a rewarding experience. I was able to talk to so many people and learn details about our community that have never been recorded. But the writing of this book has been unbelievably difficult. I faced tough choices as to whom to include in the book and what to say about those persons. I had my thoughts, but I needed more input. As I interviewed locals, I listened to their thoughts and suggestions. My list grew, but I also learned which people were considered important to our community. Between my interviewees and myself, you see the result.

The families and friends of the people who are included in this book shared not only their time, but also their treasured photographs. The photographic collections of the Prairie du Chien Historical Society provided an additional wealth of images from which to choose. In a few instances, locals allowed me to take their photographs.

There are so many men and women I wish I could have included, but space did not allow it. Though their names are not here, they are just as special as the people you will recall and meet in this book.

Thank you to the many people who shared stories and images about themselves, family members, and friends. This book would not have been possible without your generous help and interest.

INTRODUCTION

The river . . . the whole valley from bluff to bluff . . . and the towering hills covered with grass and scattering timber, and precipitous rocks, all these surrounding and environing one of the most beautiful prairies the eye of man ever beheld, gives the whole scenery a most charming and romantic appearance.

—Rev. Alfred E. Brunson, 1857

There is a quiet seductiveness about Prairie du Chien; a seductiveness that works upon people. Is it caused by the majesty of the Mississippi River, with its many islands and its backwaters teeming with fish and waterfowl, flowing past the prairie? Perhaps the allure comes from the limestone bluffs covered in trees that turn brilliant reds, oranges, and yellows in the fall, bluffs that are the other boundaries of the prairie. Maybe the cause is the rich history that occurred and is still preserved at Prairie du Chien. Or, possibly, the seductiveness comes from the people of Prairie du Chien.

The history of Prairie du Chien and its residents and the water of the Mississippi River are inseparable. The early Mississippian cultures traveled the length of the river and gathered food from its waters, creating geometric and effigy mounds along the banks and bluffs. The Mississippi brought the first Europeans to the prairie. By canoe, pirogue, and bateau, Frenchmen and Indians gathered at Prairie du Chien to trade, while some of the Canadians settled with their families on the prairie. William Clark led soldiers up the Mississippi River to build the first American fort at Prairie du Chien, leading to a battle with the British in the War of 1812. The same Mississippi River flooded the American fort built in 1816 so many times that the US Army moved Fort Crawford to higher ground on the mainland. The river challenged steamboats after the *Virginia* arrived in 1823, but steamboats still maneuvered the snags and sandbars, bringing more and more settlers from the East. Then, when the first railroad was built to connect Chicago and Milwaukee to the Mississippi River, more people made Prairie du Chien a destination.

While the population of the town grew throughout the 19th century, the community did not become the metropolis some promoters envisioned. Not all the people who stopped at Prairie du Chien stayed. The Mississippi took many farther north and west, feeling a need to seek fortunes, invest in the development of newer cities, or purchase some of the unending virgin prairie offered by the United States. In the first 60 years of the 20th century, the population of Prairie du Chien almost doubled. But the river and towering bluffs limited expansion. Since 1960, the number of residents living in the city has remained much the same, though the greater Prairie du Chien area has increased in population. The people who decided over the years to make Prairie du Chien their home resolved to make their community special. They became involved in and invested in Prairie du Chien in a personal way.

These pages present men and women who in many ways have committed themselves to make Prairie du Chien a good community in which to live and raise children. They have worked in professions providing services to all. They have started businesses that offer food, clothing, entertainment, housing, and enjoyment of life. Others dedicated themselves to children, striving to impart an education beyond books and testing. Many of the educators, wishing their students to excel, also worked to create sports programs that challenged young men and women. In the midst of the community lived men and women who looked beyond the infrastructure of a small city, back to their heritage and around to the natural beauty. Some promoted the history and river and bluffs, attracting visitors. Others made sure there was a continuum of the past into the present. Many of these residents and others have volunteered time, knowledge, and material goods, joining with one another in clubs and organizations to not only enhance Prairie du Chien, but to be neighbors in the full sense of the word.

A community is its people; the people interacting with their natural surroundings, institutions, and one another, making sure this interaction is preserved for future generations. Regrettably, many young people have left Prairie du Chien since the 1960s, drawn to cities where there are institutions of higher learning, an active cultural life, and opportunities for professional advancement. But as the time came to raise children, some who had left remembered the carefree childhood they had experienced in Prairie du Chien. They came back and again lived with neighbors whose families proudly list the generations who were and are part of the community, and neighbors who came to Prairie du Chien as young adults to stay "just a little while" and were drawn by whatever causes the seductiveness of Prairie du Chien, and stayed.

These, the generational families, the returnees, and the committed newcomers, make up the community of Prairie du Chien. They all become involved in their community to improve and promote it. Each in their own way has made Prairie du Chien a place to call home.

CHAPTER ONE

A Lasting Impression

Opposite the Wisconsin, stands Pike's hill, lofty and abrupt, and just above this place, on the eastern bank of the river, begins the low prairie ground on which Fort Crawford, and the village of Prairie Du Chien stand. . . . Originally settled by the French, it was once a place of some importance.

—Caleb Atwater, 1829

From 1673 until the 1870s, events of national and international importance occurred at Prairie du Chien. During that time, the Indian nations, France, Great Britain, and the United States competed for economic and political control of the prairie. Whoever held dominance at the prairie commanded influence over the entire Upper Mississippi watershed. In attempts to exert or maintain dominance, Prairie du Chien was the site of significant events.

In 1673, Jacques Marquette and Louis Jolliet entered the Mississippi River, leading to the arrival of Frenchmen intending to trade with the tribes of the Upper Mississippi. The Fox/Mesquaki nation fought the French, inconsequentially, it turned out, as Britain gained control of all French-held land in North America. The British fought to keep the land Indian country and thus continue the fur trade. But the United States sought to build a permanent military installation on the prairie, sending Zebulon Pike to determine a site. An American fort was erected in the Main Village, behind the residents' homes. A British force laid siege to the fort during the War of 1812, forcing the American commandant to surrender. Now, the United States was more determined to establish a fort at Prairie du Chien and, in 1816, built Fort Crawford. In 1825, William Clark used the fort to convene the Great Council and Treaty with all the Indian nations of the Upper Mississippi. Then, two years later, the Winnebago Uprising begun by Red Bird reinforced the importance of the fort. Zachary Taylor and Jefferson Davis were assigned to Fort Crawford when the Black Hawk War began, and they accepted the surrender of the Sac chief, Black Hawk. More Indian treaties at Prairie du Chien assured the opening of the Mississippi Valley to settlement, and entrepreneurs and immigrants arrived. Prairie du Chien became a bustling scene, a depot for steamboat and railroad travel westward.

By the 20th century, the Prairie du Chien that these men and women had experienced no longer existed; only a few of the buildings that were part of these important events persisted. And, for those that did, their conditions were quickly deteriorating. In 1933, *The Courier* printed an article with the headline "Tourists Hauling Old Fort Away." Then, two groups came forward to make sure that the few remnants of the rich history of Prairie du Chien were preserved and restored to help residents and visitors visualize the town's importance in the early history of the United States. Others made sure that statues were erected, streets and parks renamed, and pageants held to honor the men and women who played important roles in the history of North America, the United States, and Prairie du Chien.

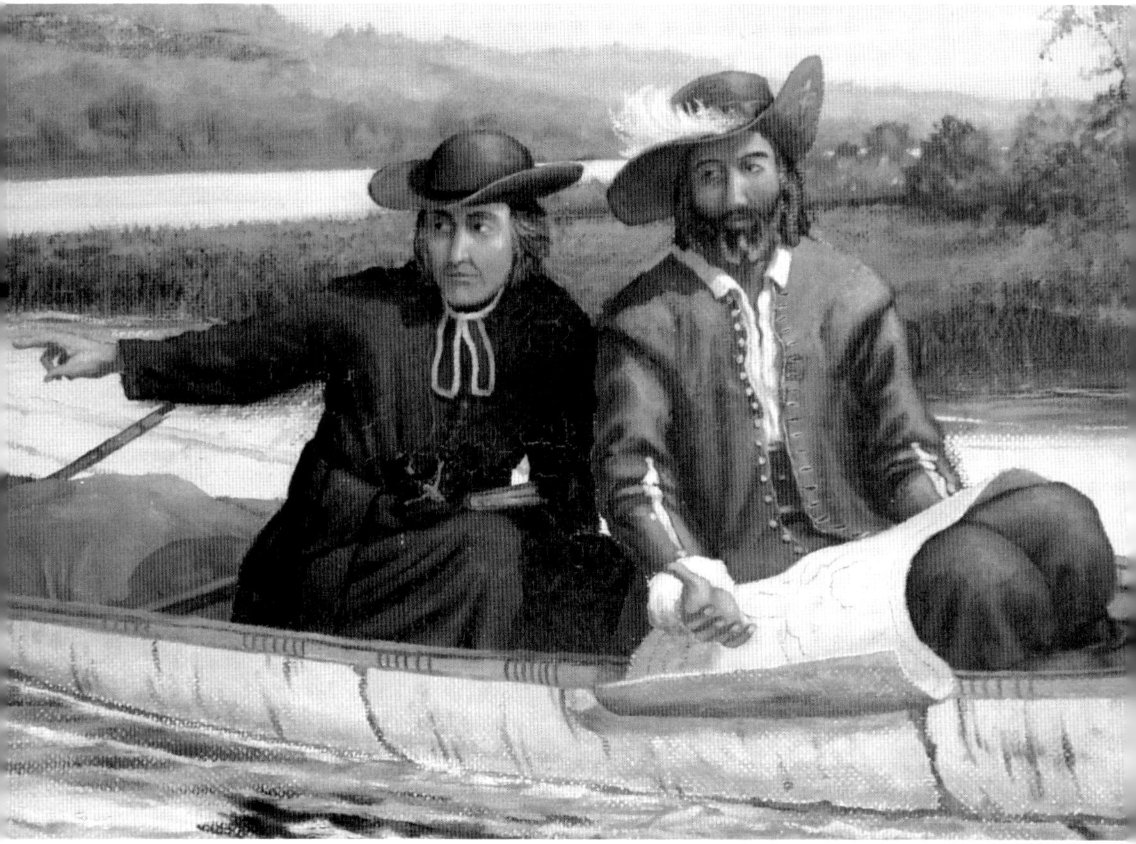

Jacques Marquette and Louis Jolliet

When Jacques Marquette and Louis Jolliet left St. Ignace in May 1673, they were in search of the river the natives called the Messipi, "the Great Water." Jolliet (right) wished to learn if the river offered a possible water route to the Pacific Ocean. Marquette (left) wanted to spread the word of God among the people they would meet. Paddling the Fox-Wisconsin waterway, they entered the Mississippi River on June 17, 1673. As they chose to turn south and travel with the current to the mouth of the Arkansas River, they never beheld the large prairie that lay to the north. With their voyage of exploration, Marquette and Jolliet established a French claim to the Mississippi Valley, opening the Upper Mississippi to French explorers and fur traders. In time, French-speaking men settled on the prairie, and Catholic missionaries resided among the Indian tribes. (Courtesy City of Prairie du Chien and Wisconsin Historical Society.)

Michel Brisbois and Joseph Rolette

Among the Frenchmen from Canada who settled at Prairie du Chien were Michel Brisbois and Joseph Rolette. The fur trade drew them to the village. Brisbois acquired much land and, working with the British, helped the residents gain title to their lots in 1781. When the United States questioned this ownership in 1820, Brisbois was instrumental in ensuring that all the residents retained their land.

Rolette had arrived at Prairie du Chien in 1808. Aggressive in business dealings, he soon established himself as a major fur trader. When the American Fur Company desired to trade in the Upper Mississippi River Valley, it had to acknowledge Rolette's control. He became an independent trader within the Northern Department.

Brisbois and Rolette were neighbors, connected through the marriage of Brisbois's niece, Jane Fisher, to Rolette. What friendship they may have had was gone by the time of Brisbois's death in 1837. In his will, Michel Brisbois requested he be buried on the bluffs so he could look down on his beloved prairie (and perhaps on Joseph Rolette?). (Both, author's collection.)

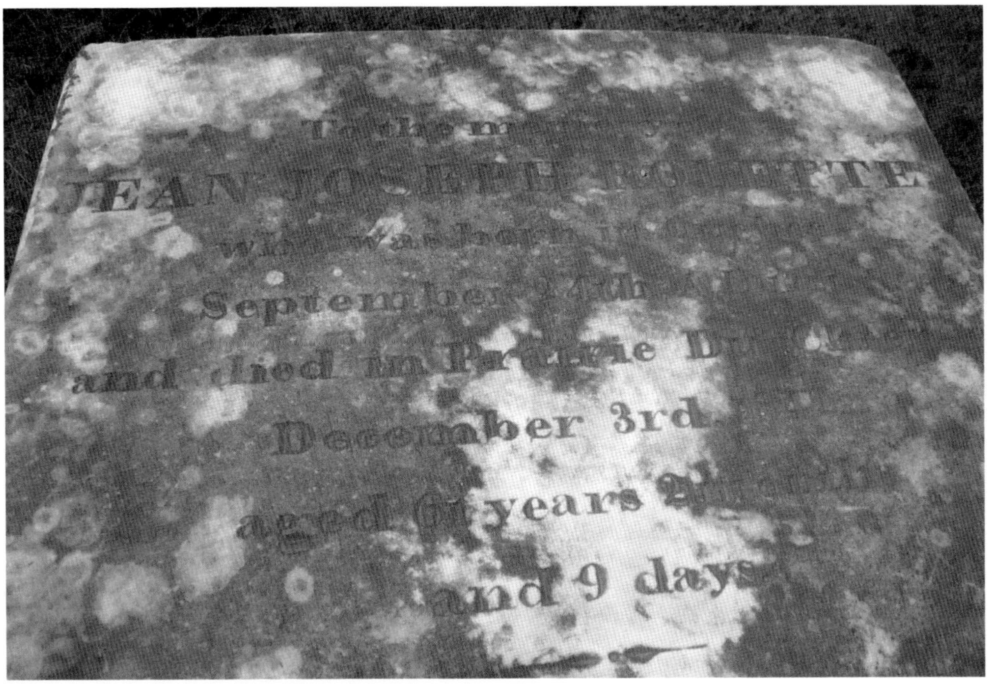

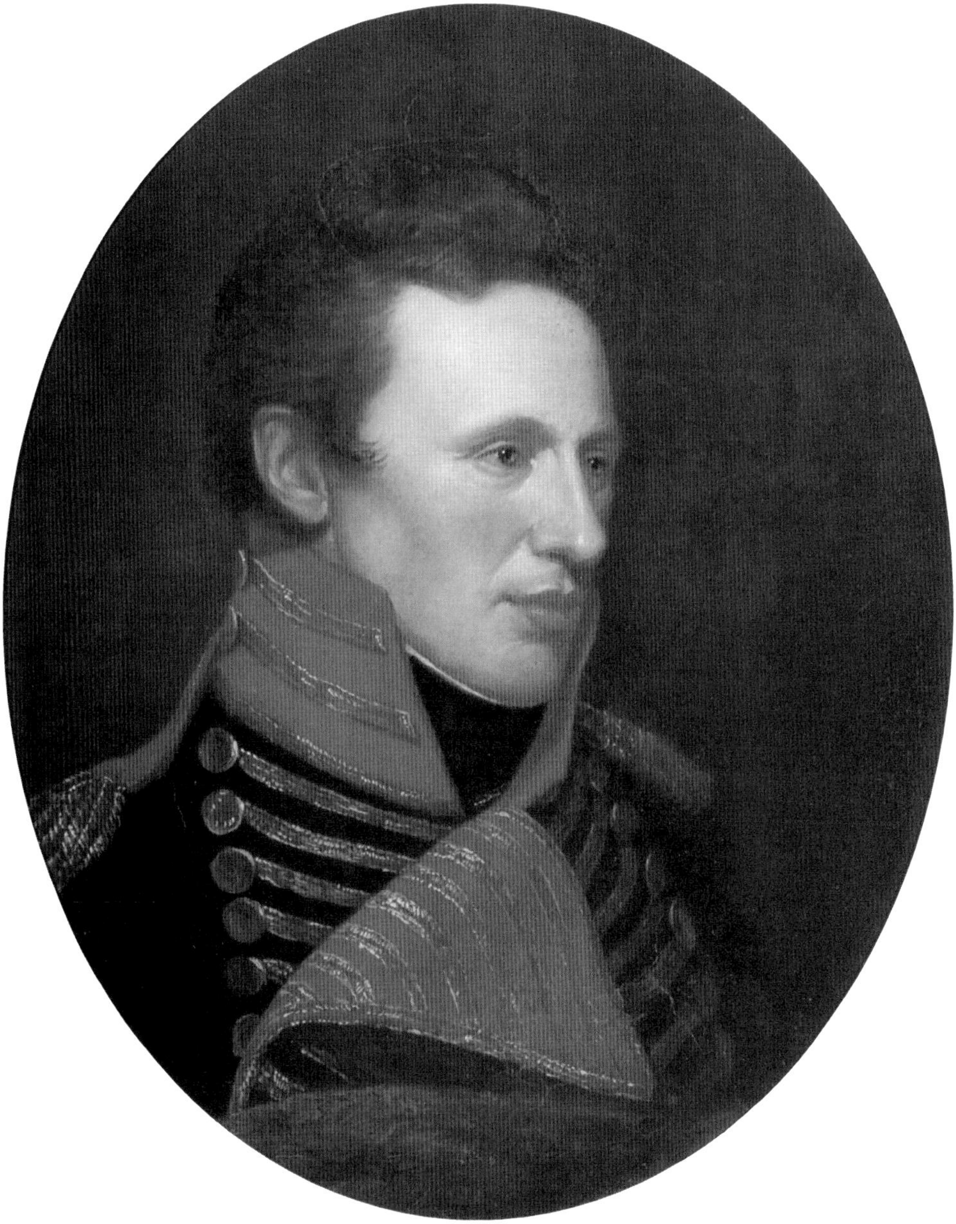

Zebulon Montgomery Pike
While Meriwether Lewis and William Clark led the Corps of Discovery across the Rocky Mountains, Lt. Zebulon Pike directed an expeditionary force up the Mississippi River. Pike was to explore the river to its source, locate sites for fortifications, determine British influence, and meet with the Indian tribes to engender their loyalty to the United States and to create peace between the Sioux and Ojibwe. When he arrived at Prairie du Chien in early September 1805, Pike immediately explored the area around the confluence of the Wisconsin and Mississippi Rivers, seeking a suitable site for a fort. He ascended a bluff on the west side of the Mississippi, across from the mouth of the Wisconsin River. He chose this spot for a fort, as it was level on top, had a spring, and "commanded a view of the country around." The site Lieutenant Pike selected was named Pike's Peak. (Courtesy Independence National Historical Park.)

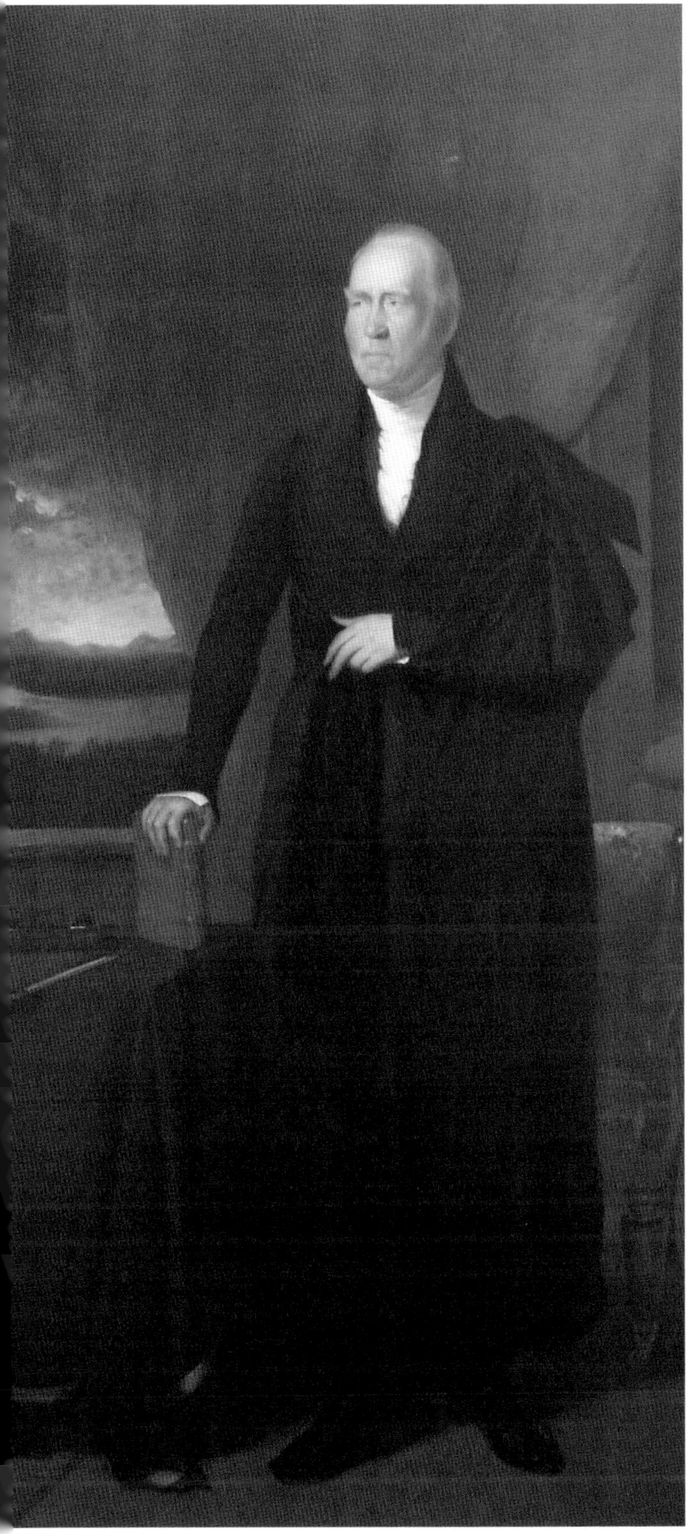

William Clark

In May 1814, William Clark arrived at Prairie du Chien to build a fort based on Zebulon Pike's recommendation. The United States was at war with Great Britain, and Clark knew the importance of Prairie du Chien and the Upper Mississippi River Valley to the American cause. He ordered the fort be built in the Main Village of Prairie du Chien on a mound behind the homes of British fur traders. Clark returned to St. Louis. In mid-July, the British captured the fort in the Battle of Prairie du Chien, the only confrontation in the War of 1812 fought in what is now Wisconsin.

In 1825, Clark came again to Prairie du Chien, to conduct a Great Council and Treaty with all the Indian tribes of the western Great Lakes and Upper Mississippi River. For two weeks in August, Governor Clark and Gov. Lewis Cass met with chiefs who spoke for the thousands of Indians in attendance. The discussions produced a general treaty of peace among all the tribes and established boundaries between white settlers and Indians. Clark and Cass signed the treaty as commissioners of the United States. Signing for the Indians were chiefs of the Sioux, Ojibwe, Sac and Fox, Menominee, Iowa, Ho-Chunk, Ottawa, and Potawatomi nations. (Courtesy St. Louis Mercantile Library–University of Missouri, St. Louis.)

James H. Lockwood

Lockwood was one of the first US citizens to settle at Prairie du Chien. He arrived in 1816 and clerked for fur traders until he began trading himself. Having studied law as a young man, he returned to the profession and was one of the first attorneys is what is now Wisconsin. In 1824, he was appointed county prosecutor and postmaster. Lockwood served as a justice of the peace for Crawford County. In 1830, he was appointed associate justice of the county court for Crawford County, a position he held for many years. When Wisconsin Territory was formed in 1836, Lockwood was elected to the territorial legislature. Like many men, he delved into various businesses that helped frontier expansion, including a sawmill and a company that produced lead shot. (Courtesy Wisconsin Historical Society.)

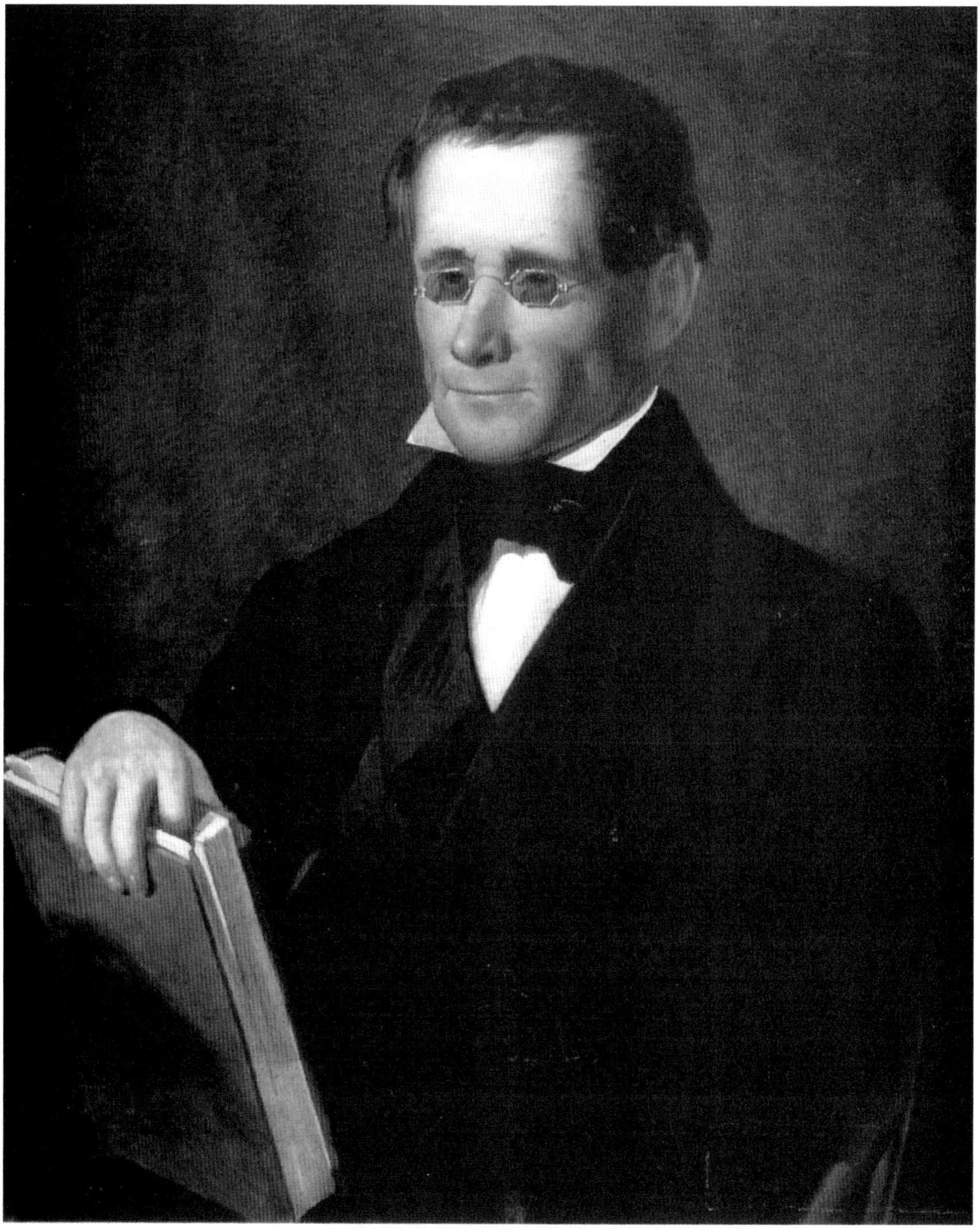

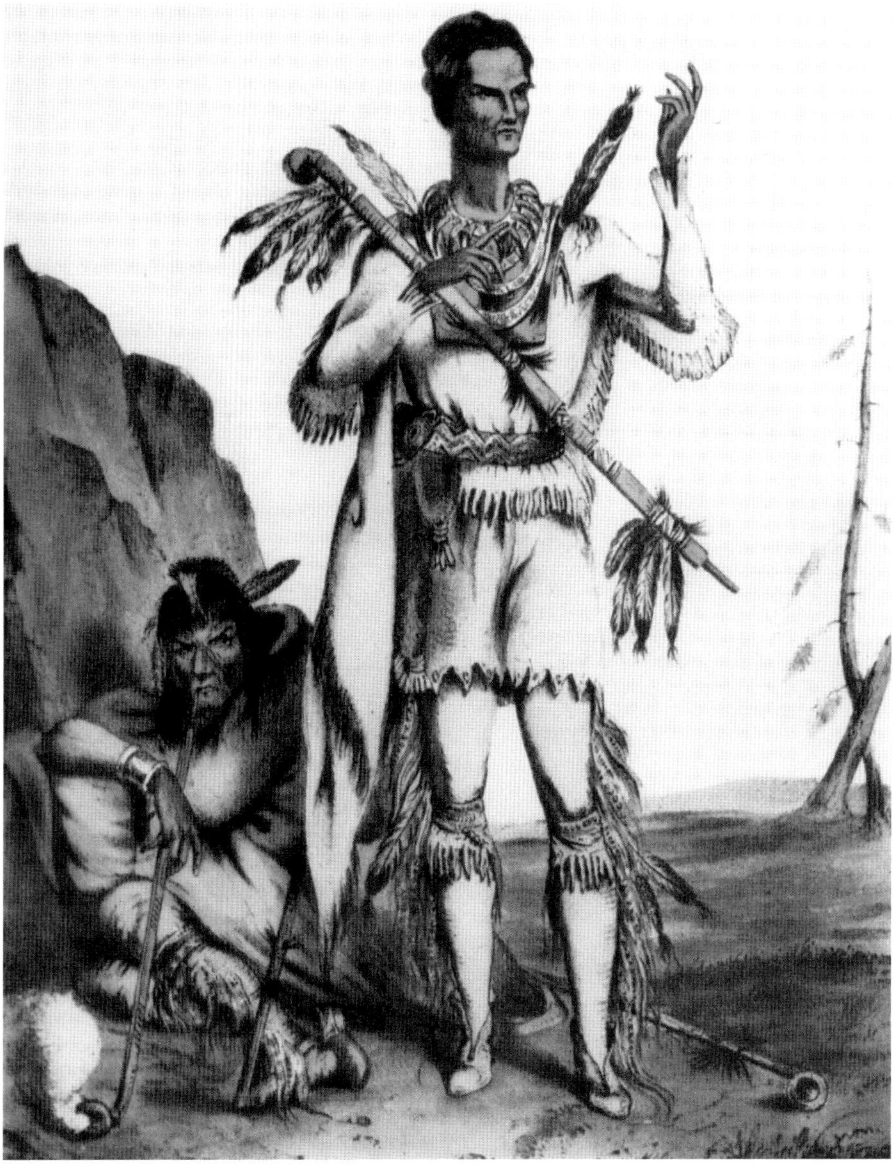

Red Bird

In the 1825 Treaty of Prairie du Chien, the United States recognized the Winnebago (Ho-Chunk) as a sovereign nation and promised to punish any whites who went upon Winnebago lands, which had deposits of lead. The lure proved too great, and men from Missouri began to mine lead found on the tribe's lands. The Winnebago complained to the US Indian agent at Prairie du Chien, but nothing was done. Then, a rumor started that two Winnebago held by the Army had been killed. In response, the Winnebago designated Red Bird to carry out a revenge raid.

In June 1827, Red Bird came to Prairie du Chien with three other warriors. They attacked the Registre Gagnier family, killing two men. Soon after, boatmen kidnapped several Winnebago women. Red Bird organized a war party that attacked the keelboats. Unable to unite his people to defend themselves against US troops, Red Bird surrendered to save his people. He was held in prison at Fort Crawford in Prairie du Chien, where he died. (Author's collection.)

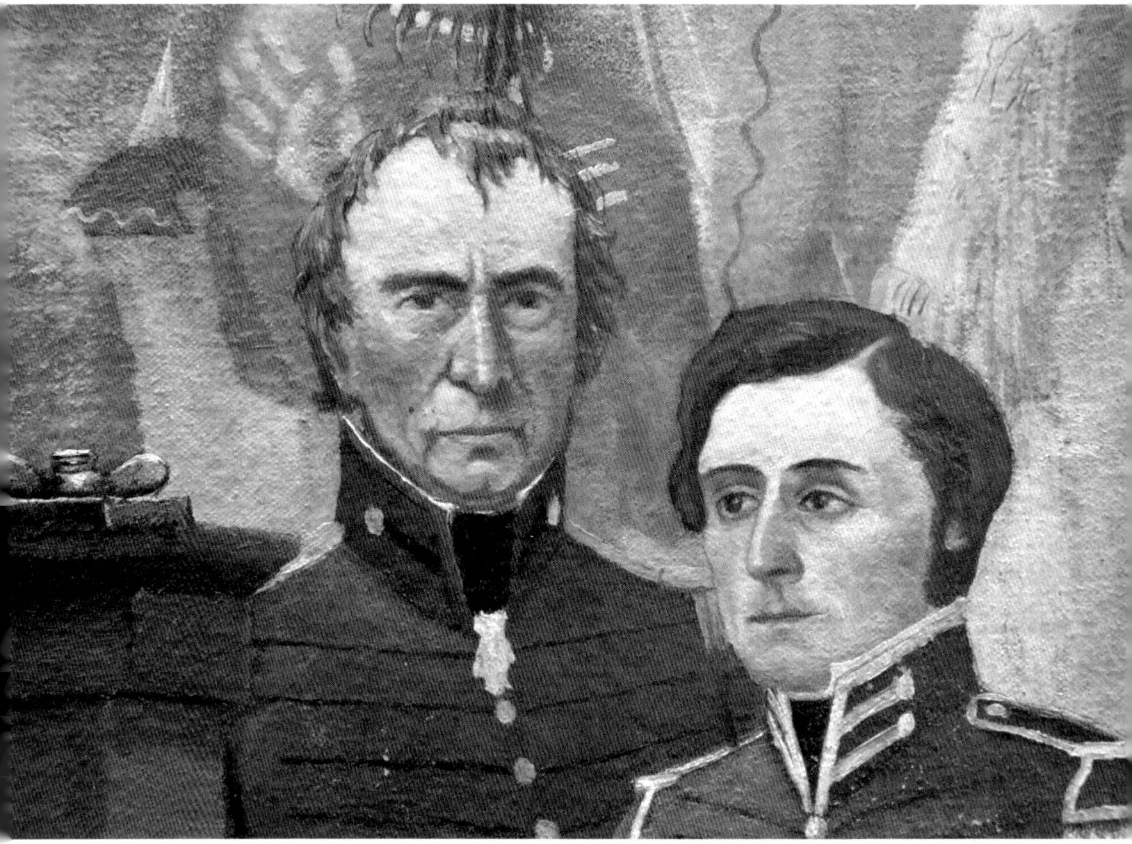

Zachary Taylor and Jefferson Davis
Lt. Col. Zachary Taylor (left) was sent to Prairie du Chien in early 1829 to oversee the construction of the second Fort Crawford. Soon after he assumed command, Lt. Jefferson Davis (right) arrived at Prairie du Chien.

With the outbreak of the Black Hawk War, Taylor campaigned to pursue and later defend Black Hawk and his forces. When Black Hawk surrendered at Fort Crawford, Taylor assigned Davis to escort Black Hawk to St. Louis, where he was imprisoned at Jefferson Barracks. Davis did much to shield Black Hawk from the curious.

During this time, Jefferson Davis fell in love with Taylor's daughter Sarah Knox Taylor. They sought Zachary Taylor's permission to marry, which he refused. Taylor respected Davis, but did not want his daughter to become a military wife. Taylor's oldest daughter had married an army surgeon, and he knew life at frontier military posts was hard on women. Davis resigned his commission in April 1835 and married Sarah in Louisville, Kentucky, on June 17. (Courtesy City of Prairie du Chien and Wisconsin Historical Society.)

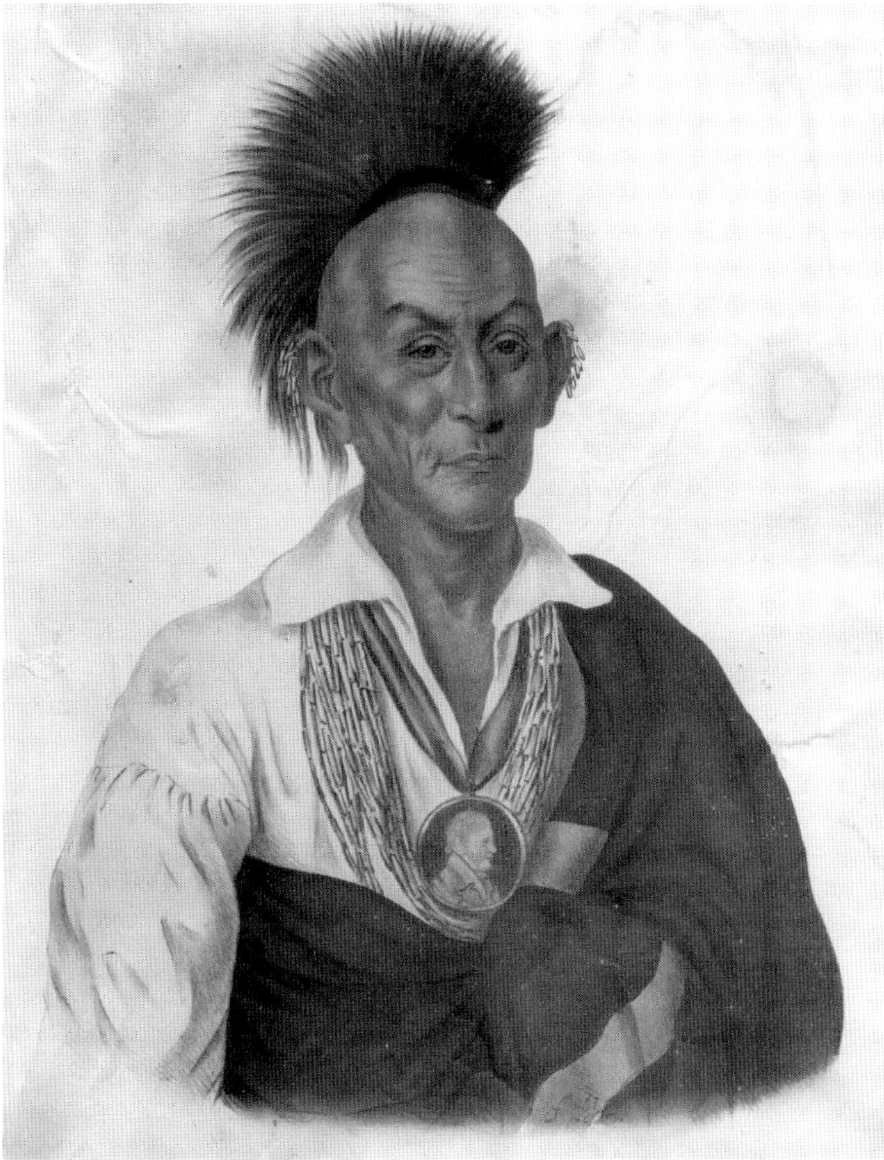

Black Hawk
One of the largest Indian villages in North America was Saukenuk, located between the Rock and Mississippi Rivers in Illinois. At one time, it included approximately 4,000 Sac and Fox people. The Treaty of 1804 ceded all this land to the United States. Black Hawk did not believe this treaty was valid and vowed not to give in to the government. He therefore sided with the British in the War of 1812 and refused to participate in the Great Council held in 1825 at Prairie du Chien. His attempt to lead his people back to Saukenuk in 1832 led white settlers to believe they were about to be attacked. For several months, Black Hawk and the Sac were pursued in what came to be called the Black Hawk War. In August 1832, Black Hawk surrendered to Joseph Street, the US Indian agent at Prairie du Chien. He was imprisoned for a short time at Fort Crawford. In his autobiography, published in 1872, Black Hawk said, "How smooth must be the languages of the whites. When they can make right look like wrong and wrong like right." (Author's collection.)

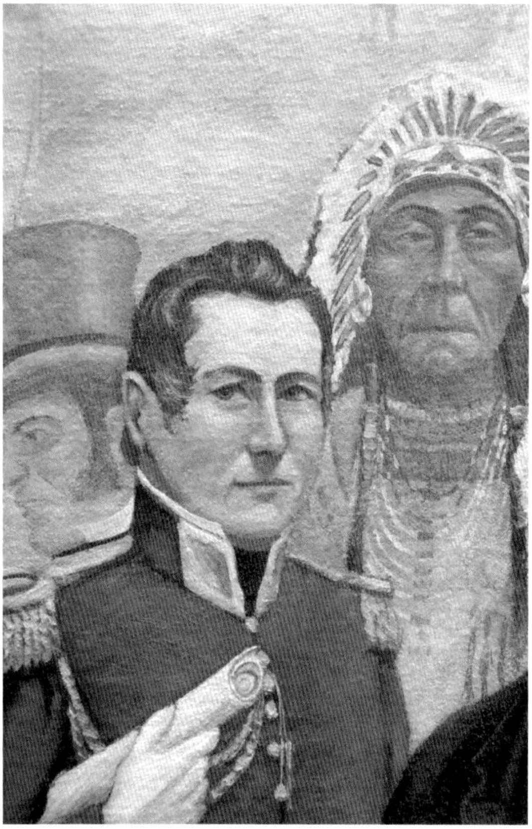

Joseph Montfort Street
Pres. John Quincy Adams appointed Joseph Street the Indian agent to the Winnebago soon after the 1827 Winnebago Uprising. Street advocated fair but firm treatment of the Winnebago. He seldom received military support and began to think that the best way to protect the Indians was to remove them to the West. During the Black Hawk War, Street convinced the Winnebago to remain neutral. The Winnebago turned Black Hawk over to Street, who surrendered the chief to Zachary Taylor. Street fought to open a school for the Winnebago across the Mississippi River from Prairie du Chien. (Courtesy City of Prairie du Chien and Wisconsin Historical Society.)

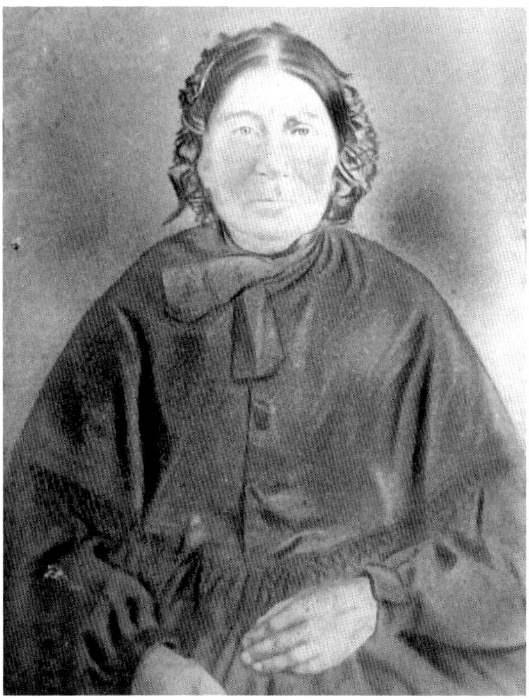

Euphrosine Antaya Fraser Powers
When Father Mazzuchelli told the residents of Prairie du Chien that he wanted to build a church for them and was in need of land, Euphrosine Powers may have offered a plot of land that had descended to her from her father, Pierre Antaya. Since Prairie du Chien was part of the United States, it was governed by laws of inheritance stipulating that a woman's property became her husband's at the time of marriage. Therefore, Strange Powers signed the deed donating four acres of land to the Catholic Church. (Courtesy the Powers-Barrette family.)

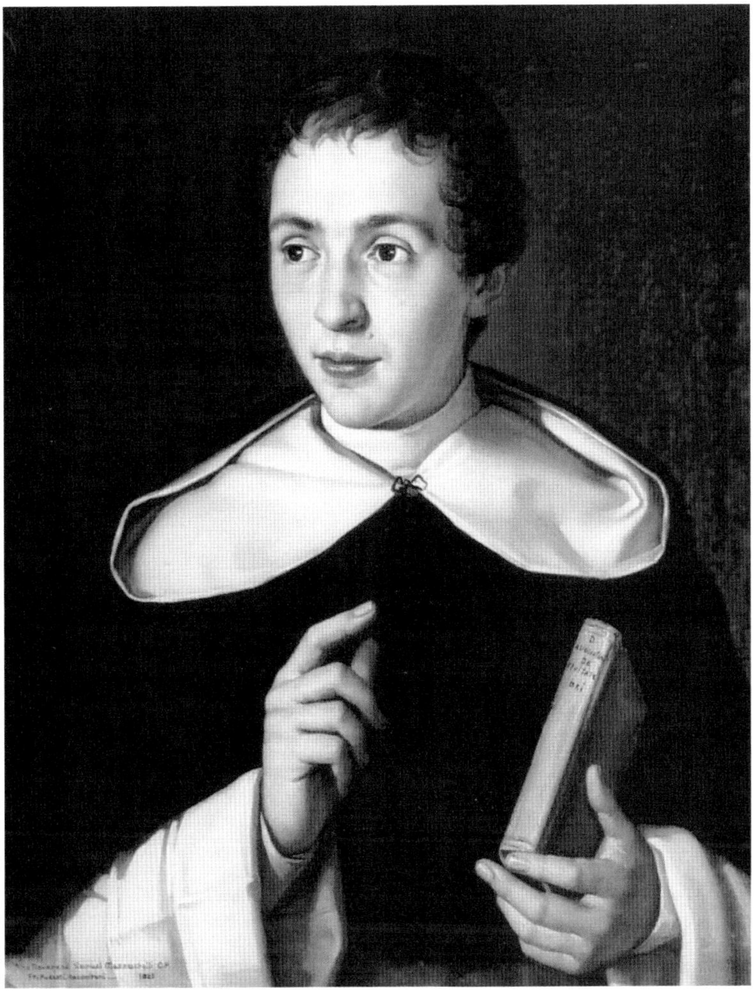

Samuel Charles Mazzuchelli
In the early 19th century, most of the residents of Prairie du Chien were Roman Catholic. In 1817, Father Marie Joseph Dunand visited the prairie, spending a month blessing marriages and baptizing children and adults. Father Francis Vincent Badin arrived 10 years later and spent over a year, off and on, ministering to the people. In 1828, the year Father Badin left Prairie du Chien, Samuel Mazzuchelli left Italy and arrived on the American frontier. After ordination, Father Mazzuchelli was assigned to be the missionary priest of the western Great Lakes and Upper Mississippi. He traveled on horseback, by foot, and in canoes to serve the people who lived in this vast area.

Father Mazzuchelli arrived in Prairie du Chien in 1832. He began planning for a church to be built for the community, to be constructed of native limestone. He did not return to the prairie until 1835, but started raising funds for the church. Strange Powers donated land the following year, and construction work began. Father Mazzuchelli designed the structure in a style he called "chaste Gothic" and worked alongside the masons erecting the stone walls. The building progressed so that, by 1839, the cornerstone was laid and the parish named St. Gabriel.

By his death in 1864, Father Mazzuchelli had established many local parish communities, designed and initiated the construction of more than 24 churches and civic buildings, and founded the Sinsinawa Dominican Congregation. The structure he designed for Prairie du Chien is the oldest church in Wisconsin. (Courtesy Sinsinawa Dominican Archives.)

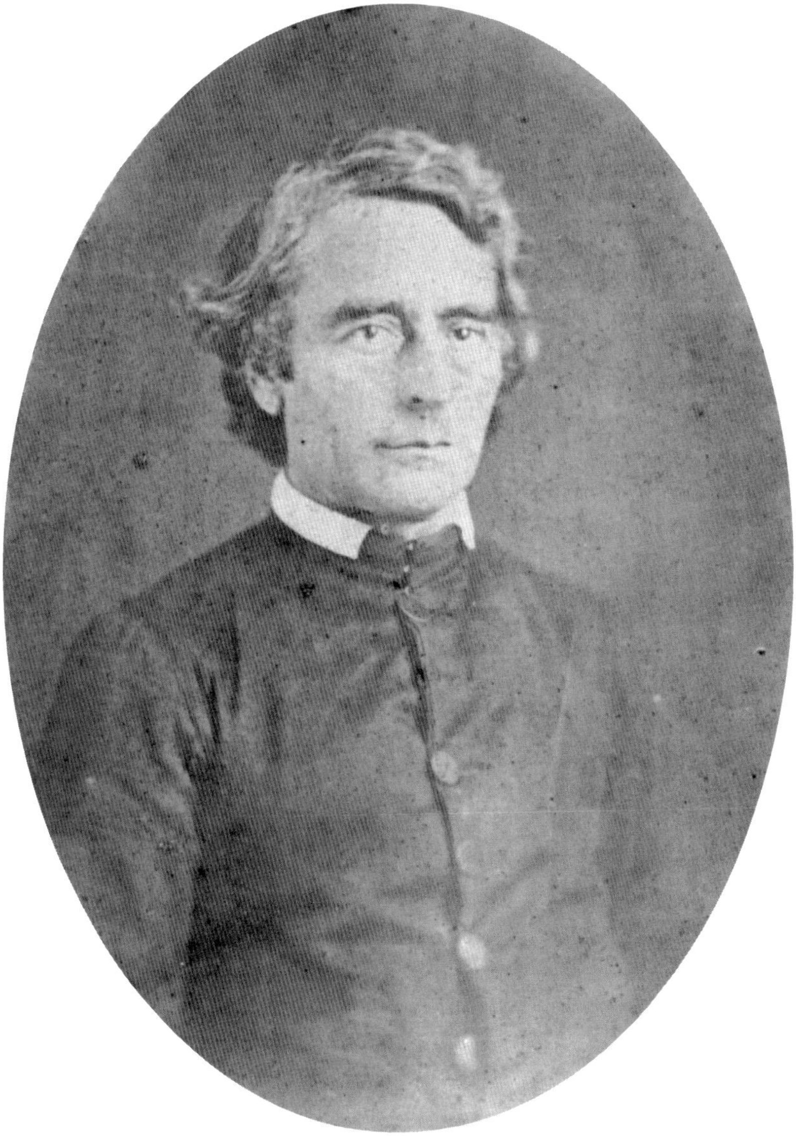

Rev. Lucien Galtier
In 1840, the first permanent pastor was assigned to St. Gabriel Parish. For the next few years, three different priests ministered to the parish. Then, in 1847, Father Lucien Galtier was assigned to be the pastor, a position he would hold until his death in 1866.

Like Father Mazzuchelli, Lucien Galtier was a builder of churches. Before coming to Prairie du Chien, Father Galtier worked among the settlers at St. Peter's in Minnesota. He selected a site for a church close to a steamboat landing on the Mississippi River, which he named St. Paul. He is therefore credited with founding the City of St. Paul. Father Galtier also built St. Peter's Church at Mendota, Minnesota, now the oldest church in Minnesota. Transferred to Keokuk, Iowa, Galtier built the first Catholic church in that community.

At Prairie du Chien, in 1858, Father Galtier installed the Stations of the Cross in St. Gabriel's Church, bringing to completion what Father Mazzuchelli had begun 18 years before. When Father Galtier died unexpectedly, he was buried in front of St. Gabriel's. (Author's collection.)

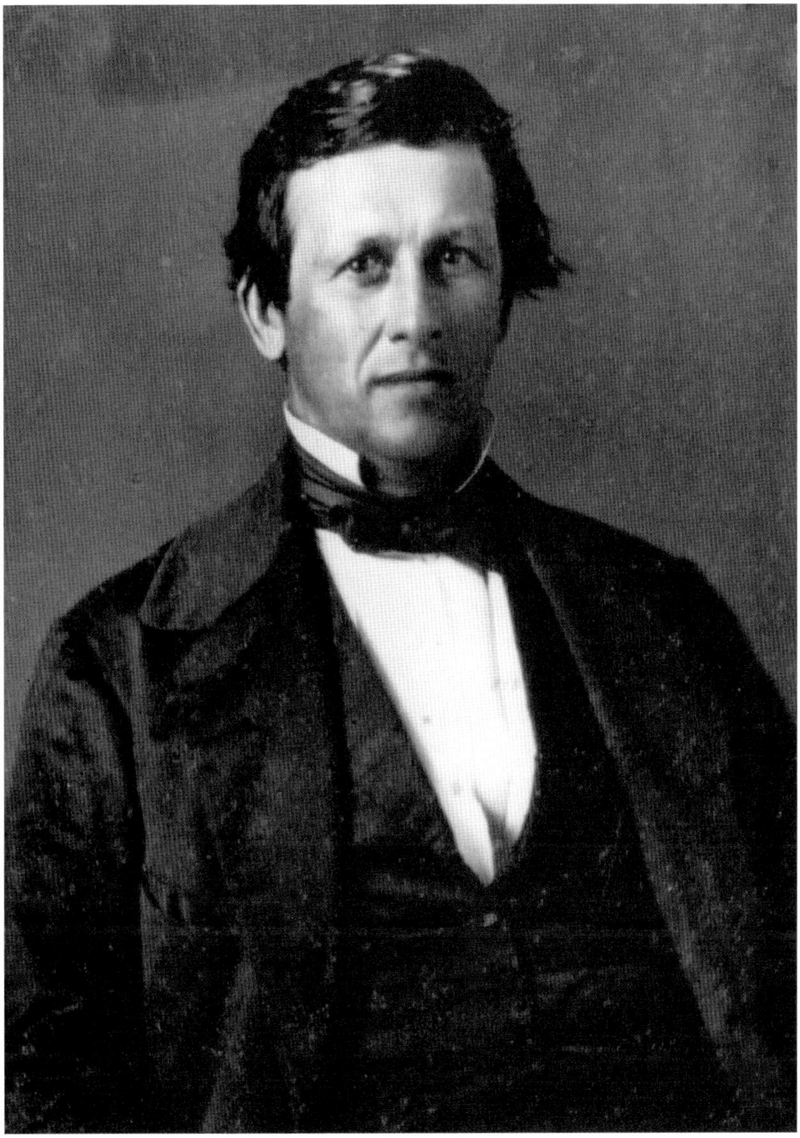

Hercules L. Dousman

In 1826, Dousman arrived in Prairie du Chien as a clerk for the American Fur Company. He quickly learned the trade, and when the company reorganized in 1834, Dousman became an equal partner with Joseph Rolette and Henry M. Sibley of Minnesota in the Western Outfit. Dousman was an astute businessman. From the fur trade, he diversified his holdings, expanding into the lumber business, steamboat and railroad transportation, and land speculation, and then shifted to stocks and securities. He acquired large tracts of land in Prairie du Chien at tax sales. As the commercial district of Prairie du Chien expanded, Dousman subdivided and sold some of the land. On other lots, he built commercial structures.

In 1843, Dousman built "the House on the Mound." The following year, he married Jane Fisher Rolette. Hercules and Jane had one son, Louis. When Hercules died in 1868, he was considered a millionaire. Louis changed the Dousman property, building a new house in 1870 and, in the 1880s, establishing a horse stud farm and race rack on the site. His widow, Nina, renamed the Dousman estate Villa Louis. (Courtesy Wisconsin Historical Society.)

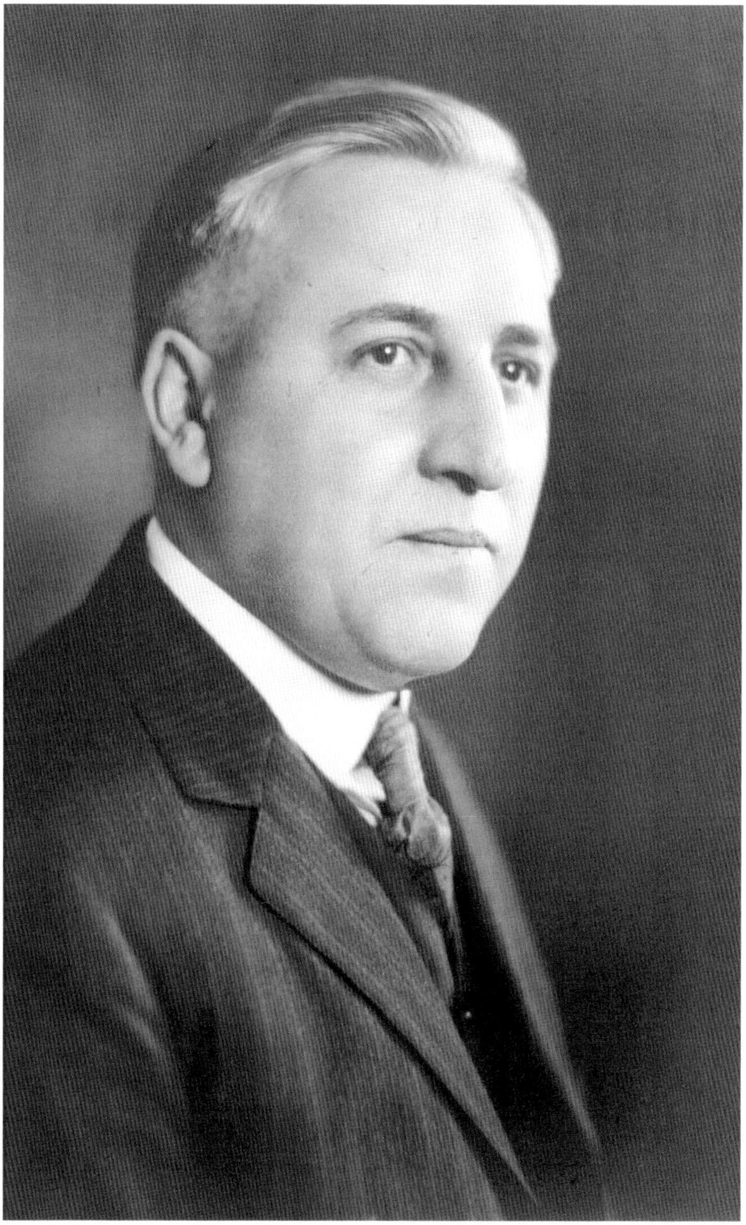

Dr. Francis J. Antoine

Francis J. Antoine had practiced medicine at Prairie du Chien since 1906. In 1930, he was elected mayor of the City of Prairie du Chien on the "Square Deal Ticket," promising to give the city a businesslike administration. As such, he paid attention to the condition of the streets, parks, and other city property. Dr. Antoine sought greater recognition in the community for persons who were part of the history of Prairie du Chien. Under his administration, the name of the major commercial thoroughfare was changed from Bluff Street to Blackhawk Avenue. York Street, which ran north and south, became Marquette Road. A member of the state and county medical societies, he assisted in the establishment of the Dr. William Beaumont Memorial, located by the Fort Crawford Hospital, which led to Church Street being renamed Beaumont Road. (Courtesy the Antoine family.)

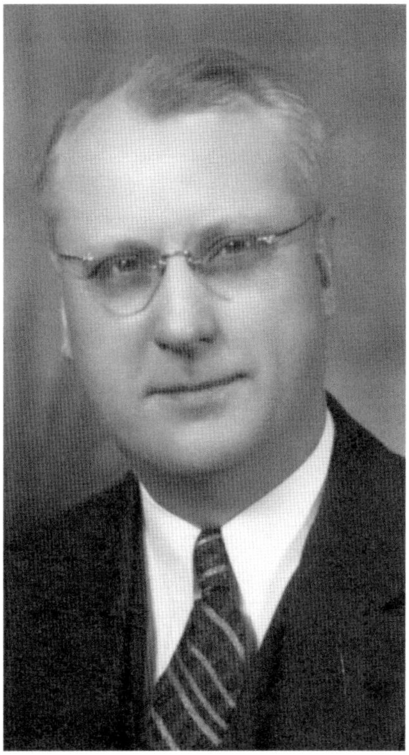

Dr. Arthur W. Thompson

In 1935, A.W. Thompson, mayor of the City of Prairie du Chien, offered the Dousman family a solution to a problem. For many years, the Dousman heirs had tried to sell the Villa Louis. Louis Dousman hired Charlie Minney to live in the house and watch the property, and he devised stories that visitors to Prairie du Chien found fascinating. The City of Prairie du Chien saw the potential in fixing up the house and opening it to the public, as well as creating a park with a swimming pool and golf course on the Villa Louis grounds. Thompson (right) and the city council made Louis Dousman an offer. The Dousman heirs agreed, giving the property to the City of Prairie du Chien. The house was repaired and opened for tours. Each year, the house opened for the season with a three-day event, Villa Louis Days.

In the late 1940s, the Dousman heirs felt that the State Historical Society of Wisconsin would do a better job promoting and preserving the Villa Louis. Ownership of the property was turned over to the State of Wisconsin in 1952. Under the society's administration, the property has been restored to its 1890s condition. Below, members of the 1947 Villa Louis Days committee are standing in the front hall of the Dousman home. (Both, courtesy Prairie du Chien Historical Society.)

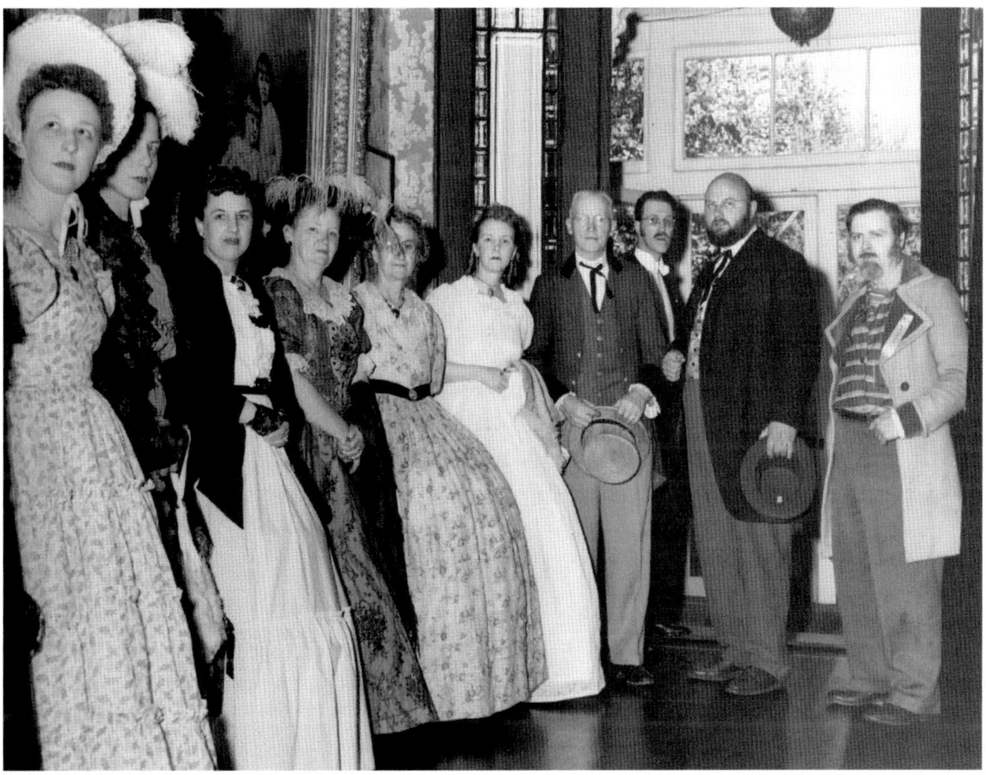

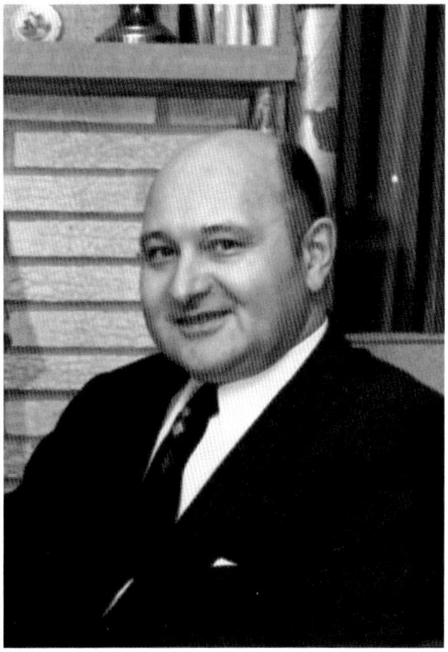

Dr. Elias Max Dessloch

Eli Dessloch began practicing medicine in Prairie du Chien in 1939 as a staff member of the General Hospital. He soon involved himself in the work being done to preserve the Fort Crawford Hospital. He was a member of the Beaumont Foundation, which acquired the hospital from the Fort Crawford Chapter of the Daughters of the American Revolution (DAR). Dr. Dessloch was instrumental in convincing the Charitable, Educational, and Scientific Foundation of the State Medical Society of Wisconsin to purchase the Fort Crawford Hospital and develop it as a museum, which opened in 1960.

Since 1996, the Fort Crawford Hospital and Museum have been owned and operated by the Prairie du Chien Historical Society. The hospital is filled with exhibits on the early events and figures of Prairie du Chien. (Courtesy Prairie du Chien Historical Society, Peckham Collection.)

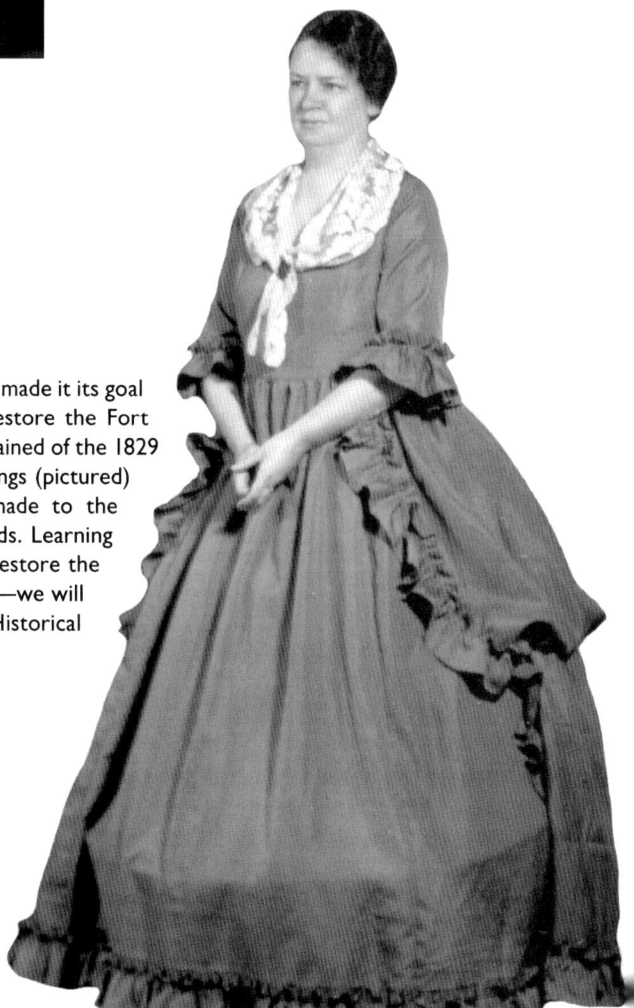

Margaret Paris Billings

The Fort Crawford Chapter of the DAR made it its goal to purchase and then raise funds to restore the Fort Crawford Hospital, which is all that remained of the 1829 military post. While Margaret Paris Billings (pictured) was chapter regent, a request was made to the Works Progress Administration for funds. Learning that over $7,000 had been granted to restore the hospital, she said, "It will be completed—we will never stop." (Courtesy Prairie du Chien Historical Society, Howe Collection.)

CHAPTER TWO

Generations of Business

We have a great deal of faith in Prairie du Chien and hope we can be a part of that progress, serving the community.

—Roy L. George, 1970

Prairie du Chien had been a center of commerce long before recorded accounts. Seasonally, Indian tribes of the Upper Mississippi gathered on the prairie to exchange wares they had produced or goods they had acquired from another Indian nation. When Europeans, first French and then British, came to the prairie, the exchange advanced as part of the fur trade. William Clark understood the economic importance of the prairie to the United States and took action to ensure the Upper Mississippi came under American control. After Fort Crawford was built on the prairie, men arrived from the East, finding value in the land. Settlers organized land companies and additions, and the prairie was surveyed into a grid of streets, blocks, and lots. To encourage settlement, these men invested in steamboats and the railroad and opened general-merchandise stores and hotels. And the settlers came, soon outnumbering the French Canadians and the Americans originally from New York, Illinois, and Missouri. The railroad brought immigrants from Ireland, Norway, Germany, and Bohemia. The Norwegians moved on, preferring farmland, but the others found comfort and opportunity in a small community.

The commercial center of Prairie du Chien had moved from the island, where the fur traders had lived, to the south end of the prairie, close to the steamboat landing and railroad depot. When both the depot and the landing moved farther north, so did the commercial district. The Upper Town grew along the street laid out from the island to the bluffs. In the 1850s, Hercules Dousman had two buildings erected in Upper Town, and he, and then his son, happily sold lots to enterprising Germans. Store structures built by Frederick, Schweitzer, and Kappel were joined by blocks of stores financed by Rauffauf, Zieprecht, Poehler, and Siegbert. Case, Garrity, Garvey, and Grace followed suit in building commercial structures, soon to be joined by Wachuta, Vondrak, and Smrcina. A downtown commercial district was born and grew. When destructive fires left only walls standing, the owners rebuilt and businesses moved back in. Into the 20th century, the building continued, the business district spreading along Bluff Street from Main Street to Ohio Street. Some of the men who had constructed the two-story brick buildings rented the space to people who foresaw a good income from their hard work. As time passed, businesses changed. In the years just before World War II, and then during the booming postwar economy, new families initiated businesses at Prairie du Chien. Several were very good at understanding consumer desires and traits, which altered as America changed. They adapted their businesses, taught their children, and their children and grandchildren successfully carried on the commercial ventures. To this day, most of the businesses in Prairie du Chien are family owned and operated, some into the third and fourth generations.

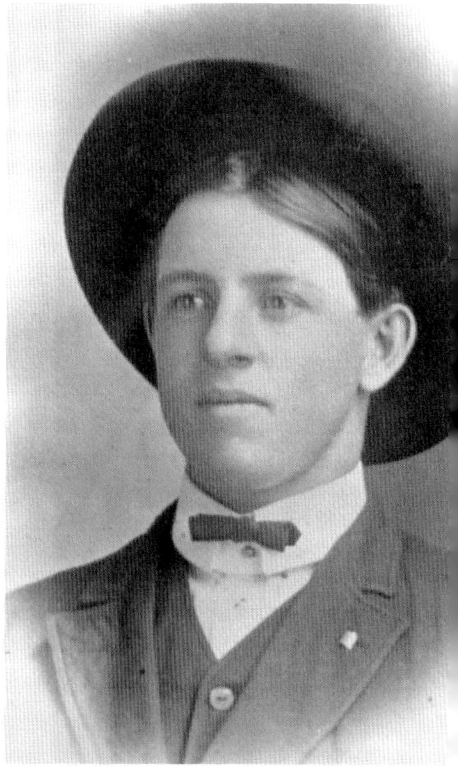

Peter E. Gokey

Pete Gokey (right, and at left below) was not thinking of the future when his friends asked him to help with the annual firemen's party in 1908. As he fried hamburgers with onions, Gokey poured a bit of water in the pan to keep the hamburgers from drying out. Those who ate the burgers remarked on how juicy and flavorful they were. The aroma of the cooking fare drew customers to the tavern. The Foleys asked Gokey to cook his hamburgers again and for many weekends to follow. The popularity of "Pete's hamburgers" grew. A cabinetmaker and sign painter, Gokey designed and built his hamburger stand, actually a trailer. In 1955, he moved his stand a half-block west on Blackhawk Avenue, where it still stands today. Pete involved his son Robert "Duster" in the business, who later took over management. When Duster died of cancer at a young age, his children started a cancer memorial. In 2014, the 40th annual Memorial Day fundraiser was held, with proceeds from the sale of Pete's Hamburgers donated to charity. Gokey's grandchildren and great-grandchildren carry on the operation of Pete's Hamburger Stand, the oldest continuous family-owned business in Prairie du Chien. (Both, courtesy the Gokey family.)

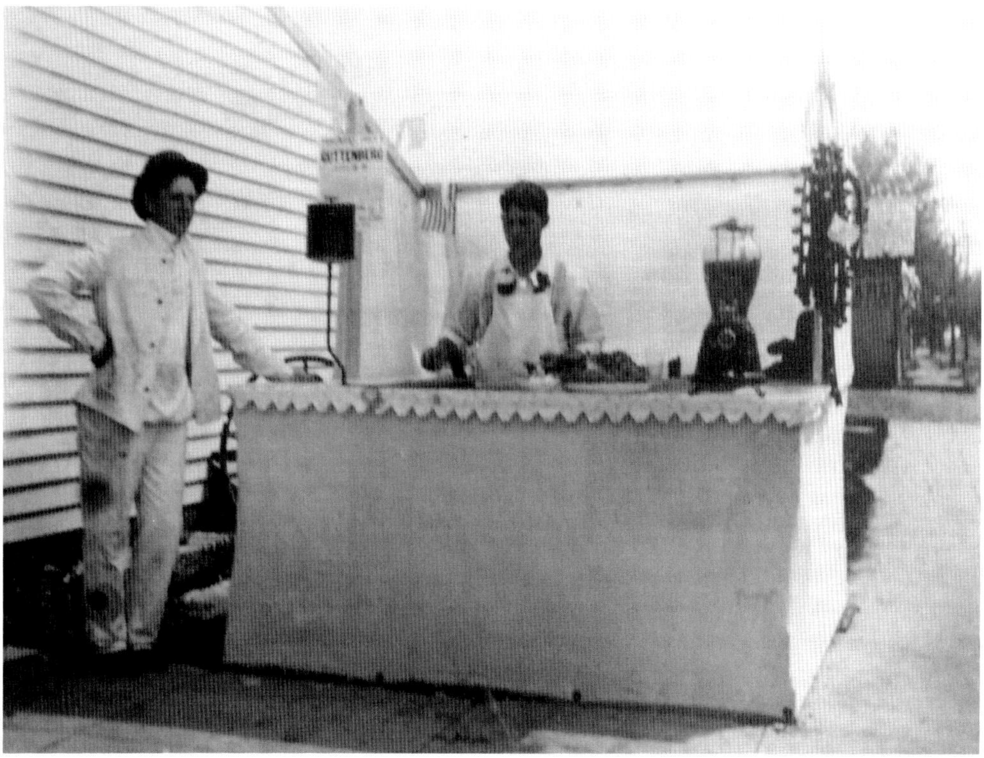

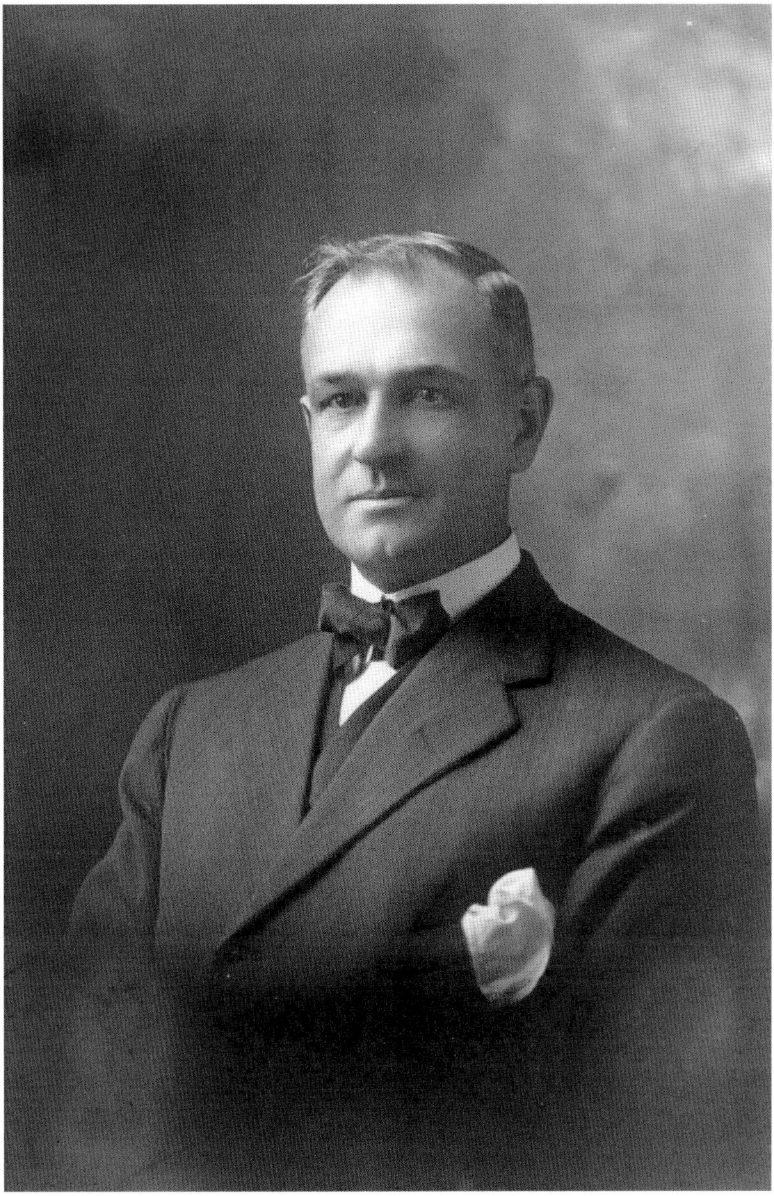

Charles Grelle Jr.

Charles Grelle Sr., a cabinetmaker and undertaker, had been mayor of Prairie du Chien for four terms. In 1900, His son, Charles Jr., and he built a new structure on the site of the original Grelle cabinet shop. Two blocks east on Bluff Street, Charles Jr. operated a dry-goods business. About 1910, Charles Jr. (pictured) began to invest in other commercial ventures. He and four other men opened the Prairie du Chien Canning Company. A few years later, Grelle, W.R. Graves, E.C. Amann, and Lawrence Swingle began the Prairie du Chien Tool Factory. Grelle became a major stockholder and officer in the woolen mill. In 1905, he became president of the Bank of Prairie du Chien, a position he held for many years. The commercial structures Grelle and his contemporaries built define downtown Prairie du Chien, and their homes are testimony to an affluent past. (Courtesy Prairie du Chien Historical Society, Grelle Collection.)

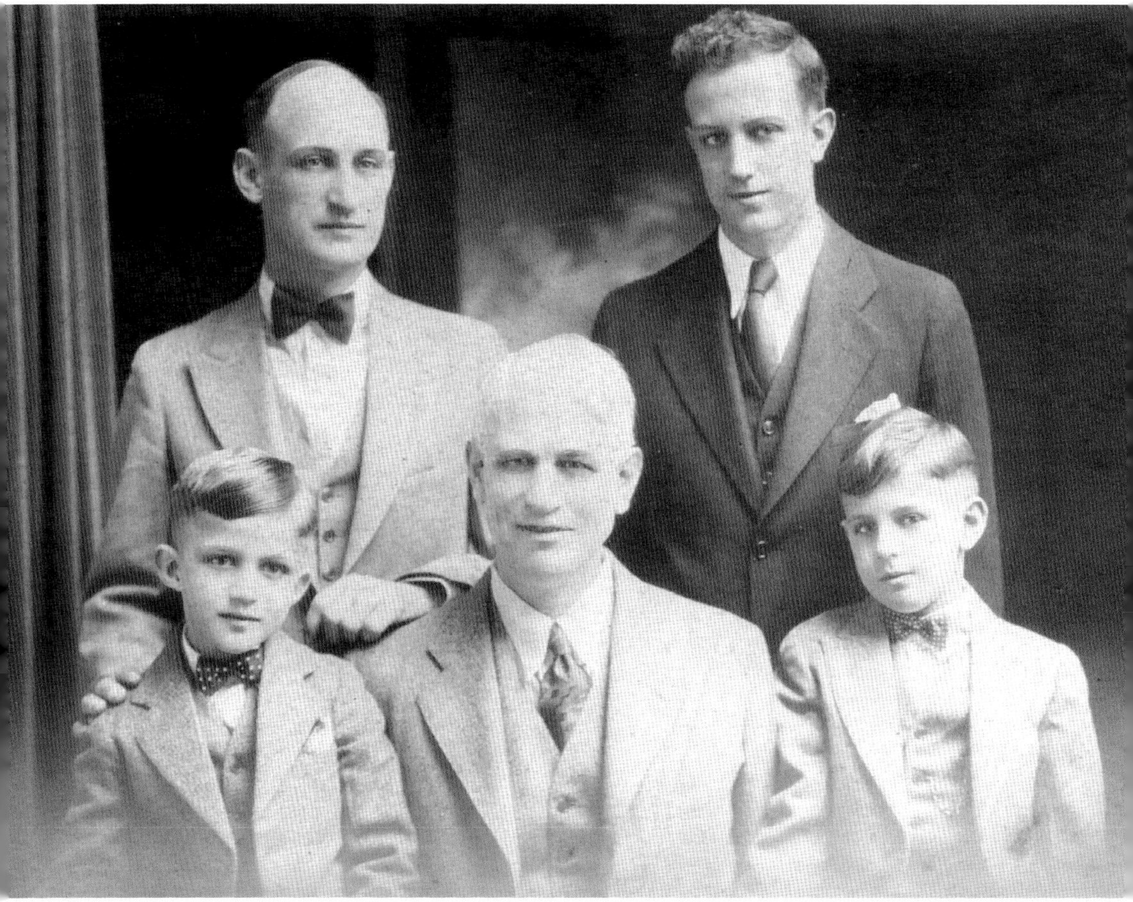

Henry E. Howe and Lyman J. Howe Sr.

For over 100 years, the Howe family name has been synonymous with the newspaper and printing industries in Prairie du Chien. With experience in editing a newspaper, Henry Howe (seated at center) came to work for William Merrell, the owner of *The Courier*. When Merrell died in 1911, Hank purchased the newspaper, moving it to a new location. Hank's son, Lyman (standing at left), was made a partner in the business after he returned from the war in April 1919. When Hank died, Lyman became publisher. Lyman died at a young age in 1949. His two sons had assisted him with the publishing of *The Courier*, so, along with their mother, Eliese, Lyman Jr. ("Jack," seated at right) and William ("Bill," seated at left) took over the operation of the newspaper and a commercial printing business that had grown from publishing. Eliese and her sons ran the business until 1973, when Jack's and Bill's sons, John and Gary, entered the company. Jack died in 2010, and Bill has retired. Howe Printing Company Inc. publishes *The Courier* and several other local newspapers the Howe family has acquired. The company also offers a vast line of printing services and products. John directs the commercial printing component of the family business, and Gary manages the newspapers. (Courtesy the Howe family.)

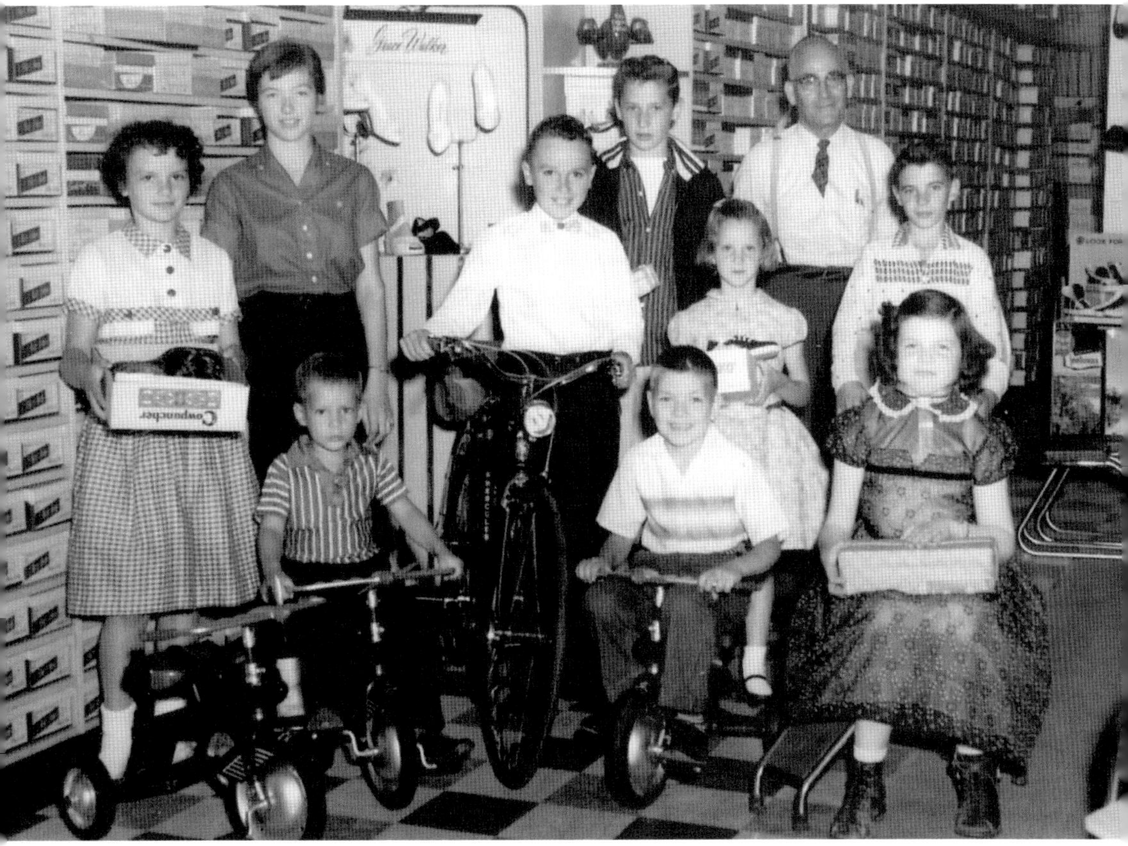

Peter A. Panka

Peter Panka (standing at right rear) was one of nine children. Like his brothers, he worked on the family farm at the east end of Bluff Street. His father, John, an immigrant from Bohemia, wanted more for his sons. In 1913, he purchased from the Frank Smrcina estate the Metropolitan Block, containing several businesses and a theater. Then, six years later, John built the Panka Building on the adjoining lot to the east. Peter had just married, so he and Antoinette "Nettie" opened a shoe store. Pete and Nettie brought their daughter, Toni, into the business. For many years, Panka's and Kozelka's were the only shoe stores in Prairie du Chien. Through good management, Toni continued to keep the shoe store operating, hiring Theresa Mezera as her assistant. When Toni retired, she passed Panka's Shoe Store to Mezera. The business Pete Panka began almost 100 years ago still offers a selection of shoes. (Courtesy Prairie du Chien Historical Society, Howe Collection.)

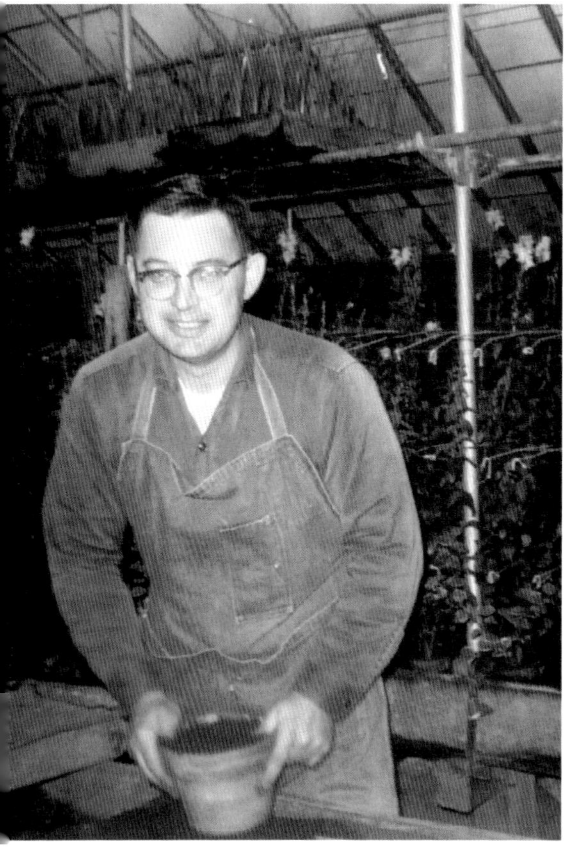

Christopher and Stanley Garnsworthy

In 1915, Charles C. Case decided to indulge in a hobby. He built a large greenhouse behind the family home and filled half of it with ferns, palms, potted plants, and flowers. The other half he devoted to the growing of "commercial green foods." But Chicago drew Case, and he left, allowing the business and plants to die. Herman Knudson of Mason City, Iowa, owned a large commercial greenhouse. Working for him was Christopher Garnsworthy, who had greenhouse experience from the time he was a young boy in England. Garnsworthy and Knudson formed a partnership and purchased the greenhouse built by Case. A grand opening introduced Prairie du Chien to Garnsworthy & Knudson and its fine stock of plants and blooming flowers, including "ornamentals of hardy recognized stock." At some point, the name of the enterprise was changed to Kembles' Greenhouse. Christopher and Nellie Garnsworthy developed the business, and their son Stanley (left, and second from left below) joined them. The business expanded, and additional growing houses were built on the property. Stanley Garnsworthy made sure that Kembles', located in a residential neighborhood, added to the attractiveness of the block. The same beauty and neighborliness persists with the present owners. (Both, courtesy the Garnsworthy family.)

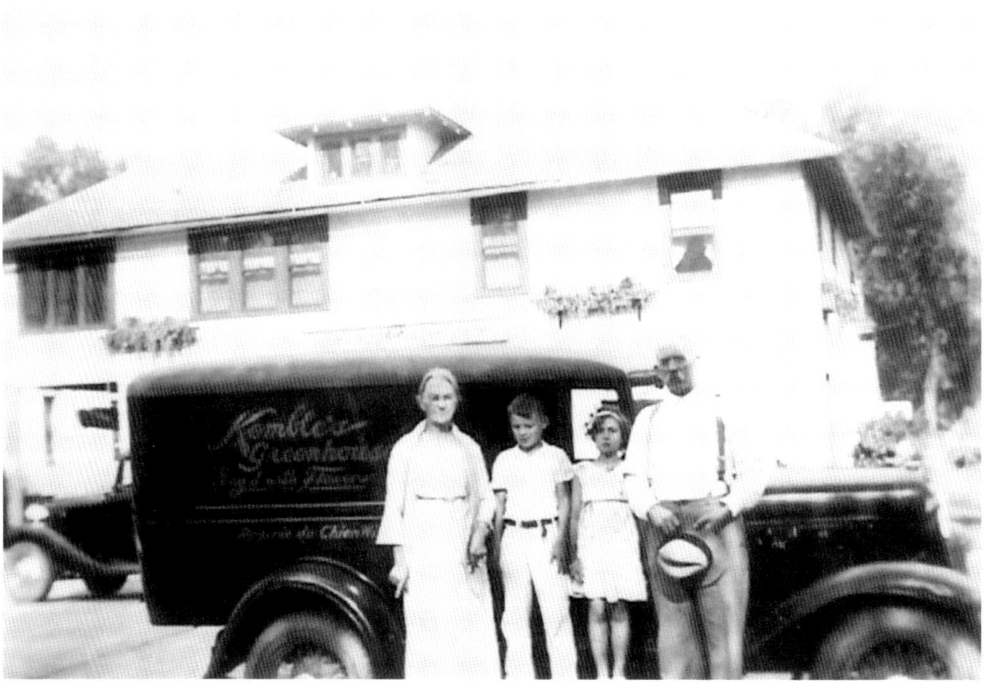

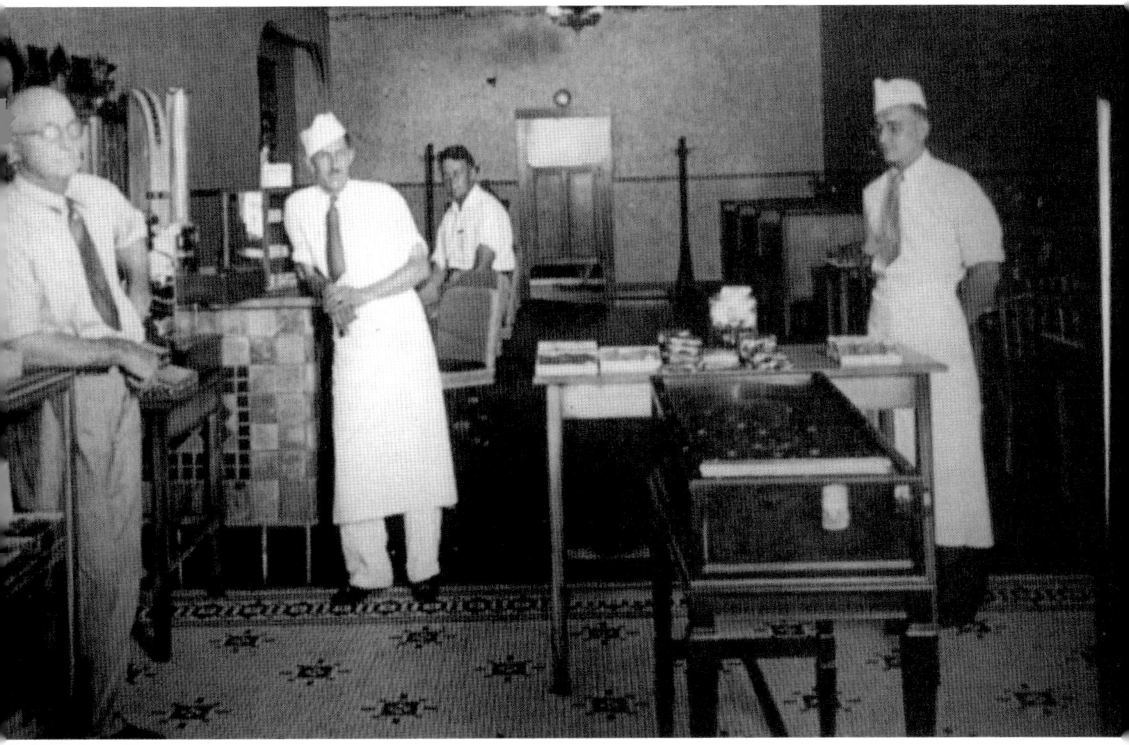

Henry J. and Clifford F. Kaber, with Russell Kieser
Henry (far left) and Emma Kaber took over the Uptown Café in 1925, liking its location near the busy intersection of Church and Bluff Streets. With so many patrons, the owners looked for a place to expand. The Kabers purchased an old livery stable farther west, closer to the newly opened bridge. They renovated the building, installing a black-and-white tile floor and a soda fountain. Their son Cliff (second from left) and son-in-law Russ Kieser (far right) were brought into the business. When Prohibition ended, the soda fountain disappeared, replaced with a bar. After World War II, Cliff and Russ enlarged the restaurant into the adjoining building, installing an oval bar with a stage in the center and renaming their eating establishment Kaber's Nite Club. In the 1950s, Cliff's two sons, Rex and Terry, became part of the operation. Of all the musical entertainment, the favorite was Elwood "Bud" McElroy, "the Blind Organist." As patrons walked into the bar, Bud, playing the organ on the stage, would hear the newcomer's voice and change what he was playing to that person's favorite song. In 1965, Kaber's expanded farther east and became Kaber's Supper Club. Jon, Rex's son, started working in 1978 and took over full management of the family restaurant in 1999. His son joined, making it five generations of the Kaber family. (Courtesy the Kaber family and Kathleen Novey.)

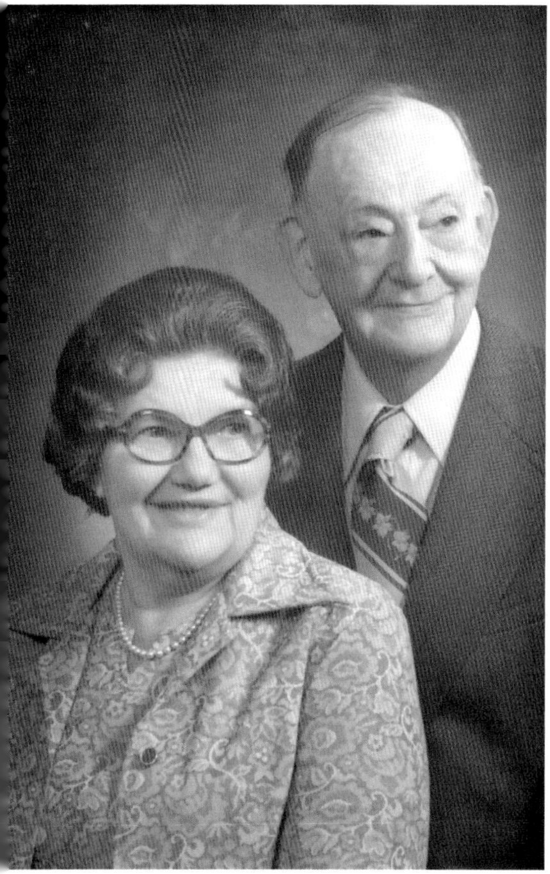

Ralph and Albina Kozelka

Ralph Kozelka was working with his brother Henry in their hardware store when Ralph decided he would venture into selling men's work clothes. Opening during the Great Depression, he often received wood or food in trade for the clothing. The business went well, and after the Korean War, Ralph and his wife, Albina (left), constructed a new building on North Beaumont Road. Kozelka's Men's Wear was a family business. Ralph, his sons Thomas and Richard, and daughter Marie Wall were all kept busy waiting on customers. Albina and Joseph Wall tailored, and Ralph's brother Emmanuel operated Kozelka's Shoe Store. Kozelka's Men's Wear moved across the street 14 years later. In the new structure, the grandchildren learned about salesmanship. Another store was opened in Dodgeville, Wisconsin, and Joe and Marie's sons entered the clothing business. Working with Marie for a few years, Bill and Leesa Wall purchased the Dodgeville store in 1983 and changed the name to Kozelka-Wall. Ken and Judy Wall had opened a women's clothing store in Prairie du Chien in 1981, calling it Wall Street. All three stores still offer a fine selection of clothing.

Shown below are, from left to right, Marie Kozelka Wall, Ralph Kozelka, Albina Kozelka, Richard Kozelka, Ivan Heisz, Thomas Kozelka, and Joseph Wall. (Both, courtesy the Kozelka-Wall family.)

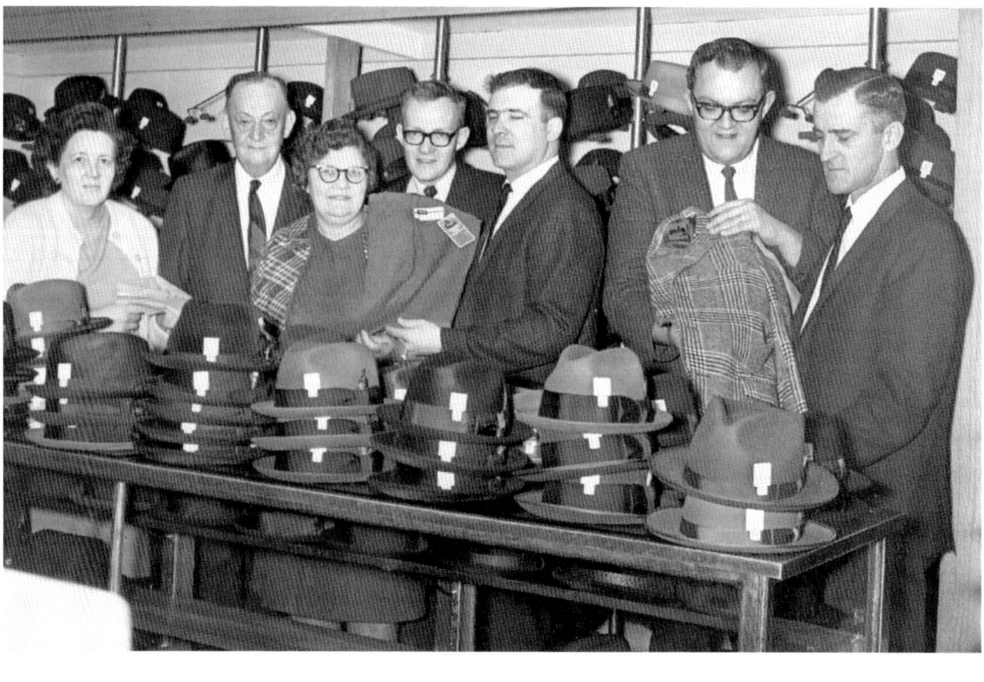

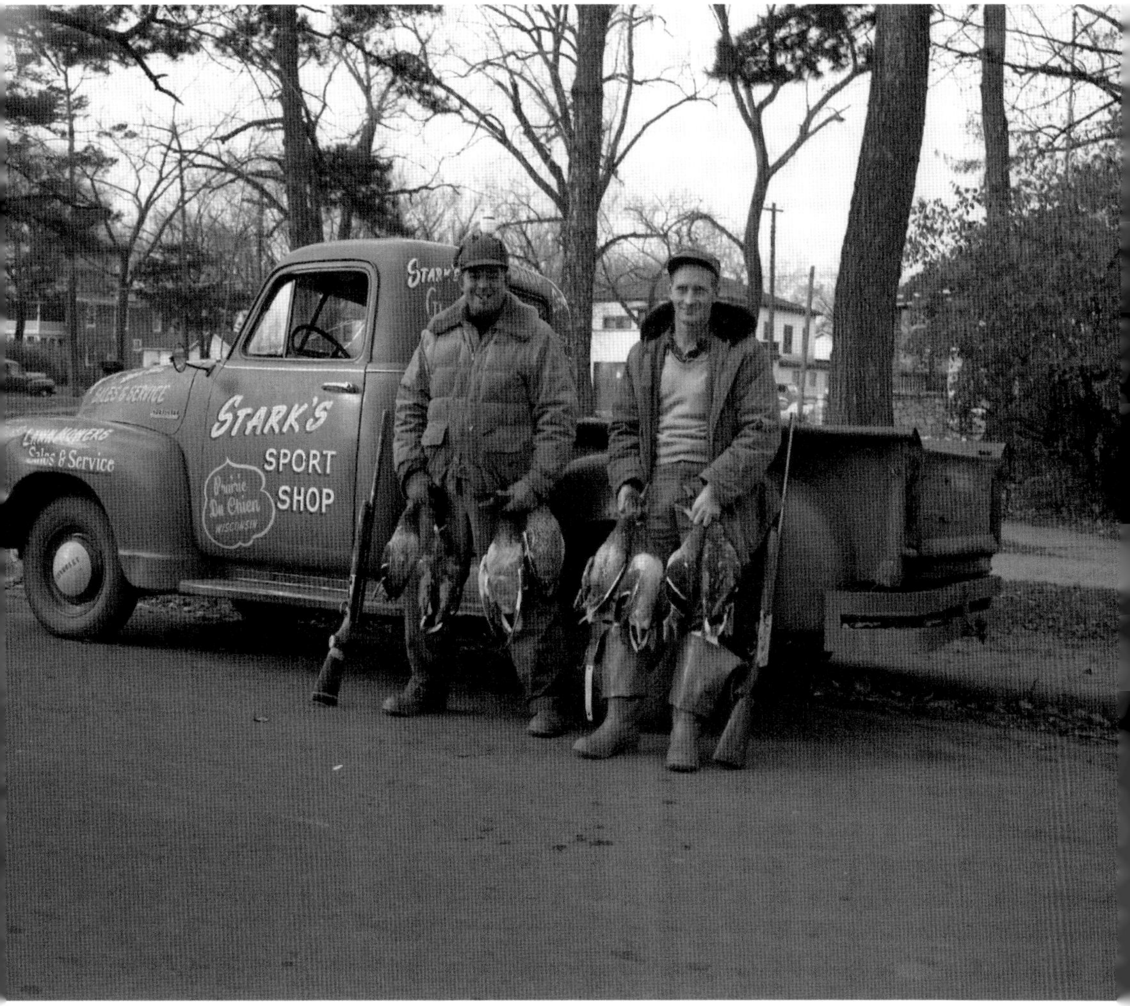

Frank C. Stark

Having operated a fresh-fruit stand in Platteville, Wisconsin, Frank Stark (left) moved to Prairie du Chien for his wife, Blanche, who had family in the community. Stark opened The Sweet Shop in 1937, making candy and ice cream. It did so well he moved twice, always expanding. He had never fished or hunted until the late 1940s, but took to the sports immediately, so he decided to open a sporting-goods store. It was the end of World War II, and supplies were hard to get, so one of his business neighbors encouraged Stark to also sell liquor. Thus, Stark's Sport Shop was born. Stark, wanting sporting goods to be his main stock, began to build wooden flatboats in the basement of the building he rented. When he built a new store in 1955 and moved across the street, Frank's son Dick was already an experienced salesman and assistant manager. In the 1970s, Stark's was one of the largest Honda dealerships in the nation. At Stark's, one could purchase boats and motors, hunting rifles, and liquor. Under Dick's sons, Randy and Ron, Stark's has evolved into one of the area's largest fishing-boat outlets. Pictured with Frank Stark is Jack Buschbom, three-time world champion bareback bronco rider. (Courtesy the Stark family).

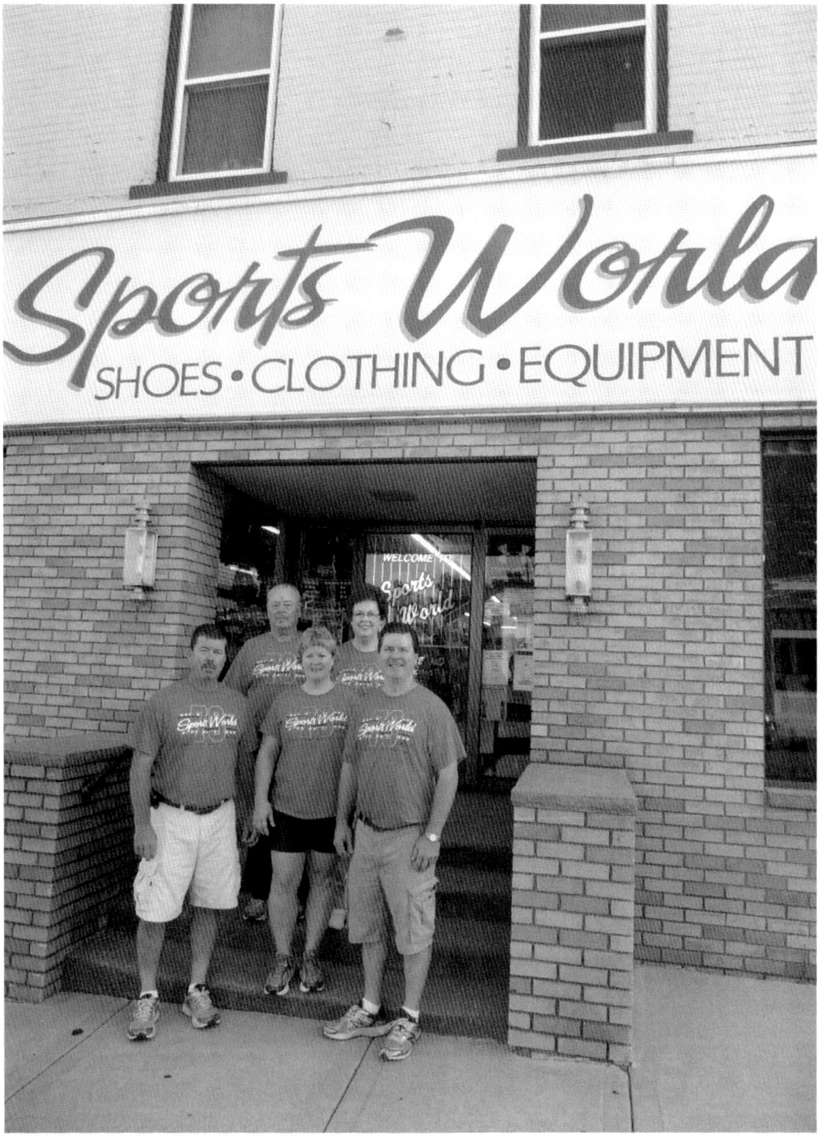

Larry Yeomans and Family
Cy Yeomans began to manage his father-in-law Jack Curry's Tiger Store in the 1920s, selling everything from guns and fishing rods to plumbing and electrical supplies. In 1940, the store became part of the Gamble's franchise. With Larry (rear left) and Rich Yeomans and their mother, Aleda, running the business, the store became the best in the chain. In the late 1970s, Gamble's stores were closing. Larry realized that people were becoming more conscious about physical fitness. Since there were no local options for people to purchase sports clothes, Larry and his wife, Phyllis (rear right), decided to open Sports World, focusing on the specific interests and needs of individuals and teams. Sons Scott (front left) and Todd (front right), daughter Penny (front center), and son-in-law John Cejka learned screen-printing. Custom-designed clothing led to engraving of trophies, awards, and advertising products. Sports World then broadened into custom embroidery. The latest expansion is Dyesport, the first domestic company in the United States to use dye-sublimation in all sports products. The fifth generation of the Yeomans family is now employed in the business. (Courtesy *The Courier Press.*)

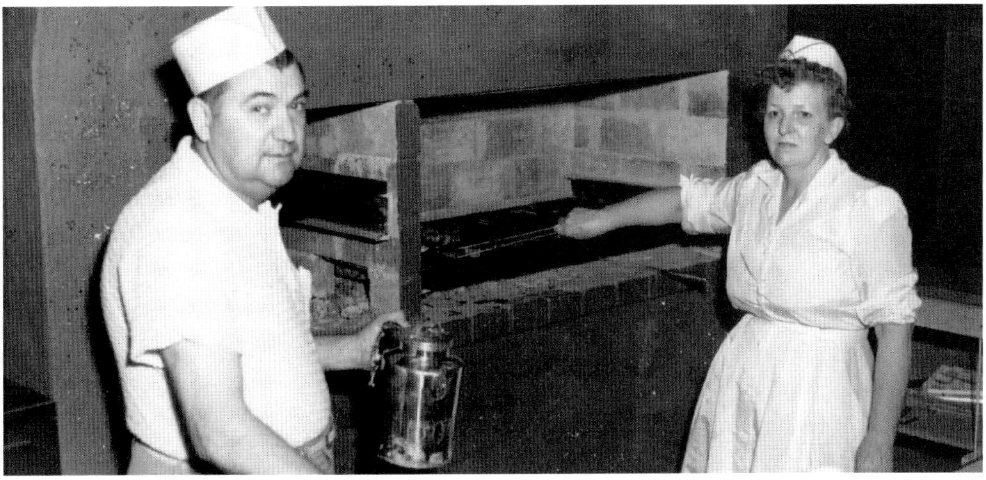

Lawrence and Lauretta Geisler

Lawrence and Lauretta Geisler (above) opened a restaurant in 1940 as a roadhouse on the highway south of town. Patrons came up with the name Red Rooster based on the establishment's sign, which indicated that it served chicken and fish. After five years, the Geislers sold the property to an employee, George Jeffers. But cooking for and mingling with people were in their blood. Lawrence and Lauretta bought Foley's Tavern two years later. They built a large addition and named their restaurant Geislers' Blue Heaven, because they liked the song "My Blue Heaven." The slightly sloping ceiling was lit with 365 stars, including the North Star and the Big Dipper constellation. A stage was built for floorshows, and professional acts from Milwaukee were booked for each weekend. Amateur hour was held during the week, with Tom and Rich Kozelka playing the steel guitar and singing, or Pete Gokey doing lively French Canadian clog dancing. Geislers' Blue Heaven was a family operation; Mary Jean and the Geislers' daughter Jeri helped prepare food and waited tables, and their husbands, Don and Jack, became part of the business. The family also catered railroad tours from Chicago. With the end of the railroad passenger trains and the relocation of the bridge across the Mississippi River, Geislers' Blue Heaven could no longer support two families, and closed. For a while, Zach's attempted to fill the void.

Below are, from left to right, John "Jack" and Geraldine "Jeri" Kluesner, and Mary Jean and Donald "Don" Tichenor. (Both, courtesy the Geisler-Kluesner family.)

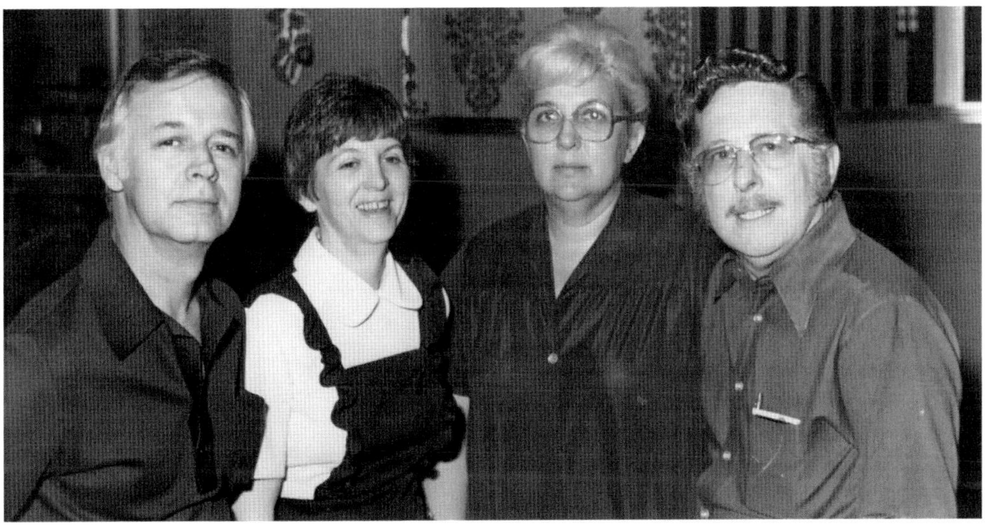

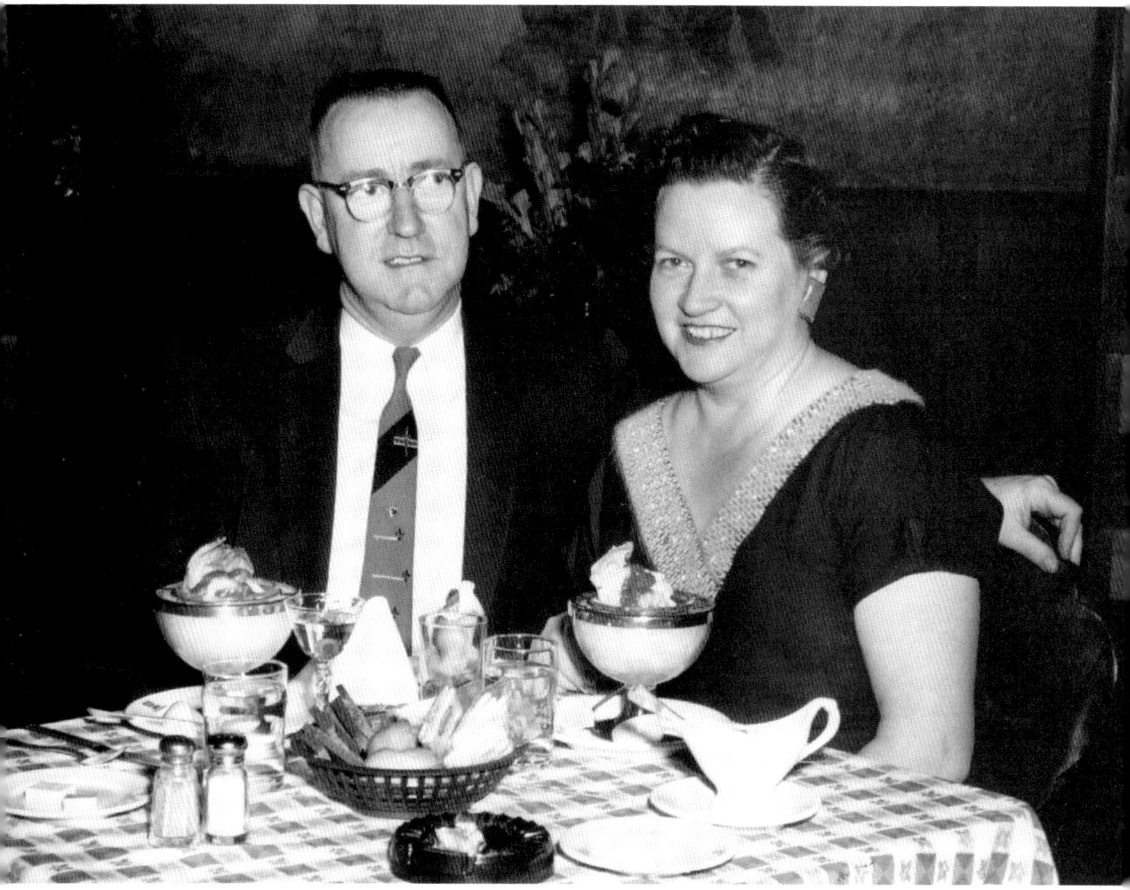

George and Dorothy Jeffers

George Jeffers went to work for Lawrence and Lauretta Geisler when he returned from service in World War II. When the Geislers decided to sell their restaurant, George and his wife, Dorothy, purchased it, renaming the business Jeffers' Nite Club. It was open only at night, serving until 11:00 p.m. Although the structure was a small frame building, it had a dance floor. Under George and Dorothy's management, Jeffers' became known for its live music and dancing. People came, ate dinner, and then had a second meal at the end of the evening. The dance era was coming to an end when a fire destroyed the entire building in November 1965. The restaurant remained closed for two years, reopening with a charcoal grill in 1967 as Jeffers' Black Angus. The only restaurant on the highway south of Prairie du Chien, Jeffers grew as it attracted out-of-town customers. A second dining room was added. George and Dorothy's daughter Ginger grew up in the restaurant, as the family home stood where there had once been cottages. Ginger's husband, Zeke DesRocher, tended bar. In 1978, Ginger and Zeke purchased Jeffers' Black Angus, adding another dining room and expanding the bar and lounge. They continued to operate the restaurant until it was time to retire, selling it to Steve and Angie Jones. The restaurant is still the first non-chain eating establishment to greet visitors as they enter Prairie du Chien. Now called Jones' Black Angus, the restaurant was one of 50 featured in the book *Wisconsin Supper Clubs: An Old-Fashioned Experience*. (Courtesy the Jeffers-DesRocher family.)

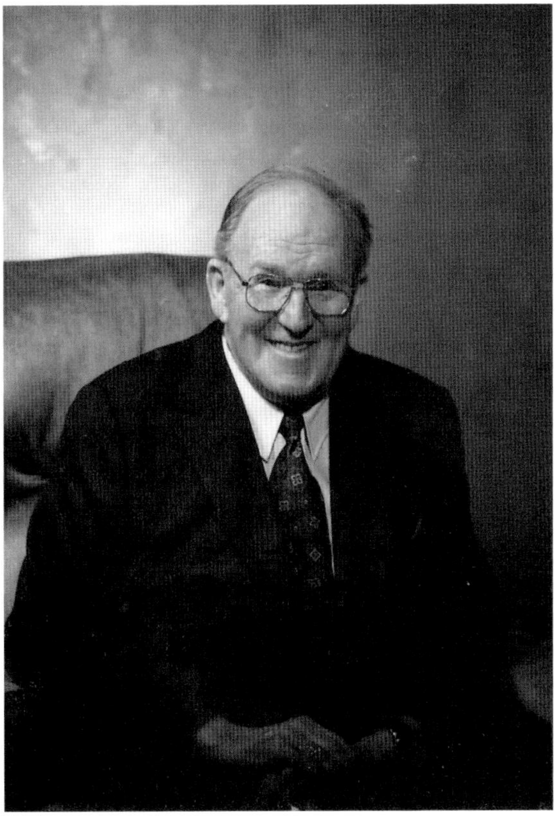

Robert P. Garrity
Bob Garrity was part of the fourth generation of his family to live in Crawford County. His father, William, owned several businesses in Prairie du Chien, and he expected his sons to work. Bob got a job at Lake's Funeral Parlor. The profession interested him, and he studied for a degree in mortuary science. In 1946, Ernest Otteson opened a new funeral home, and Garrity returned to Prairie du Chien, in time becoming a partner in Otteson & Garrity Funeral Home. The new Mississippi River bridge forced the demolition of the Otteson home, so Garrity built a new facility in 1973, which he and his wife, Marian, operated. He was later joined by two of his sons, Daniel and Michael. With a positive and mellow demeanor, Garrity treated everyone like family. Michael continues to direct Garrity Funeral Home. (Courtesy the Garrity family.)

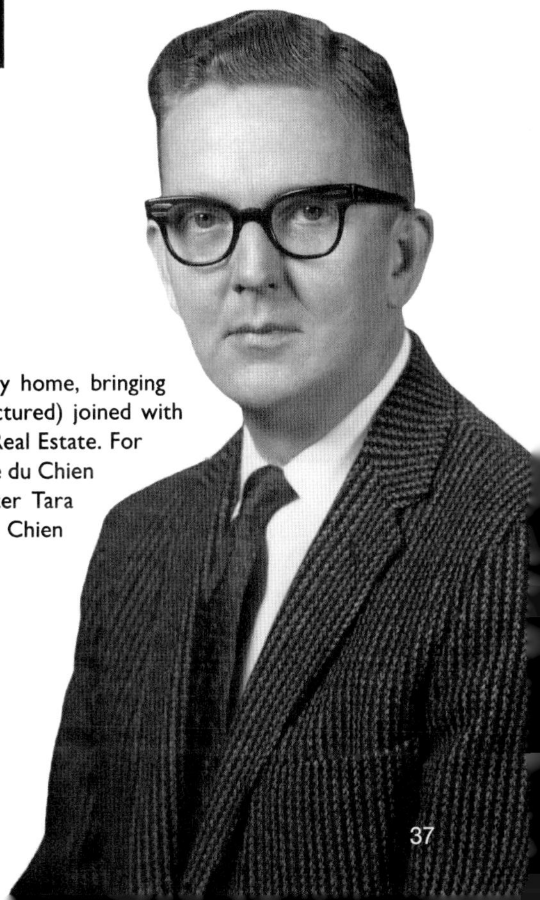

George Sutton
Amos Sutton opened a real-estate agency in the family home, bringing his son George into the business. In 1967, George (pictured) joined with Gordon Kieser to establish Kieser-Sutton Insurance & Real Estate. For 30 years, George served as a commissioner of the Prairie du Chien Housing Authority. George's son Bob and granddaughter Tara now operate Sutton Insurance Inc. (Courtesy Prairie du Chien Historical Society, Peckham Collection.)

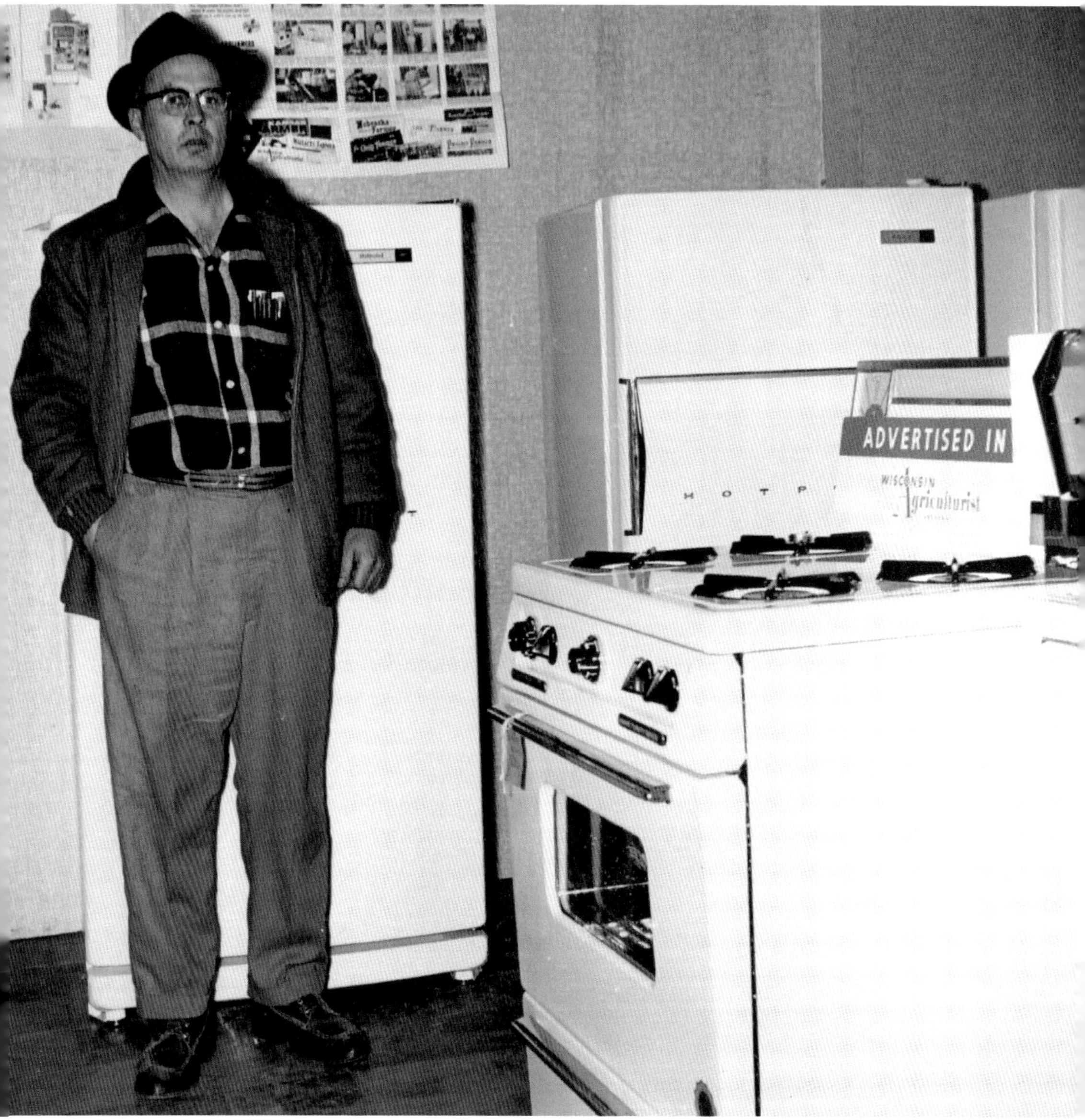

Seymour J. and Dorothy Horsfall Edwards

In 1946, Seymour Edwards started Edwards' Better Home Service, but, like many companies started by an individual, there was a family story. Edwards had married Dorothy Horsfall. Frank Horsfall, Dorothy's father, owned a lumberyard in Bridgeport. Prairie du Chien was expanding, and there was a need for new houses. Edwards used his contacts at Johns-Manville, where he had worked, and lumber from Horsfall's and started building saltbox houses in the new Mondell development. Seymour Edwards did everything—building, plumbing, heating, and electrical. In a small community, one could not specialize and hope to survive. The family lived next to the new shop, which included a store selling appliances. Though busy, Edwards was active in bringing leisure activities to the community, helping found the Prairie du Chien Country Club and the Prairie du Chien Flying Club. Brian, Seymour's son, returned to Prairie du Chien and now owns Edwards' Plumbing and Heating. Seymour and Dorothy's daughter, Rita, was one of the first female master plumbers in Georgia. (Courtesy the Edwards family.)

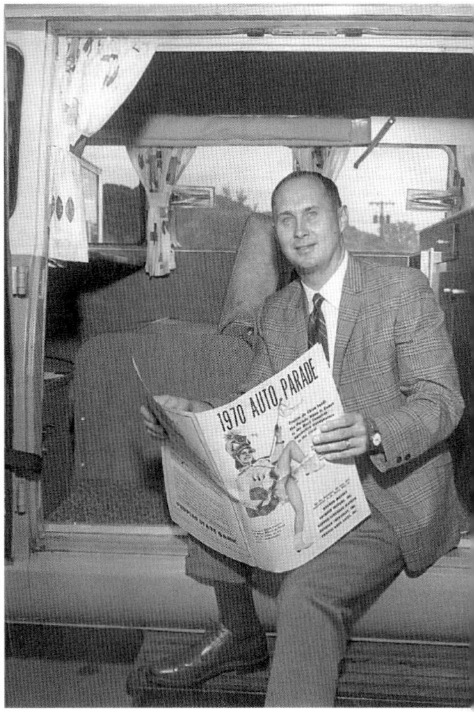

Frederick G. Huebsch Jr.
Frederick Huebsch's father opened a Chevrolet dealership in McGregor, Iowa, in 1938. Fred, though only nine, was part of the business, and continued to help throughout high school and while getting his degree from the University of Iowa.

After college, Fred joined the US Air Force, planning to make the military his career. In 1948, his father opened a dealership in Prairie du Chien. Business boomed, so he informed Fred that he was to return home and work at the family business. Within a few years, Fred took over the dealerships, closing the one in Iowa. His positive personality, active participation in community organizations, and honesty kept his customers returning. Under Fred's management from 1957 to 2000, Huebsch Chevrolet accounted for over 50 percent of the new-car sales in town.

Fred served as mayor of the City of Prairie du Chien from 1979 to 1980, welcoming Jimmy Carter to the city when the president arrived on the *Delta Queen*. Fred helped found the Prairie du Chien Historical Society in 1996, and served as the leading force on the board of the Prairie du Chien Memorial Hospital as it raised funds for the construction of a new facility. (Courtesy *The Courier Press*.)

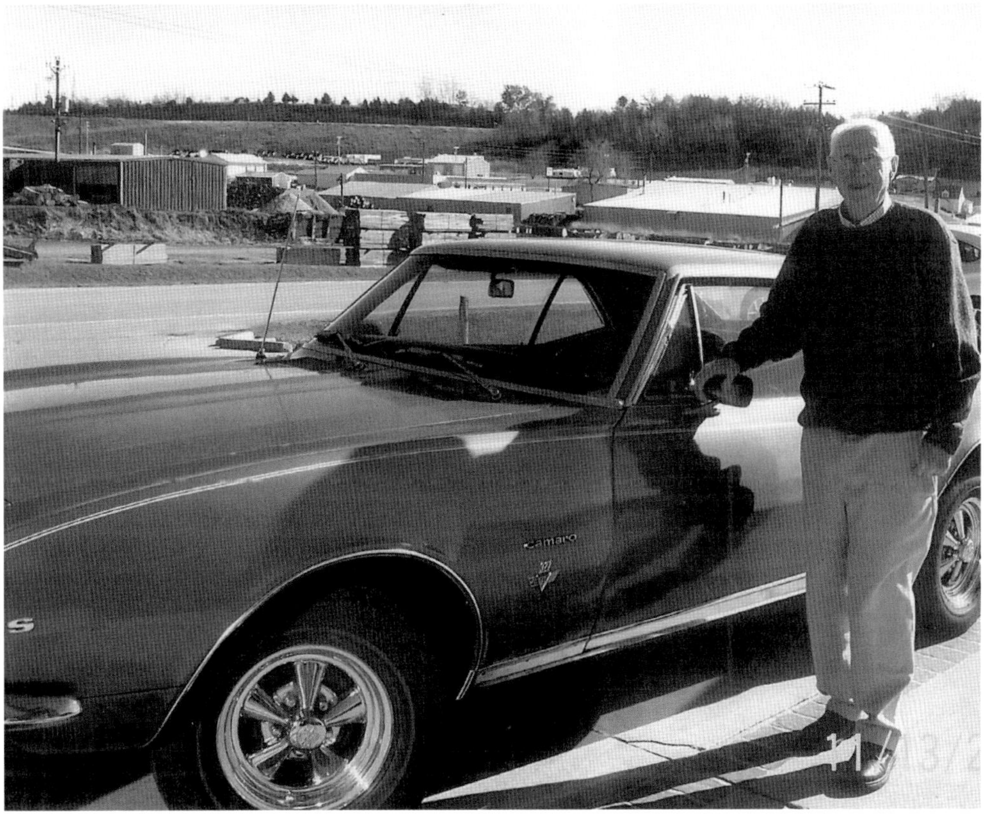

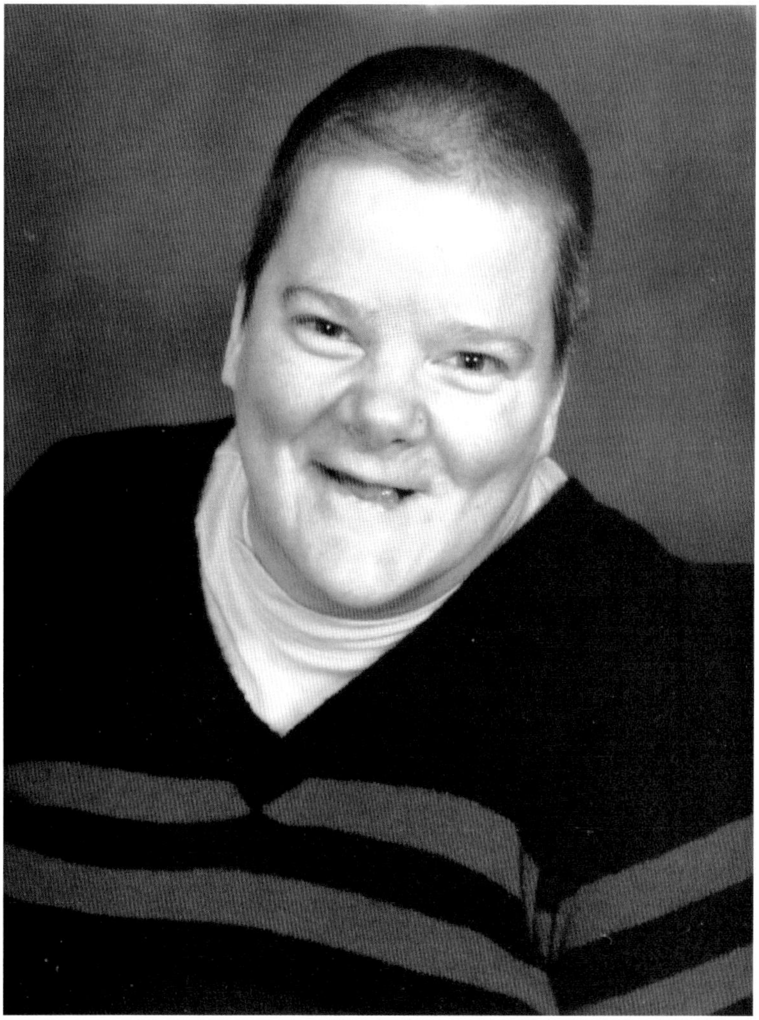

Lori Jane Knapp

When Lori Jane Knapp entered the world in 1959, little did she or her family realize the impact she would have on the lives of so many people. Due to complications at birth, Lori was born with cerebral palsy and developmental disabilities. Lori lived at home with her parents and two older brothers, but as she grew, her parents, Don and Bette, were advised to move Lori to a state institution. There, she would receive "better care." At the age of five, Lori entered Central Wisconsin Colony and became one of hundreds of children in the facility.

To keep the family connected, Don and Bette drove to Madison every other weekend. They stayed in a motel, where Lori joined them, but Lori was not thriving. Don and Bette wanted something better for their daughter. They began to work with various government agencies to formulate a new kind of community living for Lori. The result was an innovative model for providing services for children with disabilities.

In November 1972, Lori moved into the Lori Knapp Home in Prairie du Chien, located only blocks from her family. She was joined by seven other disabled children. Lori's residence was the first group home in Wisconsin and one of the first in the United States. It has grown to become the Lori Knapp Companies. Run by Lori's brother Don, it continues to help disabled people and their families across Wisconsin. (Courtesy the Knapp family.)

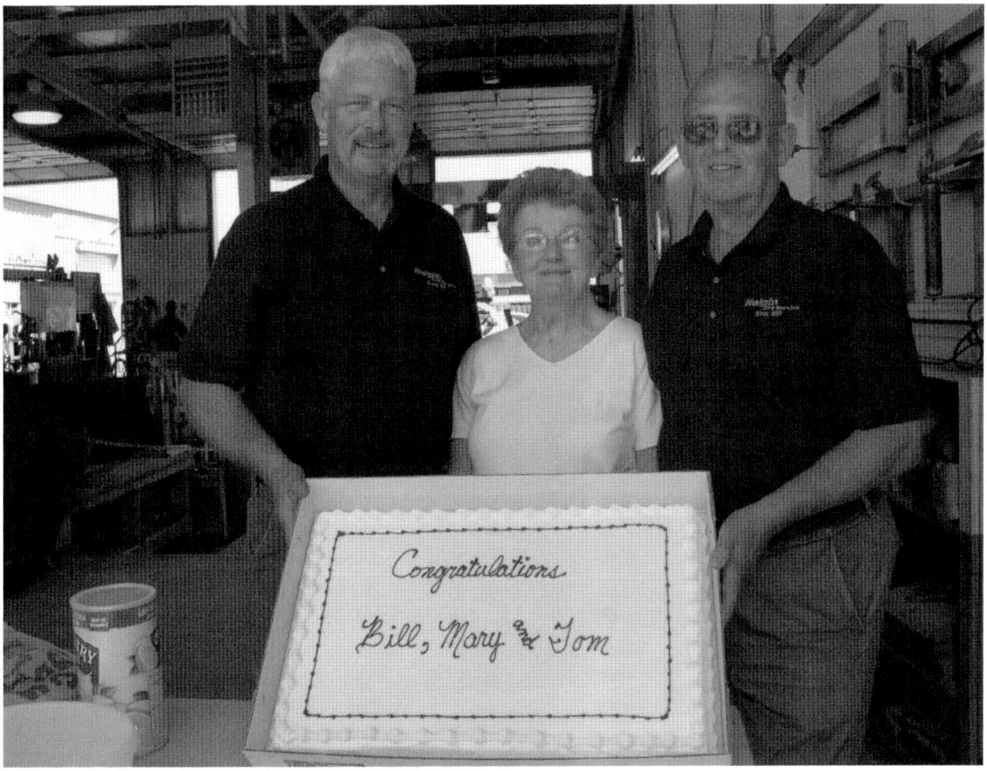

William T. and Marietta Jane Halpin
When a tornado devastated Bill and Mary Halpin's tire shop in 1958, along with much of Elkader, Iowa, they looked to Prairie du Chien to relocate. They reestablished their business in the little frame building on Blackhawk Avenue, with Bill and Herb Ellis changing tires under the shade of a cottonwood tree. Little by little, Bill and Mary (right and center) improved and expanded their facility, adapting to radial tires and adding brake and exhaust repair. They introduced more equipment to take care of commercial customers. Their son Tom (left) now owns and manages Halpin Tire Service. Bill visits occasionally to chat with customers and keep abreast of the ever-changing business climate. (Courtesy the Halpin family.)

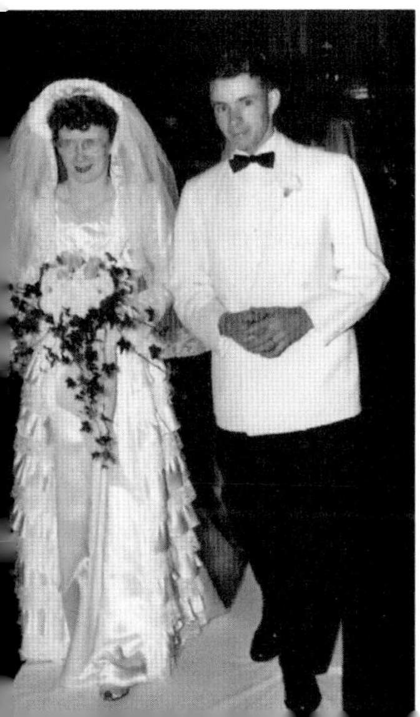

Franklin M. and Patricia A. Tiller
In 1950, Frank and Pat Tiller purchased the Grelle building and opened Tiller's Furniture Plaza, continuing a tradition of furniture sales at that location. They moved their inventory to a new building 20 years later, expanding to carry floor covering, and Frank and Pat's children carry on the business. In 2001, Frank and Pat received the C.F. LaPointe Award for their many years of service to the community. They sponsor an educational award given to a student graduating from Prairie Catholic Schools. (Courtesy the Tiller family.)

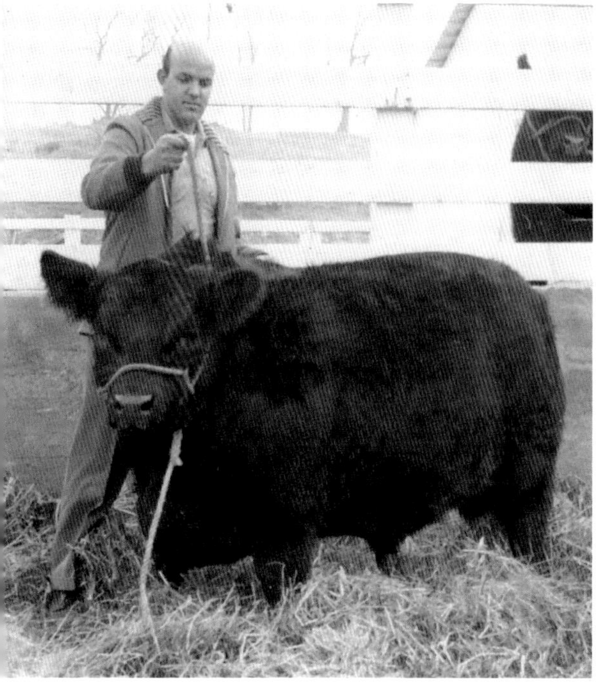

Bernard F. Pedretti
On one of his bread routes for Bohonek's Bakery, Bernard Pedretti met his future wife, Darlene. They opened their own business, Prairie Maid Bakery, in Prairie du Chien, and operated it for over 25 years. Upon learning that Frank Ahrens was selling his herd of Black Angus, Pedretti bought the cattle. He joined the American Angus Association in 1959, and the family became involved in breeding and showing cattle, focusing on performance breeding. The bulls he bred consistently ranked at the top of the Wisconsin Beef Improvement Bull Test and in bull testing in Iowa, Minnesota, Indiana, and Montana. In 1984, Bernard Pedretti was named Wisconsin's Seedstock Producer of the Year. In 2013, the American Angus Association recognized the Mill Coulee Angus with the Historic Angus Herd Award. Bernard and Darlene's sons, Mark and Tracey Pedretti, operate the farm, selling breeding stock to commercial cattlemen. (Courtesy the Pedretti family.)

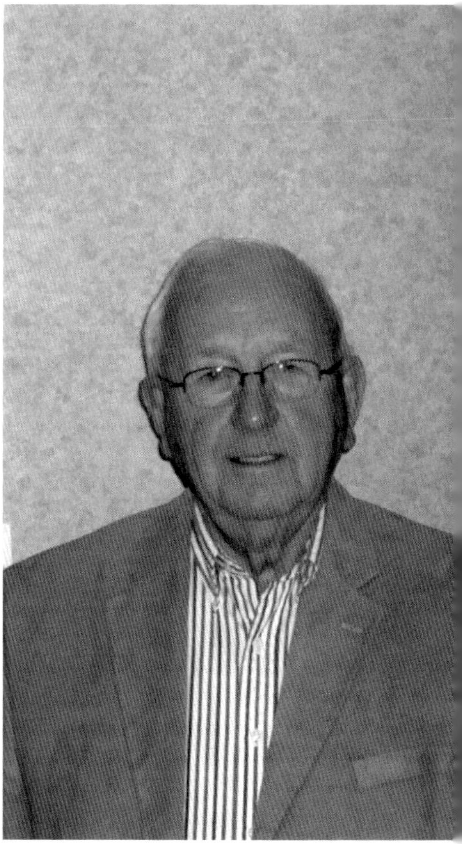

Thomas J. White
Tom White grew up learning the business of buying and selling cattle from his father, Oliver. The two formed a partnership, Oliver & Tom White Livestock, and owned a sale barn and small stockyard in Prairie du Chien. In the 1960s, Tom formed Tom White Dairy Cattle Inc., specializing in the buying and selling of Holstein dairy cattle. He established business relationships and close friendships across the United States and in parts of Canada and Central America. Tom's son Michael joined the business, learning the intricacies of cattle buying, and he now manages the family company. In 1972, Tom joined the board of directors of Peoples State Bank, a position he held for almost 40 years, serving as chairman for most of his tenure. Ron White worked with his uncle Oliver at the stock barn, the business eventually becoming Ron White Live Stock Dealers, which Ron and his son, Jeffrey, own and manage. (Courtesy Peoples State Bank.)

Franklin A. Weeks

His ingenuity and ability to foresee future markets allowed Frank Weeks to expand a modular-home business into a multidimensional company. Weeks had come to Prairie du Chien for a job on the railroad. While waiting, he started working with Valley Homes of Wisconsin and Harold "Jake" Valley. When the firm ran into trouble, Weeks bought out Jake in 1970. He reformatted and renamed the business Design Homes and began building homes of varying styles and of multiple stories. People ordering a Design Home often needed loans, so Weeks formed DH Mortgage. Buying material in bulk led to the opening of Design Building Materials, a retail store. Over the years, Frank's son Randy learned the various divisions of the modular-home business and works today with the second and third generation of men hired by his father, Frank. Daughter Lori oversees advertising, and Lori's husband Jeff handles outside sales. A hobby of Frank's was to build satellite receiving equipment, so he designed equipment to spin aluminum into a perfect parabolic dish. This grew into DH Satellite, one of the two largest manufacturers of parabolic antennas in the United States. The dishes receive satellite signals for data, television, radio, and radar. A vast majority of television stations and cable companies use DH products. With the popularity of solar energy, Weeks adapted the stands for the dishes to hold a nest of solar panels, adding another component to DH. With so much going on, Weeks began Deer Valley as a fun project for the whole family, and the fun led to a 27-hole golf course and water park managed by his granddaughter and her husband. (Courtesy the Weeks family.)

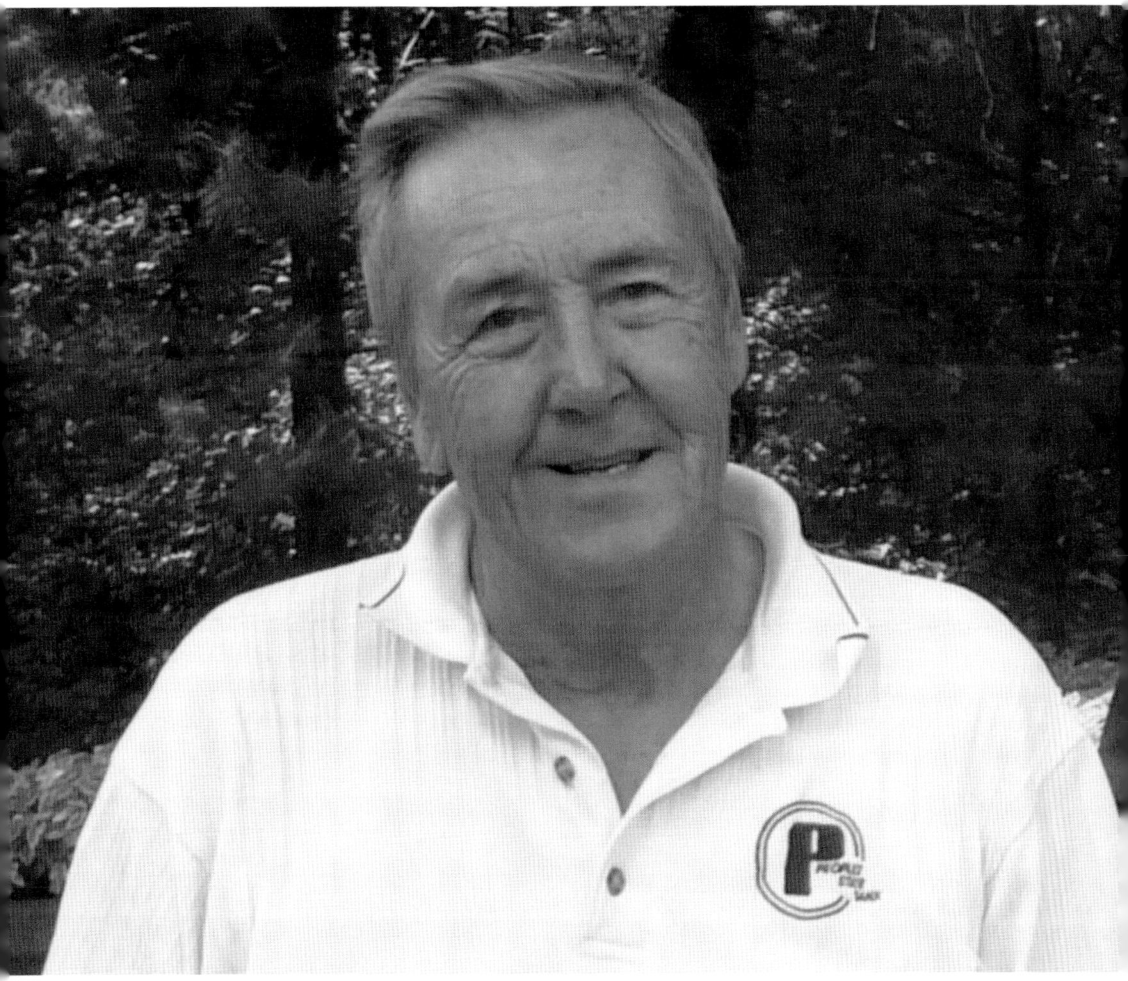

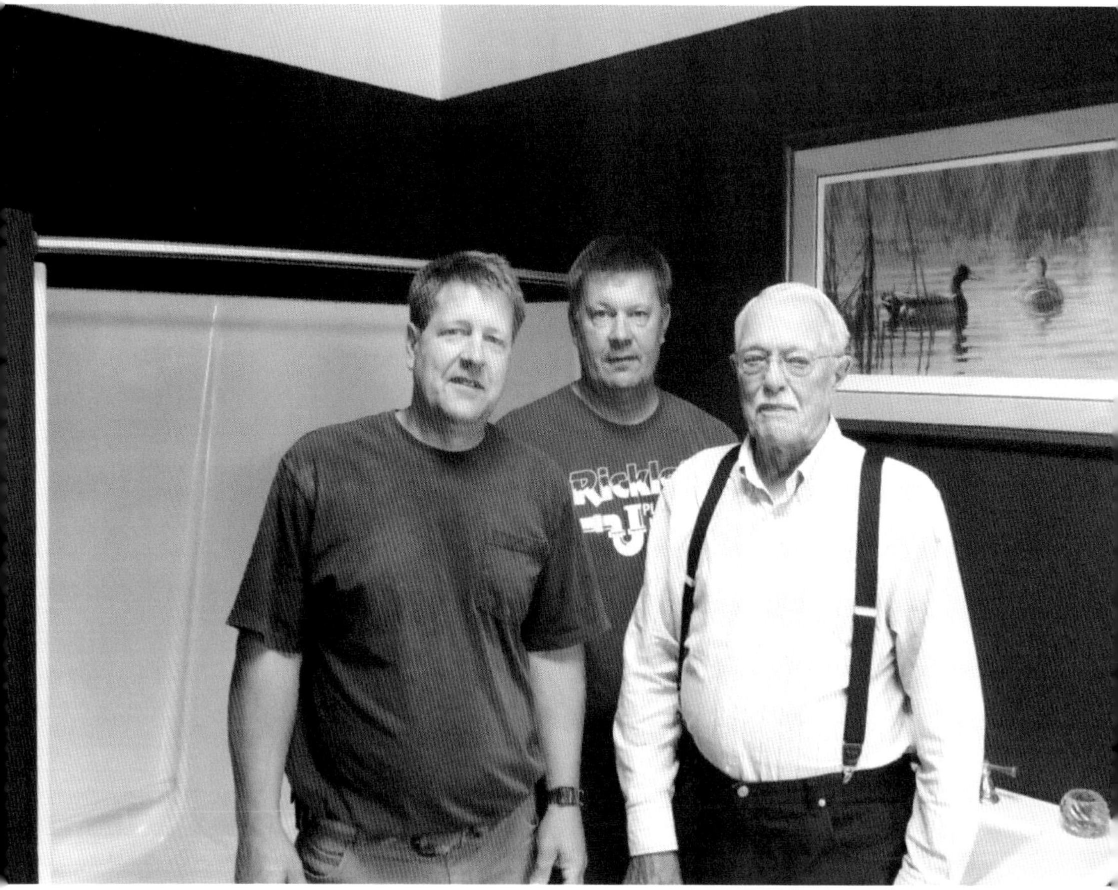

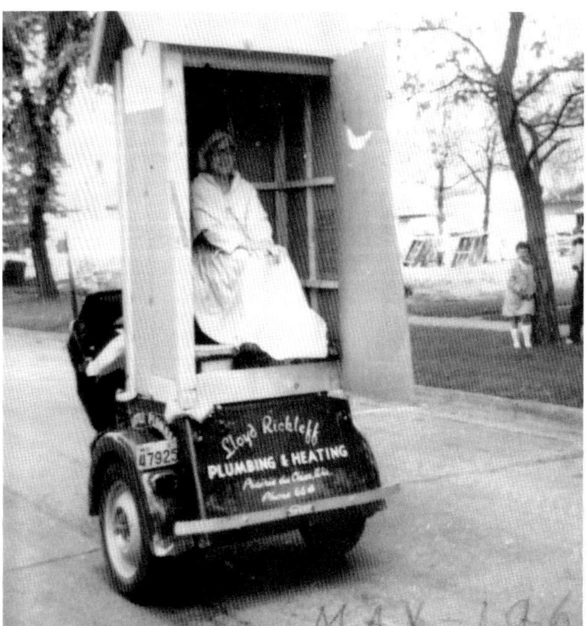

Lloyd C. Rickleff

When Lloyd Rickleff (above right) moved from the country, he went looking for a job. There was nothing available at the Prairie Cabinet Shop, so he took up an apprenticeship with John Lenhart, a plumber. He opened his own plumbing business in a warehouse owned by Peter Panka in late 1950s and then purchased Leo Woodnal's blacksmith shop. Rickleff could be seen on his cycle, "the Little Plumber," motoring from one service call to another. Doug (above left) served an apprenticeship under his father and is now the master plumber, preparing to mentor his own son. Steve (above center) takes care of the heating and air conditioning. At left is the Little Plumber with Lloyd's daughter Vicki Rickleff. (Both, courtesy the Rickleff family.)

Robert G. Dillman, Bruce A. Dillman, and Blair E. Dillman

Ernest "Doc" Dillman taught his sons the value of hard work. Bob (center) was a trumpet player who, as a high school student, began playing at area dances. For over 60 years, he led Dixieland bands. He worked as a salesman for Huebsch Chevrolet, WPRE, and Dillman Equipment. He was elected to the county board and served for 34 years as chairman, the longest-serving chairman in the county's 200-year history.

Bruce (left) entered the family business of Prairie Sand & Gravel and Prairie Ready-Mix after earning a degree in engineering. With Blair (right), they started Dillman Brothers Asphalt. In 1980, Bruce purchased the equipment construction division of Boeing Aerospace and moved it, operating as Bituma Construction. He sold the business and then, in 1994, founded Dillman Equipment, which his son Brian manages. Bruce holds many patents in the road-construction industry. (Courtesy Joann Evans.)

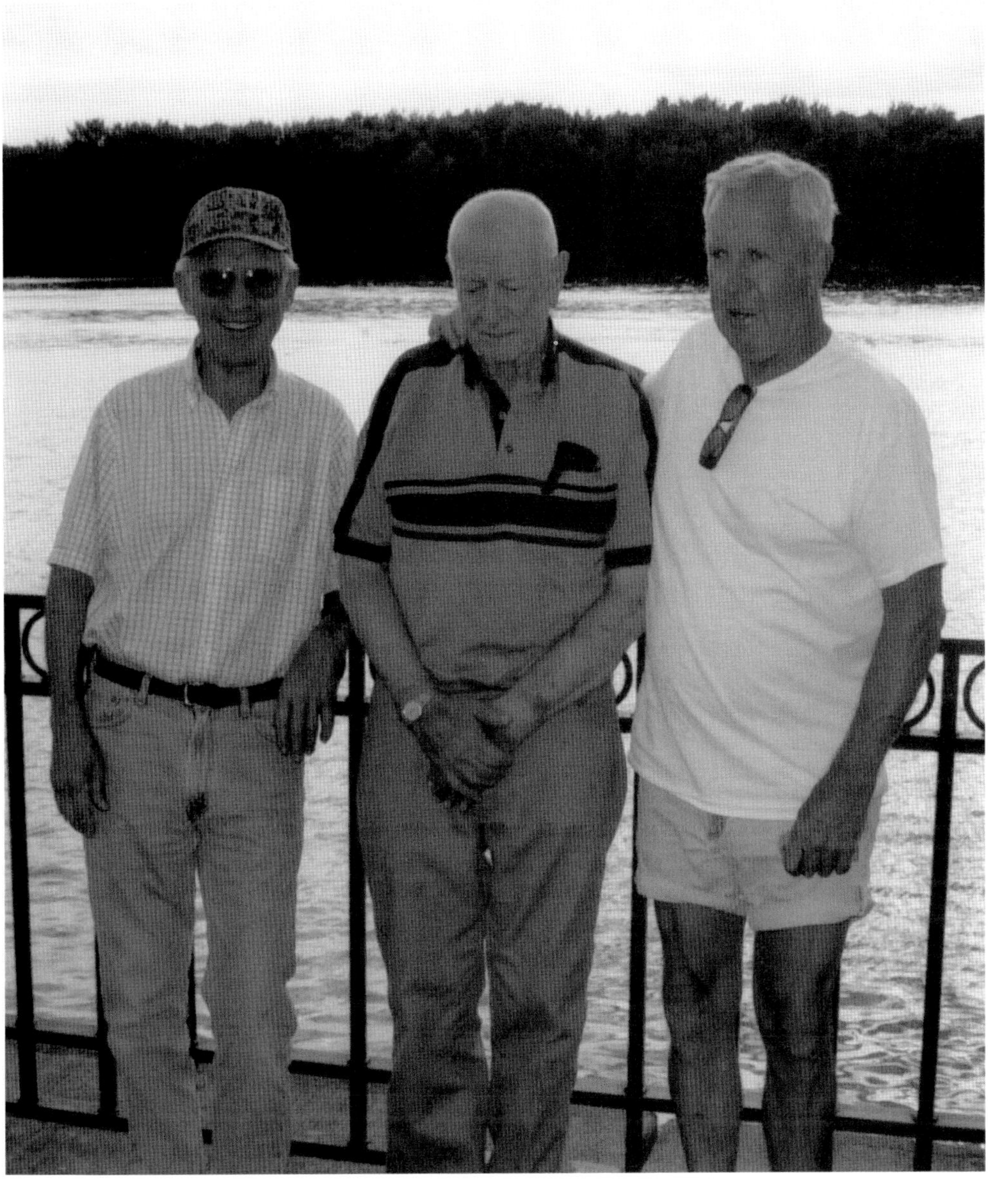

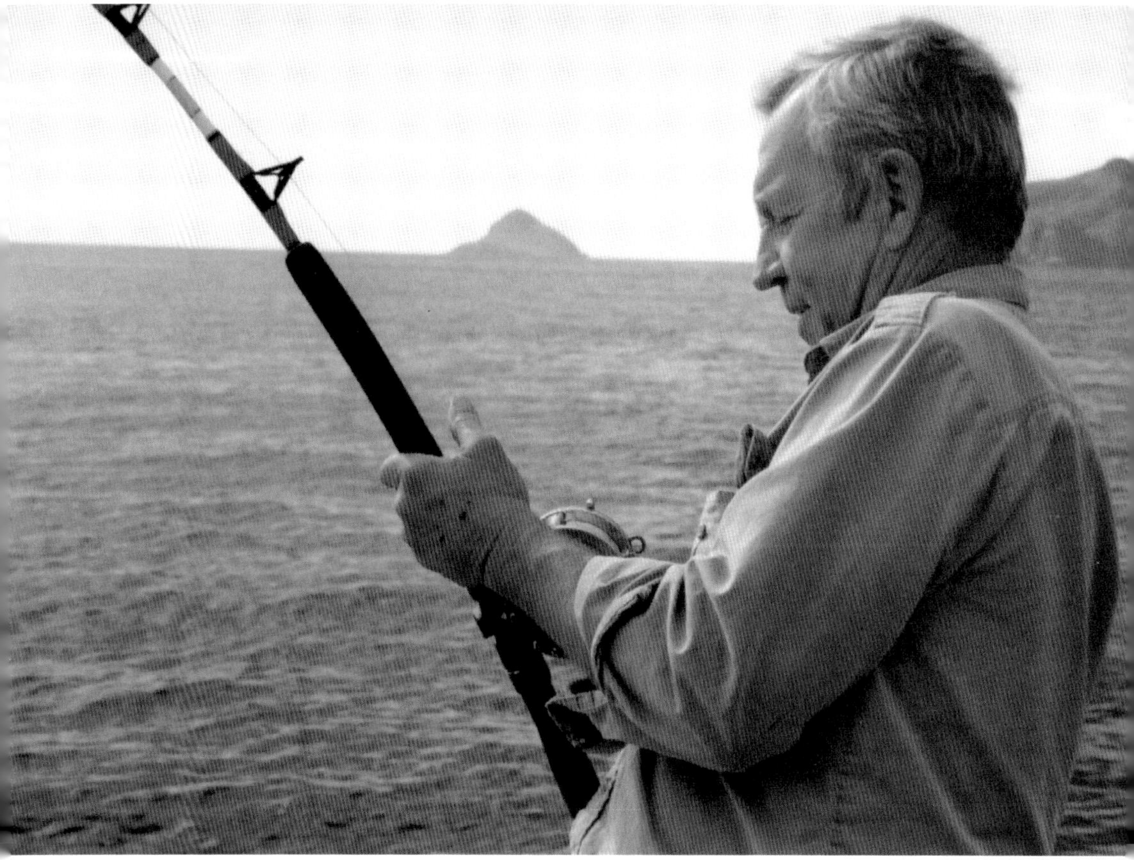

Blair Dillman

Blair continues to operate Prairie Sand & Gravel and Prairie Ready-Mix, having expanded it to the largest firm in Wisconsin. He manages and personally oversees the family corporations from the cab of his pickup truck. But it is his love of the Mississippi River and history that drive him. He constantly has numerous projects in the works, reflecting his eclectic interests. He monitors the flock of Canada geese he has adopted and the status of a Mississippi dredge boat. Through his determination, relentless energy, use of heavy equipment, and acquisition of historic building materials and elements, Blair has turned a barn into a restaurant complex and golf course; relocated a tobacco warehouse and converted it to a retail furniture store; stabilized an empty cannery into an extensive shop featuring home decor, gifts, and gourmet food; and resurrected a derelict 1864 hotel into a reception center. He restored the French Store, one of the earliest commercial buildings in Prairie du Chien, and landscaped property facing the Mississippi River into campgrounds. And he is always looking for more to do. (Courtesy Joann Evans.)

CHAPTER THREE

Educators and Active Minds

Each day we live in a world throbbing with romance, adventure, mystery, and fascination. All we need to do is open the windows of our mind.

—John M. Scott, 1963

Willard Keyes taught for a bit at Prairie du Chien in 1818. Though he had a great number of pupils, he moved on. For the next quarter of a century, private tutors educated children, or parents sent their sons and daughters to boarding schools. In 1841, a school district was organized, but the officers were unable to raise enough money for a school, so instructions were conducted in homes. Finally, a two-story stone building was erected in 1857, but only children of families living in "Lowertown" benefited from this educational organization.

About the same time, attempts were made to sustain a Catholic school. Twice, grade schools opened, taught by religious orders. But they only operated for a few years in each instance.

In December 1866, a number of German citizens met for the purpose of organizing an independent German school, where German could be taught without regard to religious affiliation. They built a small brick school, and instructions were successfully held until 1878.

Credit for the permanent establishment of education, public and private, in Prairie du Chien goes to John Lawler. In 1872, Lawler and Rev. P.M. Abbelen convinced the School Sisters of Notre Dame to send teachers from Milwaukee to open St. Mary's Academy for young women. The sisters in time assumed charge of graded schools at St. Gabriel and St. John Parishes. Lawler then purchased the building used by the failed Prairie du Chien College, which Lawler had helped to found, and gave it to the Society of Jesus for a school of higher learning for young men. Prairie du Chien had incorporated as a city in 1872; three years later, the first board of the independent Prairie du Chien school district was elected. In his first action as board president, John Lawler drew up specifications for the levying of a tax to build a high school. The school opened in 1876, along with a frame building for a grade school. The board assumed ownership of the Lowertown School for the First Ward. Within a few years, Lawler made sure grade schools opened in the Third and Fourth Wards. For almost 100 years, Prairie du Chien supported three grade schools and three high schools. St. Mary provided instruction until 1968; Campion closed in 1975. The Prairie du Chien School District has expanded beyond the municipal boundaries of the city.

Over the years, Campion, St. Mary's, and the Prairie du Chien Public School attracted men and women dedicated to teaching, in and out of the classroom. Many spent their entire teaching career at Prairie du Chien, some even coming out of retirement to teach additional years. These teachers inspired students to not only learn, but to be inquisitive and strive to excel. The students responded to these instructors and administrators' challenges and expressed their admiration in many ways, including becoming teachers.

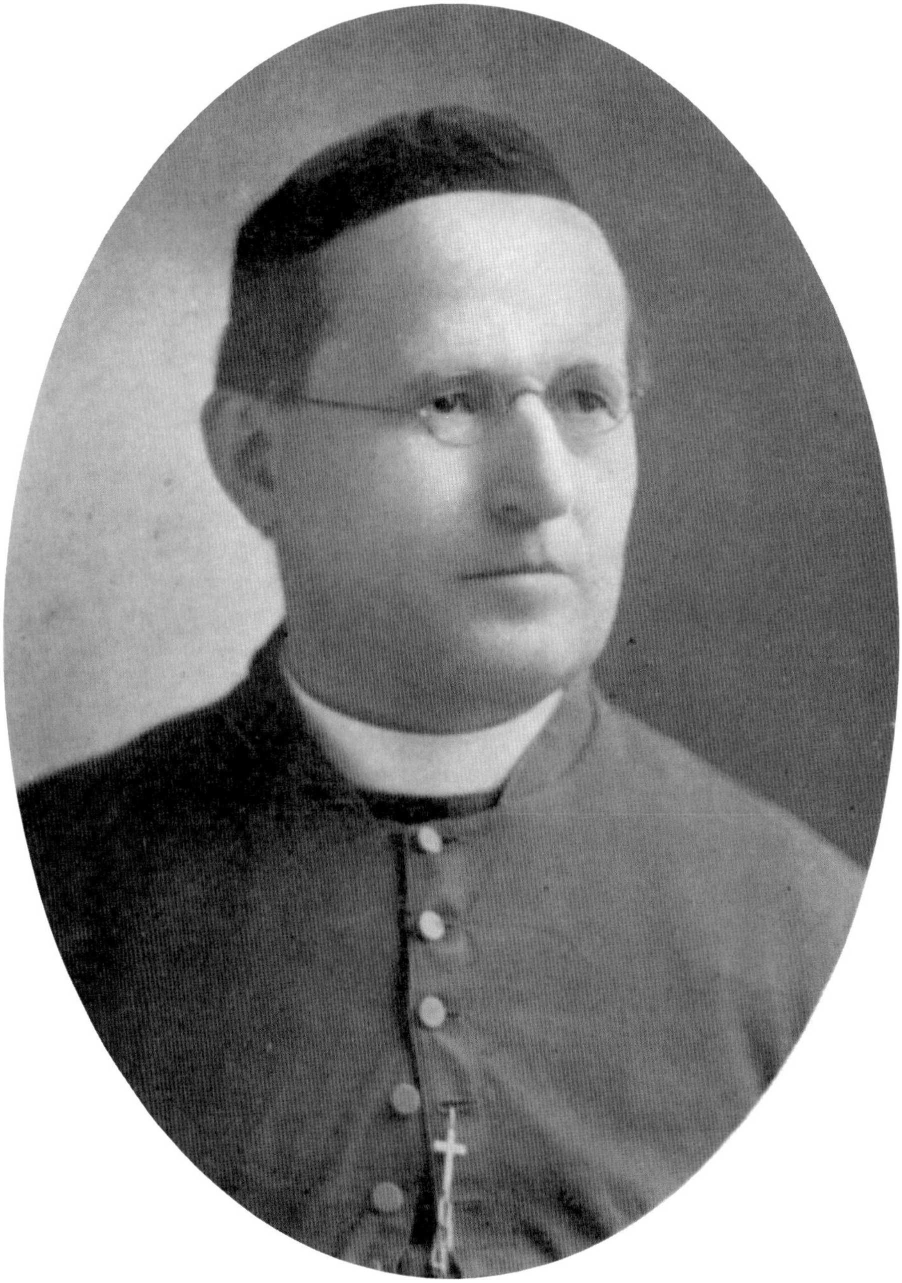

Rev. Peter Mathias Abbelen

When Peter Abbelen became pastor of St. Gabriel in 1872, he devoted much energy to the establishment of Catholic education in Prairie du Chien. He traveled to Milwaukee and convinced the School Sisters of Notre Dame to come to the community and teach. In the spring of 1872, three sisters arrived and assumed charge of the grade school at St. Gabriel. Then, in the fall, through the generosity of John Lawler, they began instructions at St. Mary's Institute. In 1888, a parish school was built on the grounds of St. Mary's for the children of St. John Parish. Because of Father Abbelen's determination and persuasiveness, Catholic education continues at Prairie du Chien. (Courtesy the Antoine family.)

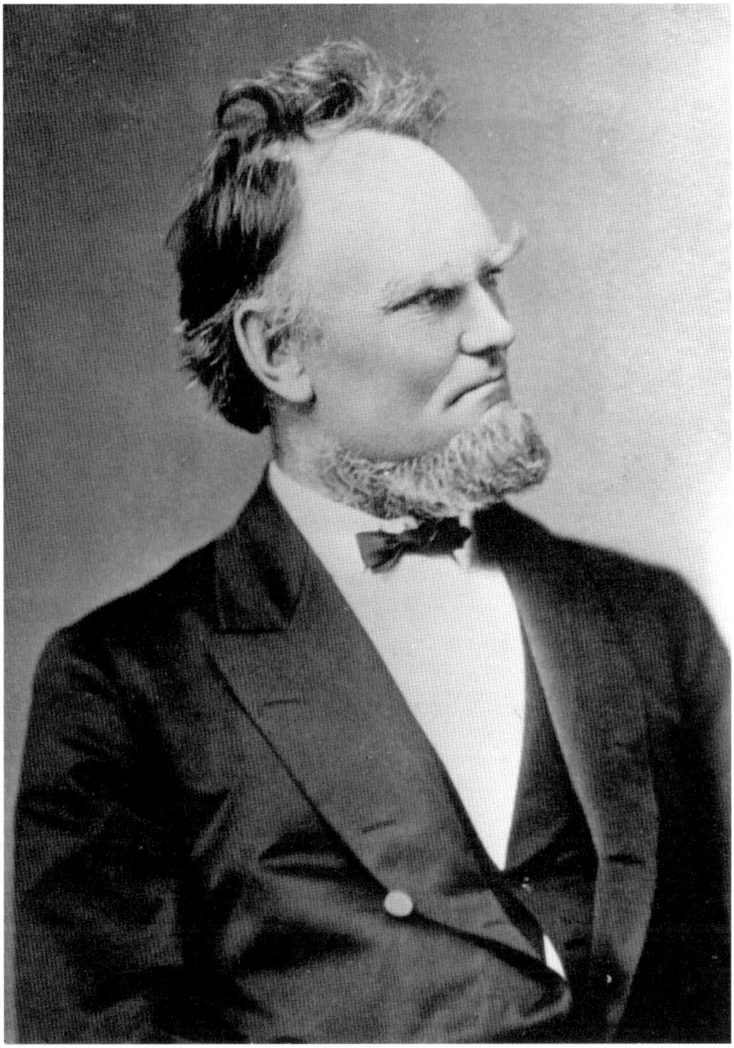

John Lawler

Lawler came to Prairie du Chien in 1857 as station agent of the Milwaukee & Mississippi Railroad. He was involved in transporting goods to the West, which led to the formation of his company and the construction of the Pile and Pontoon Bridge across the Mississippi River.

John Lawler was a devout Catholic, and Father Abbelen prevailed upon him to donate the land for St. Mary's Institute. Lawler gave seven acres to the School Sisters of Notre Dame, also bestowing funds for the construction of the first school building in 1872, and then a second in 1883. An advocate of education, Lawler was the driving force behind the establishment of the Prairie du Chien school district. When the first school board was elected in 1875, Lawler was elected representative of the citizens at large and president of the board. The following year, Lawler acquired the building that had housed the Prairie du Chien College and then St. John's College. He remodeled the structure and gave it to the Society of Jesus. They named the structure Lawler Hall; this was the beginning of Campion College, later Campion Jesuit High School. Pope Leo XIII awarded him a knighthood in the Order of St. Gregory for his work to further Catholic education.

A park, located along the waterfront north of the site of the pontoon bridge built by John Lawler, is named in his honor. (Courtesy Prairie du Chien Historical Society, Martner Collection.)

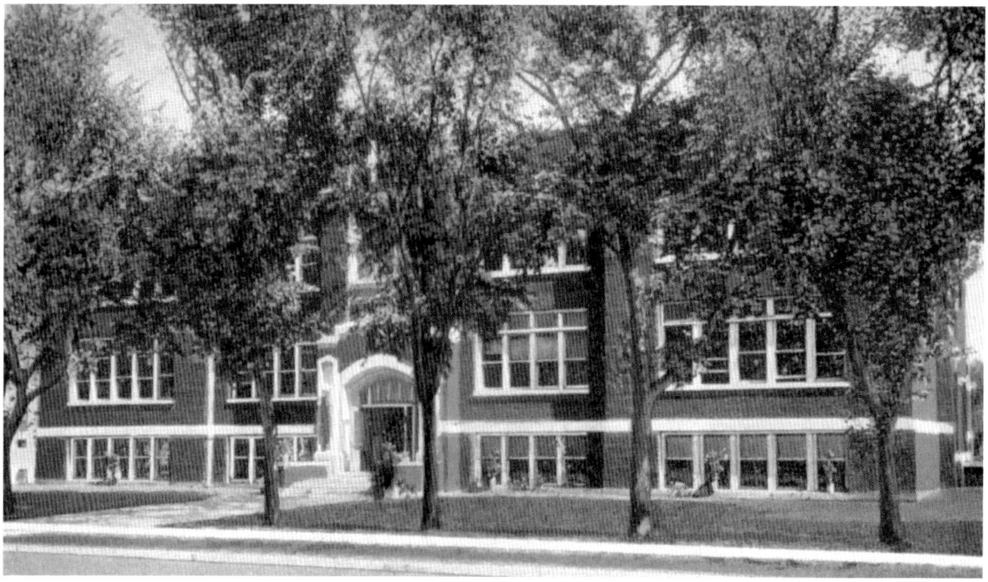

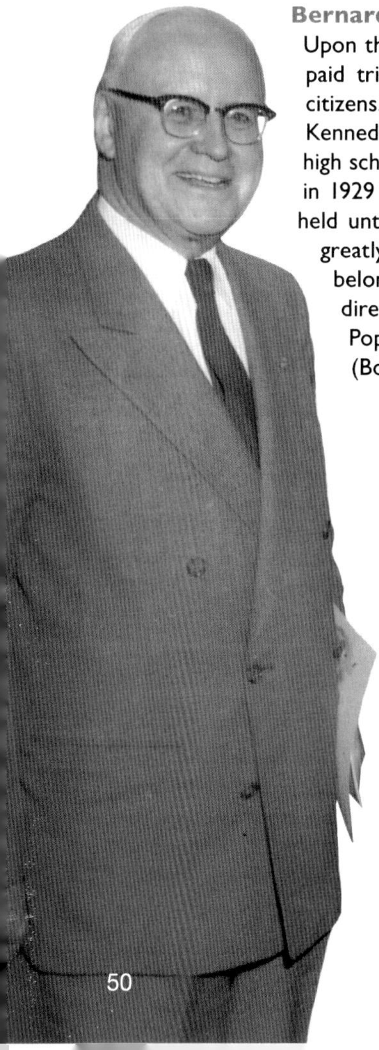

Bernard A. Kennedy

Upon the death of Bernard Kennedy, the Wisconsin legislature on April 5, 1977, paid tribute to the man cited as "one of Prairie du Chien's most prominent citizens." The Prairie du Chien School District had already acknowledged B.A. Kennedy's commitment to education in 1972 by naming the grade school and junior high school complex (above) in his honor. Kennedy had come to Prairie du Chien in 1929 from Omaha, Nebraska, to be superintendent of schools, a position he held until 1962. Under his administration, the number of high school graduates greatly increased and the education complex grew. A devout Catholic, Kennedy belonged to the Knights of Columbus and served as state deputy and supreme director of the organization. Because of his service to the Catholic Church, Pope Pius XII awarded him Knight Commander of the Order of St. Gregory. (Both, courtesy Prairie du Chien Historical Society, Howe Collection.)

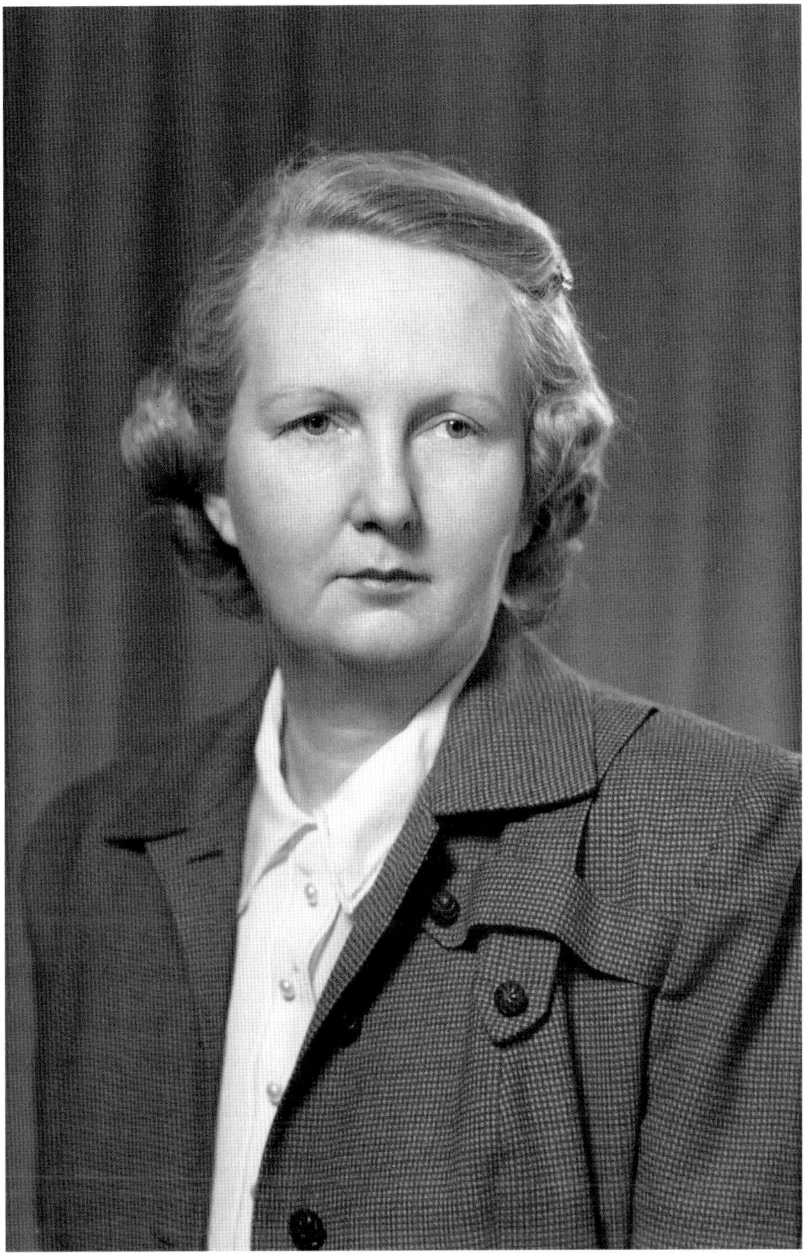

Margaret M. Garrity

In 1932, Margaret Garrity was a member of the last class to graduate from St. Mary's College in Prairie du Chien. Respecting her father's wishes, instead of accepting a job offer in Mexico, she stayed in Prairie du Chien and obtained a position teaching high school Spanish and business arts. She was made assistant principal of the high school under B.A. Kennedy, a position she held for 20 years. The Garrity house was a gathering place for teachers, where bridge games ruled. Margaret Garrity retired, then, at the age of 70, returned to teaching, devoting a total of 40 years to education. She also managed her father's businesses and, with Lila Murton, a fellow teacher, operated Garrity's Jewelry Store. (Courtesy Prairie du Chien Historical Society, Peckham Collection.)

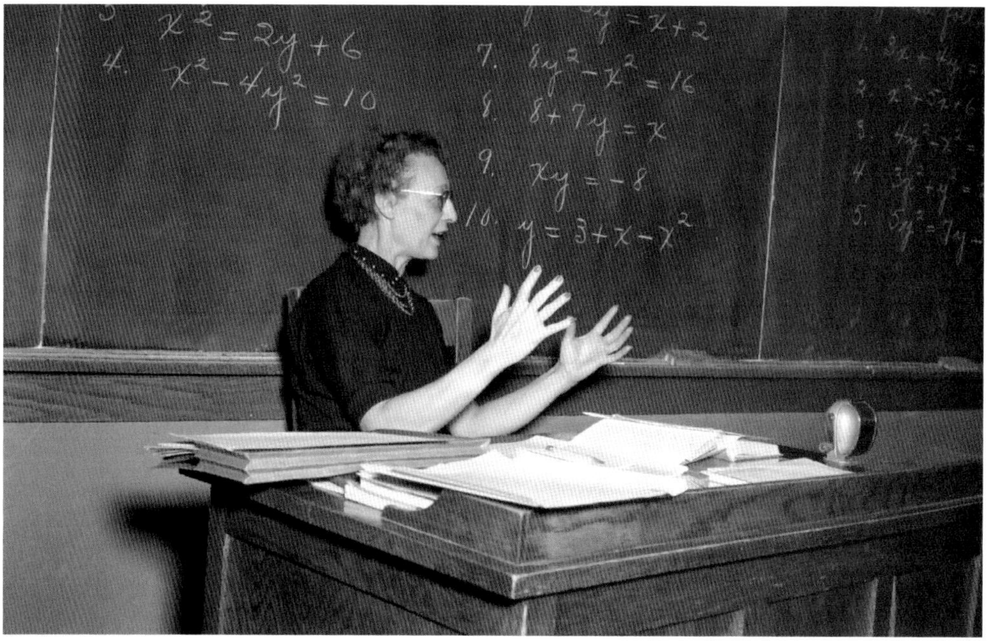

Violet E. Dohse

A graduate of St. Mary's Academy, Violet Dohse returned to Prairie du Chien after receiving her degree at the University of Wisconsin–Madison. For the next, 51 years, she taught mathematics in the public high school. Her students called her "Posey" behind her back, but Miss Dohse was a loved and respected teacher. In 1970, her students rewrote *The Night Before Christmas* in her honor.

Tom drew on the board
And was turning around;
Along came Miss Dohse
For an error she found!

A bundle of equations
She had in her mind,
She sounded like a computer
Just starting to unwind.

(Courtesy Prairie du Chien Historical Society, Peckham Collection.)

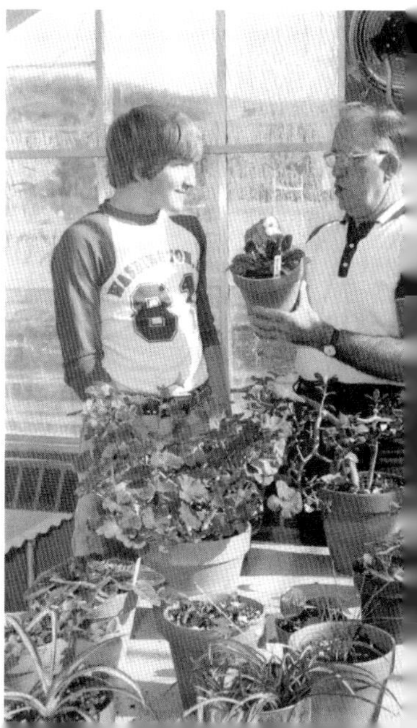

Guy C. Ralph

Growing up on a dairy farm, it was natural that Guy Ralph received his degree in agricultural education. He came to Prairie du Chien in 1946 and started the vocational-agriculture department at the high school. In 1980, he was awarded the Teacher of Teachers Gold Award by the National Vocational Agriculture Teachers' Association because of the number of students he had taught who were teaching agricultural studies in three states. Then, three years later, Ralph (right) was awarded an Honorary American Farmer's Degree at the National FFA Convention. (Courtesy Prairie du Chien Historical Society.)

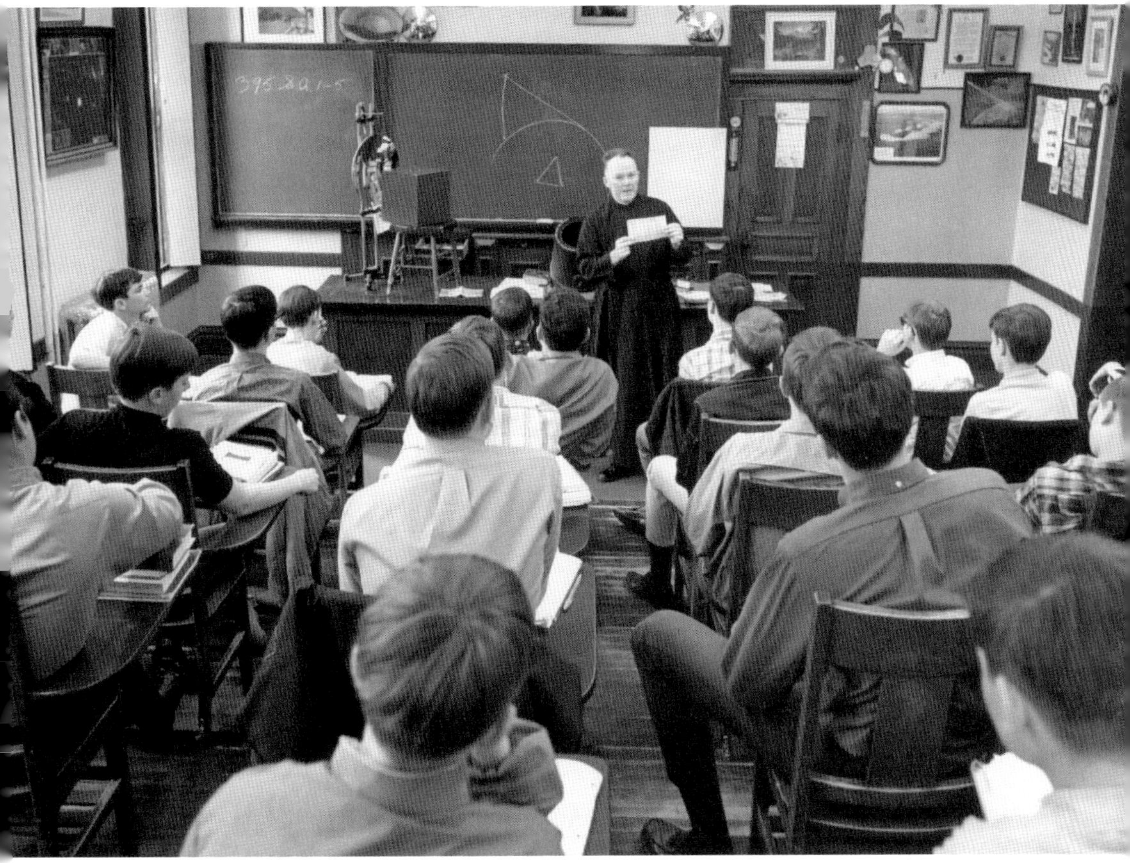

John M. Scott

A fellow teacher at Campion Jesuit High School called Father John Scott "the guru of demonstrations." With a deep, booming voice and dark hair that seemed to be charged with electricity, Father Scott was a strong presence, teaching physics with nonstop, hands-on activities in an age when most teaching involved lectures. In 1963, he wrote a textbook, *Adventures in Science*, which could be easily read and reflected his colorful use of words. Dr. Wernher von Braun wrote Father Scott, "I congratulate you on being the first priest to be the author of a textbook on general science. You have done truly yeoman service by turning the classroom into a launching pad of exciting ideas to boost the minds of the young into orbits of knowledge and inspiration." Father Scott taught and wrote all his life. In his numerous articles, his words combine a love of nature and science with the majesty of God. (Courtesy Jesuit Archives, Central United States.)

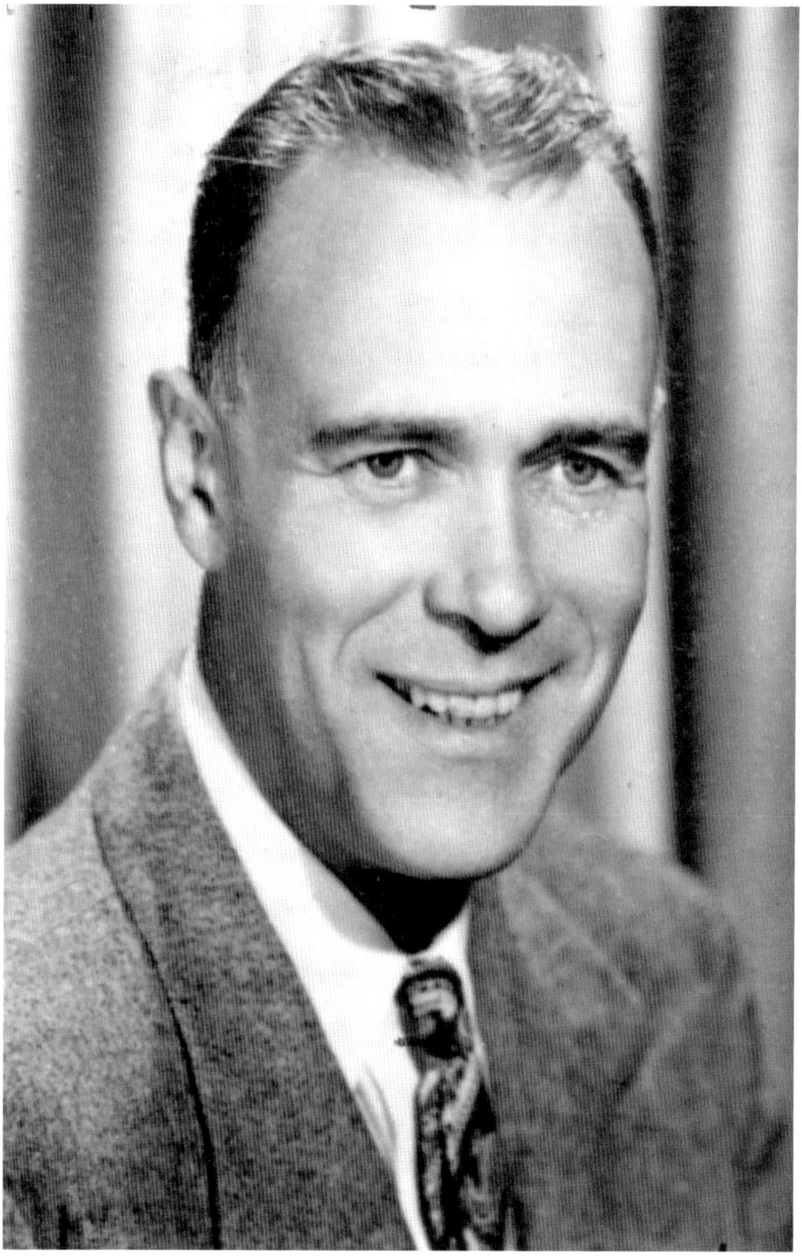

Sidney S. de Ranitz

When Prof. Sidney S. de Ranitz came to Campion Jesuit High School in 1939, he was a composer and accomplished musician. His symphony *The Creation* had been performed at the Century of Progress International Exposition in Chicago. With the construction of a new music hall, Professor de Ranitz formed a music department with a concert orchestra and a marching band, taught music theory, and gave lessons on every instrument, from drums to piano. He planned and produced biannual concerts for the Mother's Day weekend festivities. Professor de Ranitz composed the music and wrote the lyrics for "Campion Alma Mater" and wrote over 30 selections of music for the organ. (Courtesy Prairie du Chien Historical Society, Howe Collection.)

Maurice Oehler

For several years, Maury Oehler taught chemistry at Campion Jesuit High School, then left for work in the private sector. In 1976, John Mulrooney asked Oehler if he could substitute in the Prairie du Chien High School for an ill chemistry teacher. That substitution lasted for 20 years. One day, while reading *The Science Teacher*, Oehler saw an article about a teacher "out East" who had celebrated Mole Day. When the 1986 school year began, he mentioned it to his chemistry class, and the students thought it a good idea. By 1988, Mole Day was a big celebration at the high school. During an interview for a local television show, Terry Burrington suggested that Oehler start an organization for the celebration of Mole Day. Oehler put the idea to other high school chemistry teachers and received an overwhelming response. The National Mole Day Foundation began on May 15, 1991. In all, 400 teachers joined, and the first national celebration of Mole Day took place on October 23, 1991, from 6:02 a.m. to 6:02 p.m. Maury continued as director of the foundation, the leadership of which originated from his home in Prairie du Chien. He retired in 2013 and is now director emeritus, but still plans on attending the National Mole Day Foundation convention, held every other year with the Chem Ed Conference. He says, "The Mole Day breakfast is the big thing."

Oehler annually assigned his chemistry students a project: design something having to do with Mole Day. Kenny Quick and Tom Knickerbocker wrote the *Ten Commolements* in 1991, in honor of the beginning of National Mole Day. John Mundt, another of Oehler's students, drew the design for the initial Mole Day, which, along with the Ten Commolements, were printed on T-shirts. For over 20 years, Mundt created the artwork reflecting the latest theme for the T-shirts and website. (Author's collection.)

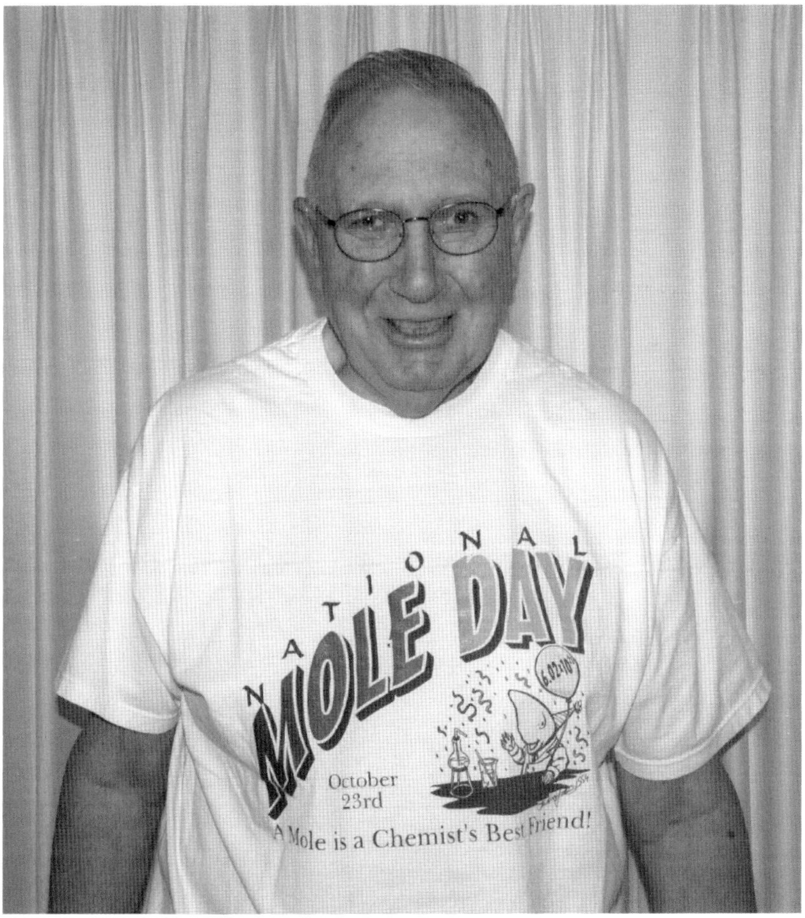

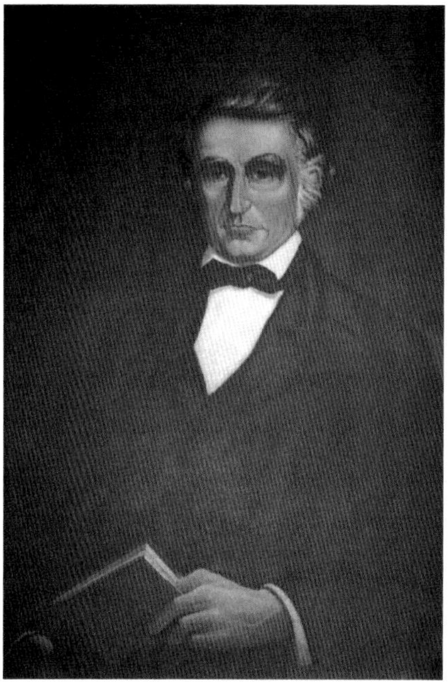

Dr. William Beaumont

William Beaumont was the post surgeon at Fort Mackinac in June 1822 when Alexis St. Martin was brought to him. St. Martin had been severely injured when a shotgun accidentally discharged. Under Beaumont's care, St. Martin survived, but the wound in his stomach never closed. Beaumont saw this as "an excellent opportunity for experimenting upon the gastric juice and process of digestion."

In 1828, Beaumont came to Fort Crawford as post surgeon. From December 1829 until April 1831, he performed another set of experiments on St. Martin, exploring the effects weather and temperature have on digestion, and comparing the digestion of vegetables to meat. When he completed his work in 1833, Beaumont published *Experiments and Observations on the Gastric Juice and Physiology of Digestion.* (Courtesy Prairie du Chien Historical Society.)

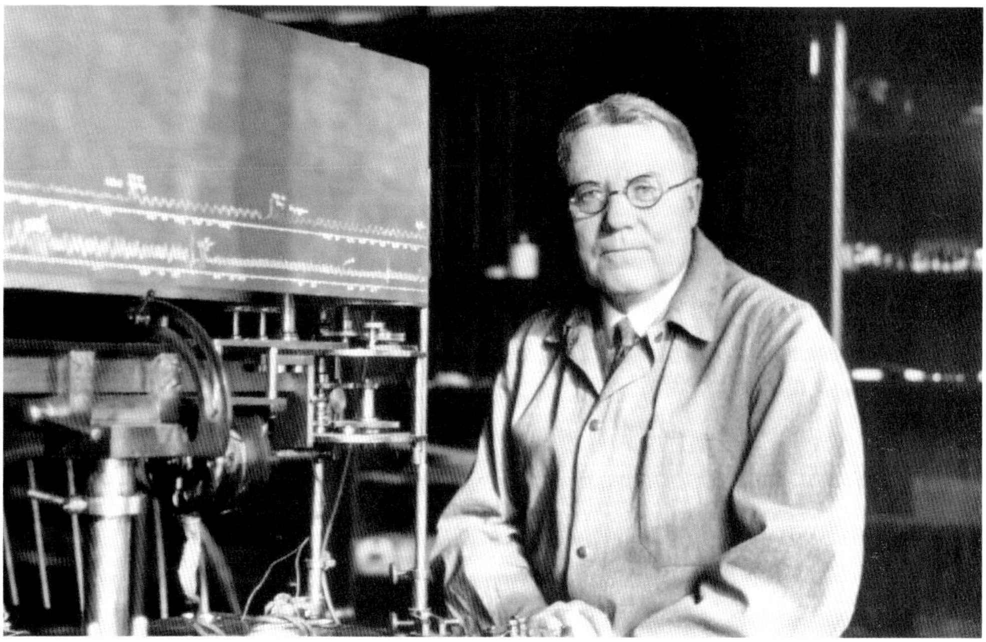

Dr. Walter Bradford Cannon

His early life in Prairie du Chien may have influenced Walter Cannon to follow in Dr. Beaumont's footsteps. At Harvard Medical School, Cannon used X-rays to explore the mechanism of swallowing and the movement of digestive organs. He noticed that fear affected digestion and first described the "flight or fight" response. In 1915, Cannon wrote *Bodily Changes in Pain, Hunger, Fear, and Rage.* During World War I, he served in hospitals, coming to realize the importance of replacing bodily fluids when a person has a loss of blood. (Courtesy the Harvard Medical Library in the Francis A. Countway Library of Medicine.)

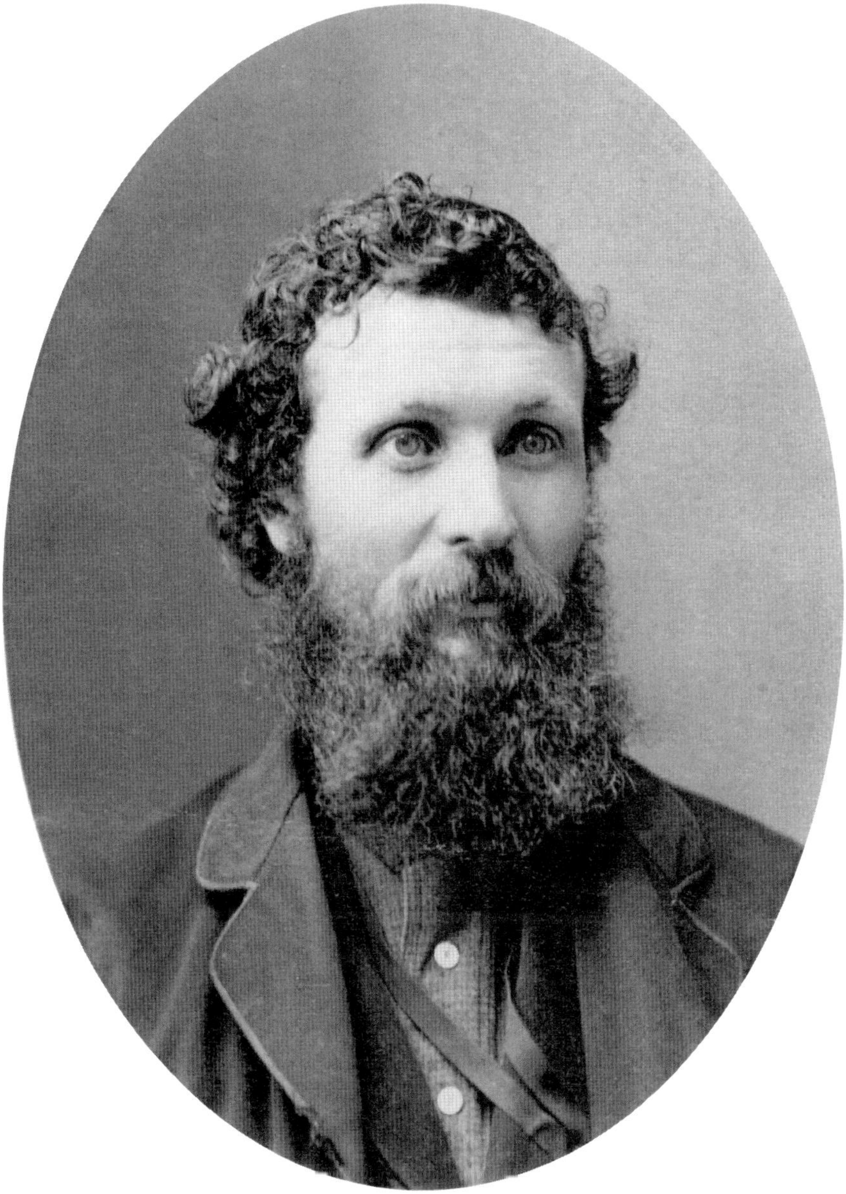

John Muir
After viewing Norman Wiard's invention, the *Lady Franklin*, at the 1860 Wisconsin State Fair, John Muir came to Prairie du Chien with Wiard to perfect the iceboat. When Wiard proved disorganized, Edward Pelton offered Muir a job as chore boy at the Mondell House. There, Muir met Emily Pelton, Edward's niece. About the same age, they developed a close friendship, and from 1864 until Muir died, they corresponded. When Emily moved to California to teach, she visited Muir in Yosemite in 1873; Muir traveled to see Emily in December the following year. Their correspondence lessened, Muir writing her an annual New Year's summary of his activities. But Muir always remembered Prairie du Chien, writing on January 1, 1883, "I once more wish you a happy New Year. About the 20th I think since the first New Year wish in the Mondell House; and many a change has taken place in those 20 years for both of us." (Courtesy Wisconsin Historical Society.)

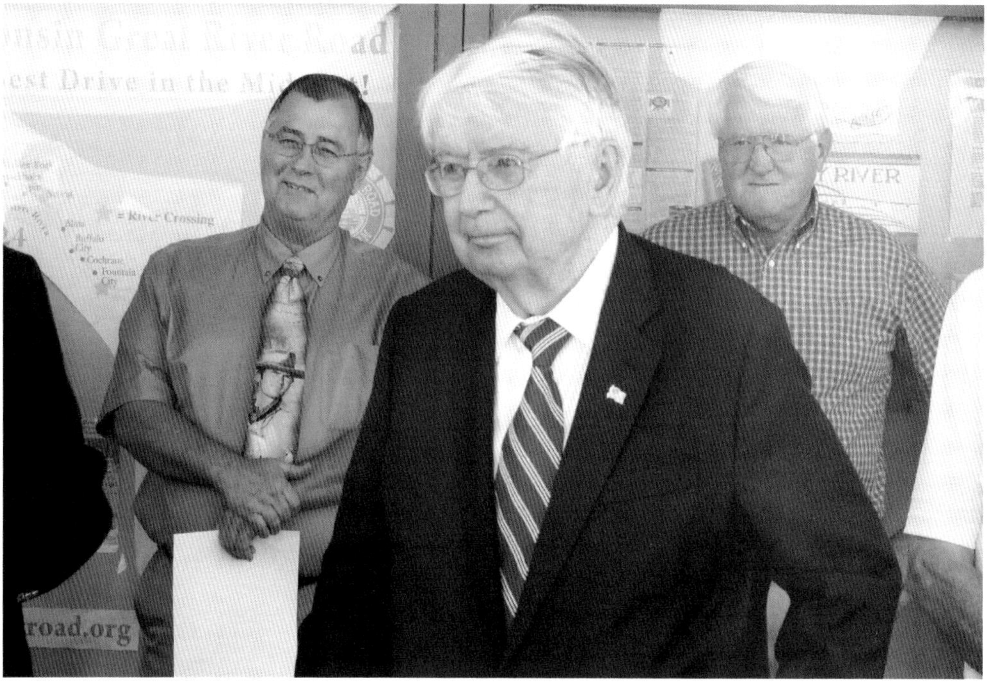

Patrick Joseph Lucey

For his education, Patrick Lucey attended Campion Jesuit High School. To return home for the weekend, he often rode his bicycle the 22 miles from Prairie du Chien to Ferryville.

After military service, Lucey began a career in politics that spanned over 60 years. He was elected governor of Wisconsin in 1971 and became the state's first four-term governor. Lucey became known for strengthening tourism and conservation efforts in the state. His far-reaching accomplishment was the formation of the University of Wisconsin system. After serving as ambassador to Mexico and running for vice president, Patrick Lucey retired. He was remembered in October 2013 when the 22-mile stretch of Highway 35 between Prairie du Chien and Ferryville was renamed the Governor Patrick Lucey Highway. (Courtesy *The Courier Press.*)

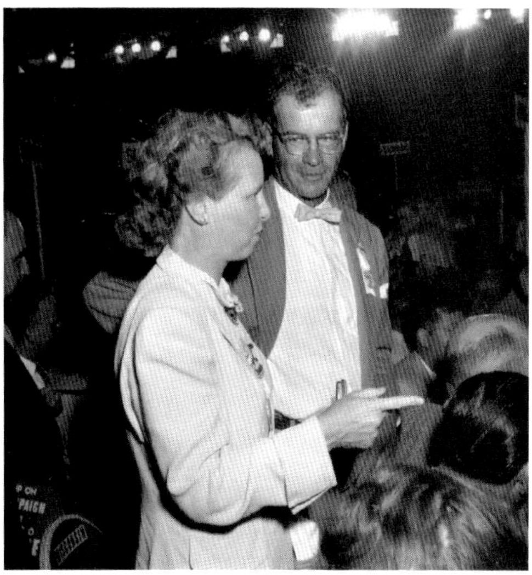

Marguerite A. Rogers

Marguerite Rogers was active in business and politics in a time when these pursuits were dominated by men. She served as Crawford County register of deeds for 13 years. During World War II, Rogers volunteered her services to the American Red Cross and continued to hold posts with the organization until 1992. An active Democrat, she ran for the state assembly and was elected to the Electoral College during the 1952 presidential campaign. She operated an abstract business, sold real estate, and built a subdivision. On the county board and city council, she served as council president. (Courtesy Wisconsin Historical Society.)

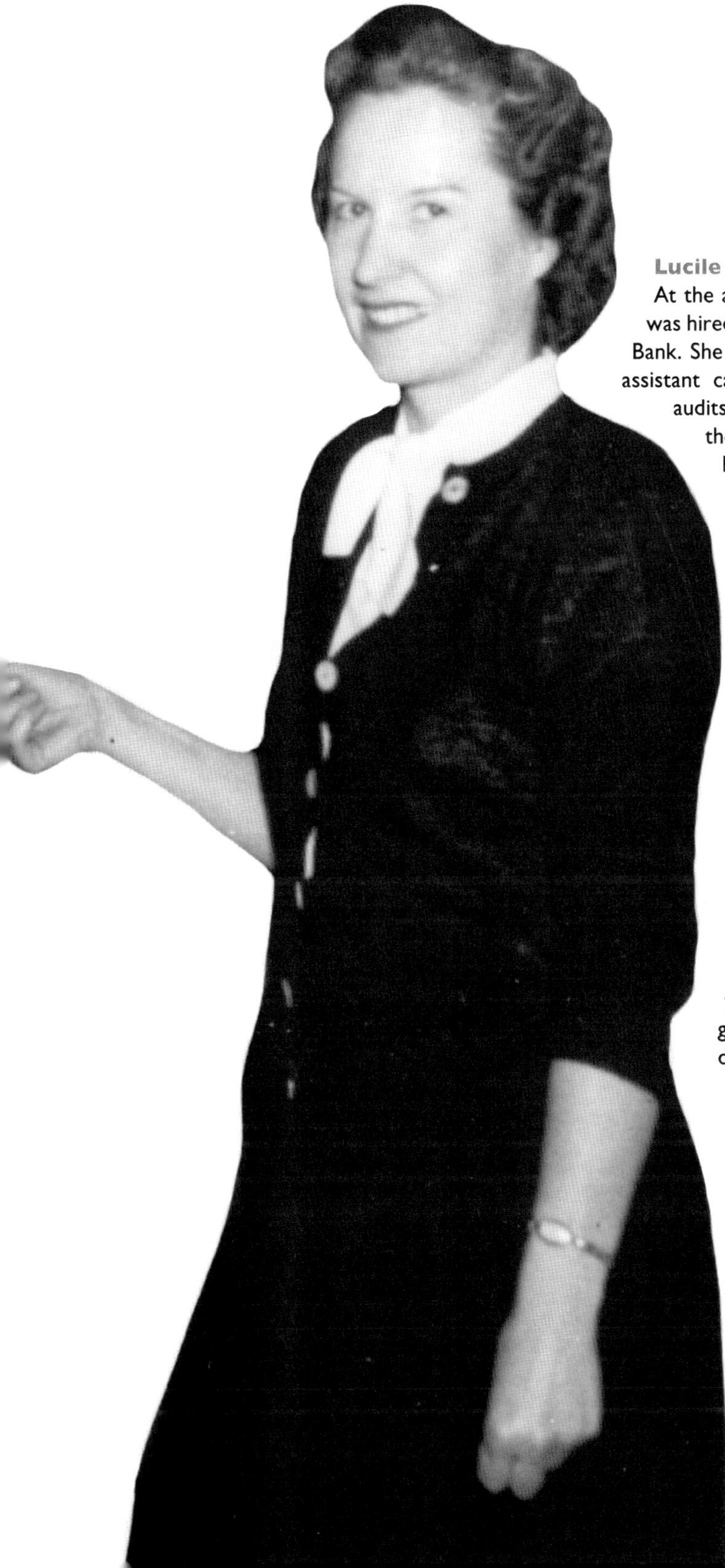

Lucile M. McCloskey Doll

At the age of 23, Lucile McCloskey was hired as a clerk for Peoples State Bank. She steadily rose in position to assistant cashier, conducting monthly audits at branch stations, and then rising to cashier. Upon her marriage to George Doll, she retired for one year, then returned as cashier. She filled in so many times as executive presidents came and went that the board of directors appointed her executive president/ CEO of Peoples State Bank. Doll was one of the first women in Wisconsin to attain that position. She became a director of Peoples State Bank until she retired in 1977. In honor of her years of service, the bank created the Lucile M. Doll Memorial Scholarship for Wauzeka high school graduates. (Courtesy Prairie du Chien Historical Society.)

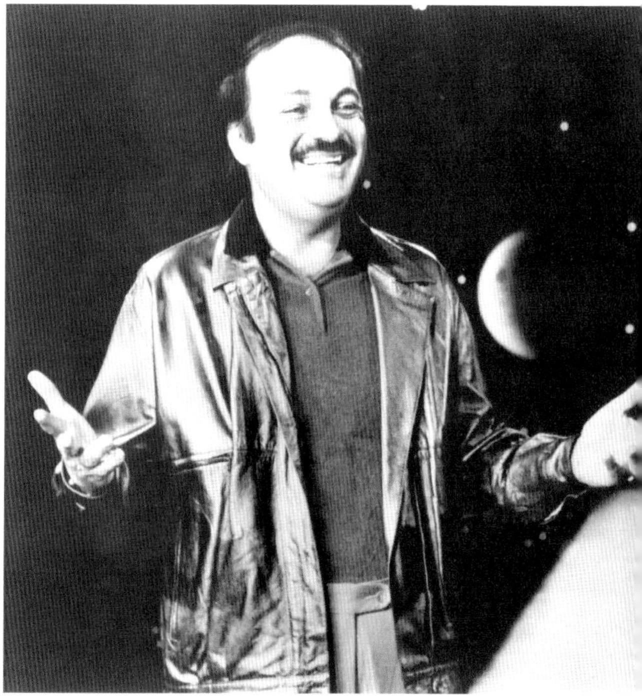

Foley Arthur Horkheimer
From Randolph, Wisconsin, Foley Horkheimer attended Campion Jesuit High School. He had a bent for being a public persona, hosting a radio show at age 15 and then traveling summers playing jazz piano and organ. He adopted the stage name Jack Foley. Perhaps inspired by Father Scott, Jack's interest in science led him to volunteer at the Miami Science Museum. There, he met astronomer Arthur Smith, who asked Foley to become director of the Miami Space Transit Museum. He turned planetarium shows into multimedia events. This led to his television show, *Jack Horkheimer: Star Hustler/Star Gazer.* (Courtesy Patricia and Phillip Frost Museum of Science, Miami, Florida.)

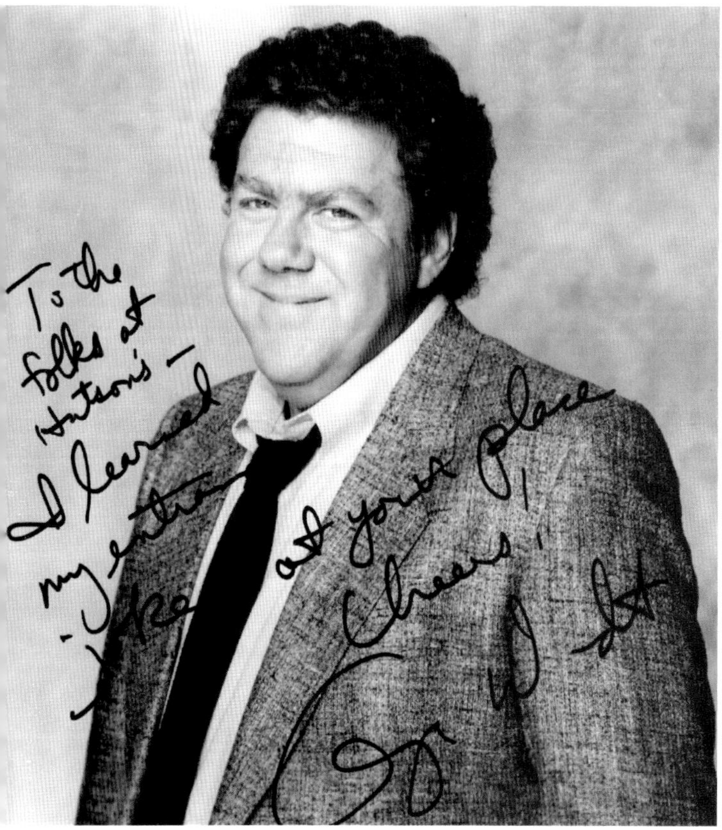

George Robert Wendt
George Wendt was one of the many boys from the greater Chicago area who was a student at Campion Jesuit High School. He returned to Chicago upon graduation from college and immediately entered the world of comedy, acting at The Second City. Wendt is best known for his role as Norm Peterson on the television show *Cheers.* He may have learned to sit at a bar and drink when, as a Campion student, he frequented Ma Selch's and ordered sodas or milkshakes. (Courtesy Harold and Gloria Hutson.)

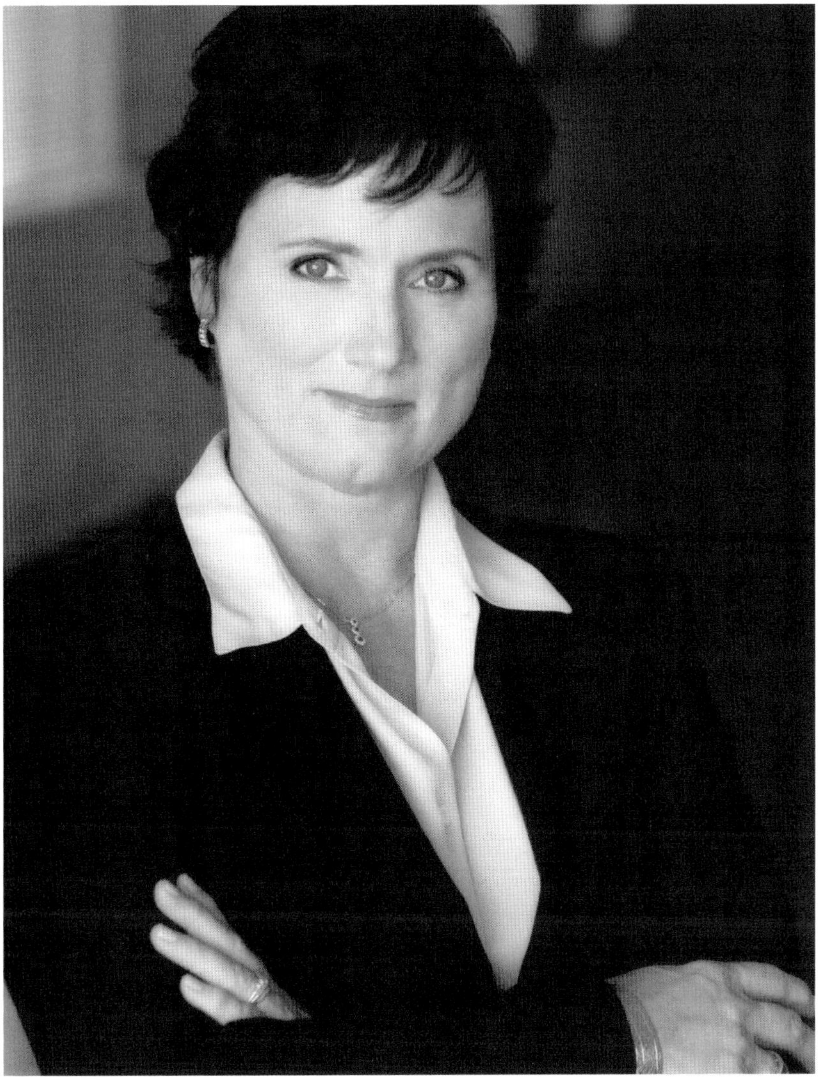

Peggy Ann Garrity

When Peggy Garrity was a senior at St. Mary's Academy, she played Mrs. Mitty in *A Thurber Carnival.* The director knew that Garrity had a strong personality and would portray Mrs. Mitty accurately. That strong personality carried Garrity through college and law school at Southwestern University–Los Angeles. Only two years after she was admitted to the California State Bar, Garrity was retained by Sara Jane Moore, who had pled guilty to the attempted assassination of Pres. Gerald Ford. Garrity filed Moore's petition to vacate her life sentence and set aside her guilty plea, arguing her case in US district court. Although the motion was denied, Garrity had established herself as a strong plaintiff's attorney. She became an advocate for women's rights.

Garrity needed all her skills in 1996, when she took on Clint Eastwood and Warner Bros. Representing Sondra Locke, Garrity argued that Eastwood and Warner Bros. had conspired to keep Locke from producing movies. Her evidence and arguments were so successful that Eastwood settled out of court. Said Garrity, "I see her [Locke] as sort of an Everywoman for the '90s." From her success in other high-profile cases, Garrity's opinion was sought regarding the needs of children and the diminished rights that employees face when forced to sign contracts. (Courtesy Peggy Ann Garrity.)

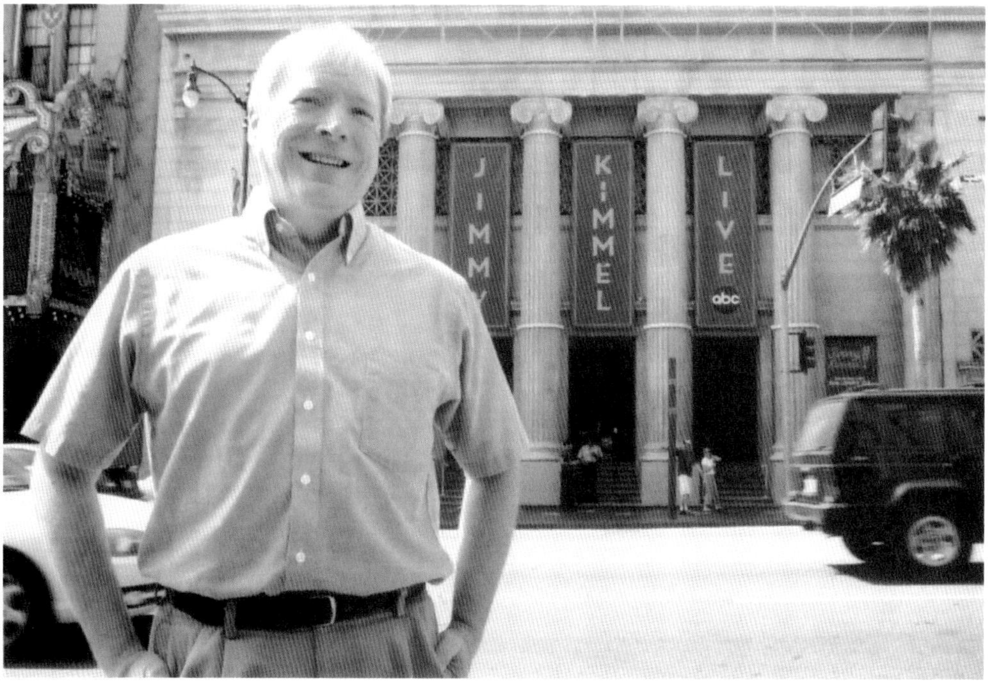

Bradley G. Williams

Brad Williams always had an ability to remember events in detail and attach a day and date to the events in his lifetime. No one considered it unusual until he and his brothers learned of one other person with that ability, and Williams underwent tests at the University of California–Irvine. Williams has hyperthymesia, or superior autobiographical memory. Once his ability became publicly known, he spent a year making the rounds of television programs. ABC dubbed him "the Human Google." The notoriety has not changed Williams; he continues to work at a radio station in LaCrosse and acts in regional theater. (Courtesy the Williams family.)

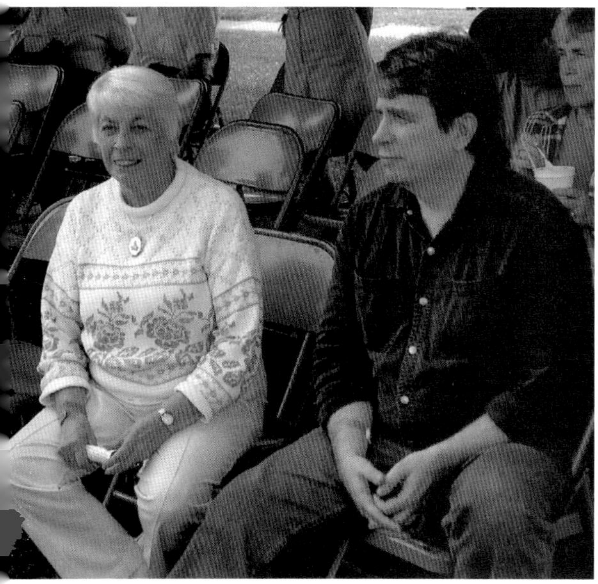

Eric Williams

While Eric Williams (pictured here with mother, Virginia) worked for many years in market research for the film and advertising industries, he quietly pursued his screenwriting goals. He had some successes, but his big break came when Warner Bros. purchased the script *Mad City*, which Williams had written with Tom Matthews. When the Williams family realized that brother Brad had hyperthymesia, Eric wrote, directed, and edited the documentary *Unforgettable*. With the help of brother Greg, Eric followed Brad's journey through one eventful year as Brad's rare mental gifts made him a celebrity. *Unforgettable* premiered at the 2010 Wisconsin Film Festival. (Courtesy William F. Howe.)

CHAPTER FOUR

Coaches and Athletes

To do what we have been able to do, I think it speaks a lot about the way we were brought up, the hard-working people around us, and the values that were instilled in us. I think there will always be a part of our hometown in us.

—Matthew Antoine, 2014

The first competitive sport held at Prairie du Chien may have been the game of lacrosse, played by Indian tribes of the Upper Mississippi. In 1805, Lt. Zebulon Pike observed a group of young Sioux and Winnebago men engaged in the game along the east bank of the Mississippi River north of Prairie du Chien. But the game vanished from the area with the removal of the Indians.

As Prairie du Chien grew from a frontier settlement to an established city, and baseball rose to prominence, social clubs organized competitive events. Men put together baseball teams, finding businesses to sponsor them. There was even a city-wide team, the Prairie du Chien Pirates. By 1909, enrollment was large enough that Prairie du Chien High School could field baseball and basketball teams; after World War I, football became part of the school's athletic program. Sacred Heart College already had sports teams, so a rivalry began between the two schools.

As in many small communities where everyone is a neighbor, sports became a big part of Prairie du Chien's social life. Whether one had a family member on a team or not, families attended sporting events. The public high school and Campion High School coordinated their schedules so that residents did not have to choose which game to attend. In football, Prairie High played on Friday nights, and Campion played on Saturday afternoons. Before the school year began, an attempt was made to coordinate the baseball and basketball schedules. Many men watched these games, reliving moments from their high school days. A few students were good athletes and received scholarships, allowing them to compete at the collegiate level. Many of their coaches attained recognition for their ability to inspire young athletes and produce winning seasons.

In the summer, baseball reigned. Many young people, though, turned to swimming and diving. It was a way to find relief from the heat and humidity and to have fun with friends. When a summer recreation program was established, swim meets, diving contests, and water ballet provided opportunities for folks to develop and demonstrate their skills.

As the world of competitive sports broadened beyond the traditional high school athletics, a handful of Prairie du Chien students and adults chose to perfect their abilities and compete in national and international venues. Their intense focus and dedication brought recognition beyond Prairie du Chien and Wisconsin to them and the community.

Daniel H. Swingle

Dan Swingle worked hard on the family farm, saving his money. When Art Roth opened an Indian motorcycle dealership in Prairie du Chien, Swingle purchased a Speedway model and became a professional motorcycle racer. The Indian Motorcycle Club of Prairie du Chien turned the old Dousman track into the Indian Speedway. Professional motorcycle racers competed, and Swingle joined them on the race circuit that took them all over the Midwest. Here, he poses with the trophy he won in May 1915. (Courtesy the Dan Swingle family.)

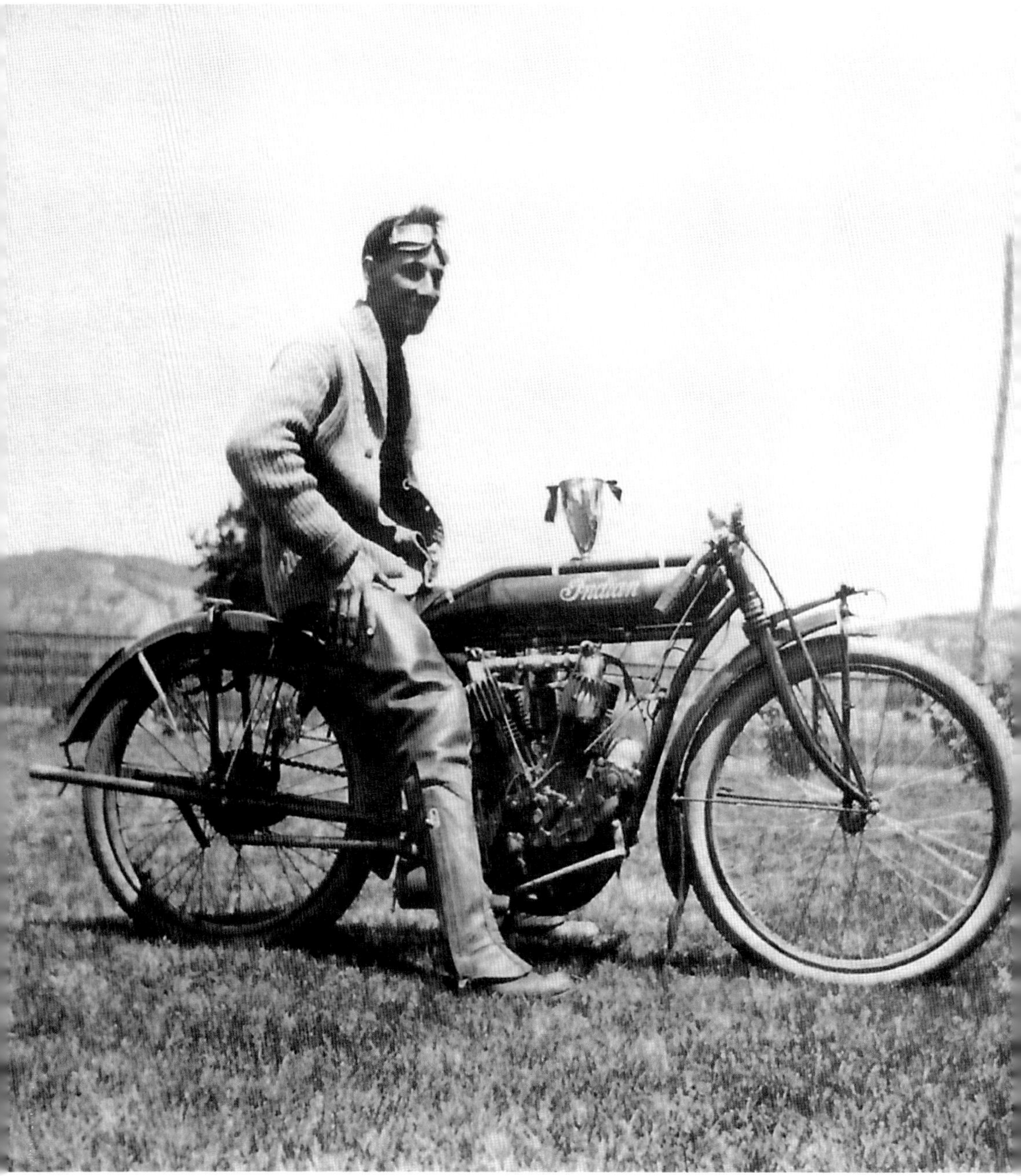

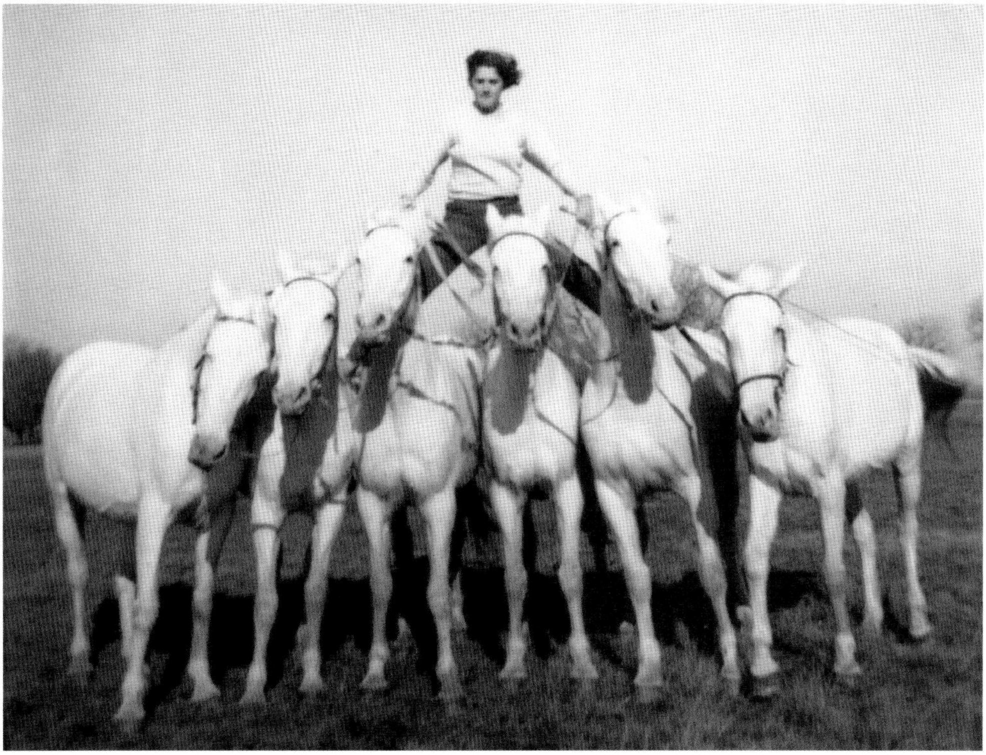

Elaine Kramer

Kramer grew up on the family farm east of Prairie du Chien. Like many area teens, she went to the Metro Theater. In 1954, she saw the movie *Ride a White Horse* and knew that she wanted to become a Roman rider. She wrote a letter to the White Horse Ranch in Nebraska, asking to train at the ranch. She received an invitation to come. Within six months of arriving at the ranch, Kramer was asked to jump six horses abreast for an injured performer. Her debut at the American Royal Show was the beginning of a 20-year career. The following year, she performed a Roman-riding act with the Flying Valkyries in Palm Springs and then joined Jinks Hoglan's All Girl Review. She toured the East Coast with women who amazed rodeo audiences with their trick horseback riding.

In 1959, Kramer knew she wanted her own Roman-riding act. She purchased and developed her team of perfectly matched sorrels, all Saddlebreds. She set up an outdoor arena on her property at Prairie du Chien. Anyone driving by could see her as she schooled her six horses, harnessed in pairs, to gallop around the arena, weave figure eights, and fly over jumps as she stood balanced on the backs of the last pair. Kramer performed from Toronto to the San Francisco Cow Palace to Madison Square Garden, thrilling spectators with the flair and fluidity of the horses and her handling. She was at the height of rodeo stardom when she retired her horses in 1972 and came back to Prairie du Chien to help on the family farm.

Kramer's friends remembered the uniqueness of her Roman riding and began a two-year campaign to have her and her feats recognized. In 2005, she was inducted into the National Cowgirl Hall of Fame and acknowledged as "one of America's most famous Roman riders." She is the first Wisconsin resident to be inducted and is one of 215 women "who shaped the West, and changed the World." In 2010, she was honored by the American Saddlebred Museum. (Courtesy Prairie du Chien Historical Society, Howe Collection.)

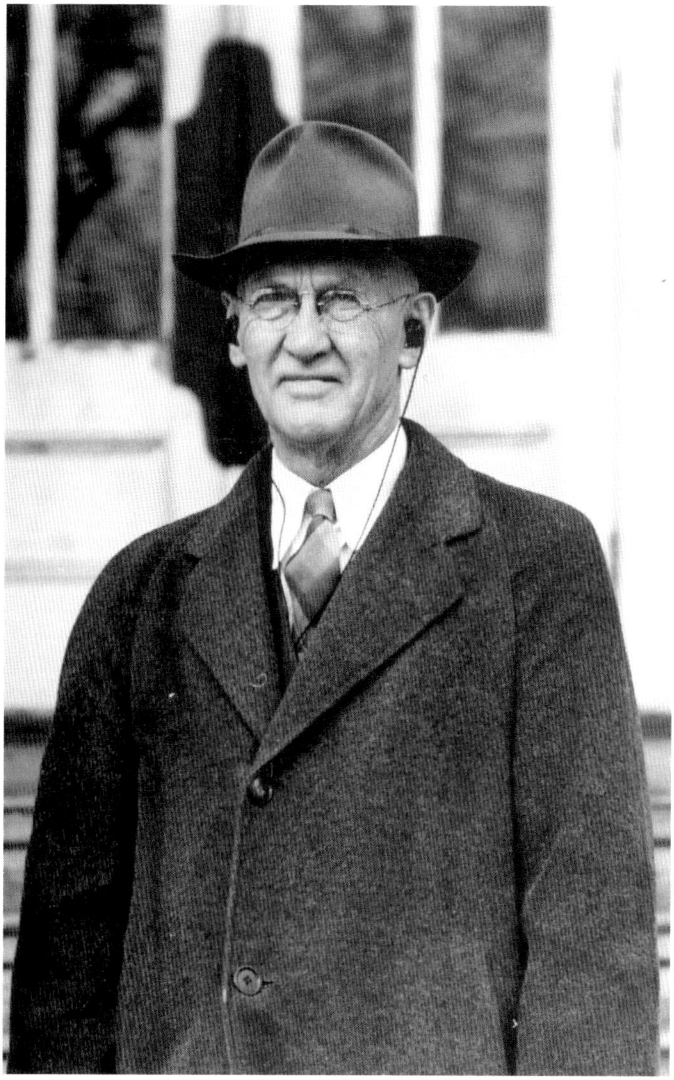

William Stanislaus Hoffman

When Bill Hoffman retired from coaching in 1952, he had been at Campion Jesuit High School for 41 years. Arriving at Campion in 1911, which at that time also had a college department, Hoffman coached football, baseball, and track, and fielded a basketball team. His coaching duties were interrupted twice. During World War I, he spent 1917–1918 as athletic director of Camp Sevier, in South Carolina, and then at the Great Lakes Training Station. In 1925, Hoffman began a coaching record that earned him the title "Dean of Mid-West High School Coaches." By the time of his retirement, Hoffman had compiled an impressive record of 685 victories, 312 defeats, and 18 ties.

Gentlemanly in his demeanor, Hoffman was known for his fedora, great overcoat, and ever-present, slight smile (even with a cigar clamped in his mouth). The Campion football field was named Hoffman Field in his honor. In 1950, the Catholic Diocese of La Crosse created the Hoffman Football Trophy, a traveling trophy awarded to the best high school football team in the diocese. In 1963, Campion dedicated its new natatorium, The W.S. Hoffman Athletic Center.

In 1981, Bill Hoffman was posthumously inducted into the Wisconsin Football Coaches Association Hall of Fame. (Courtesy Jesuit Archives, Central United States.)

Patrick Dennis Bowlen

Pat Bowlen played some sports while growing up in Prairie du Chien and later at Campion Jesuit High School, but he was not destined to be a professional athlete. Instead, he earned degrees in law and business, practicing in Alberta, Canada, and investing in the mining industry. In 1984, Bowlen purchased the majority share of the Denver Broncos; Pat and the Bowlen family acquired full ownership in July 1985. Under his ownership and as CEO, the Broncos have compiled an impressive record. Bowlen was inducted into the Colorado Sports Hall of Fame. A generous man, in 2013, Bowlen received the Mizel Community Enrichment Award. (Courtesy Eric Lars Bakke/Denver Broncos.)

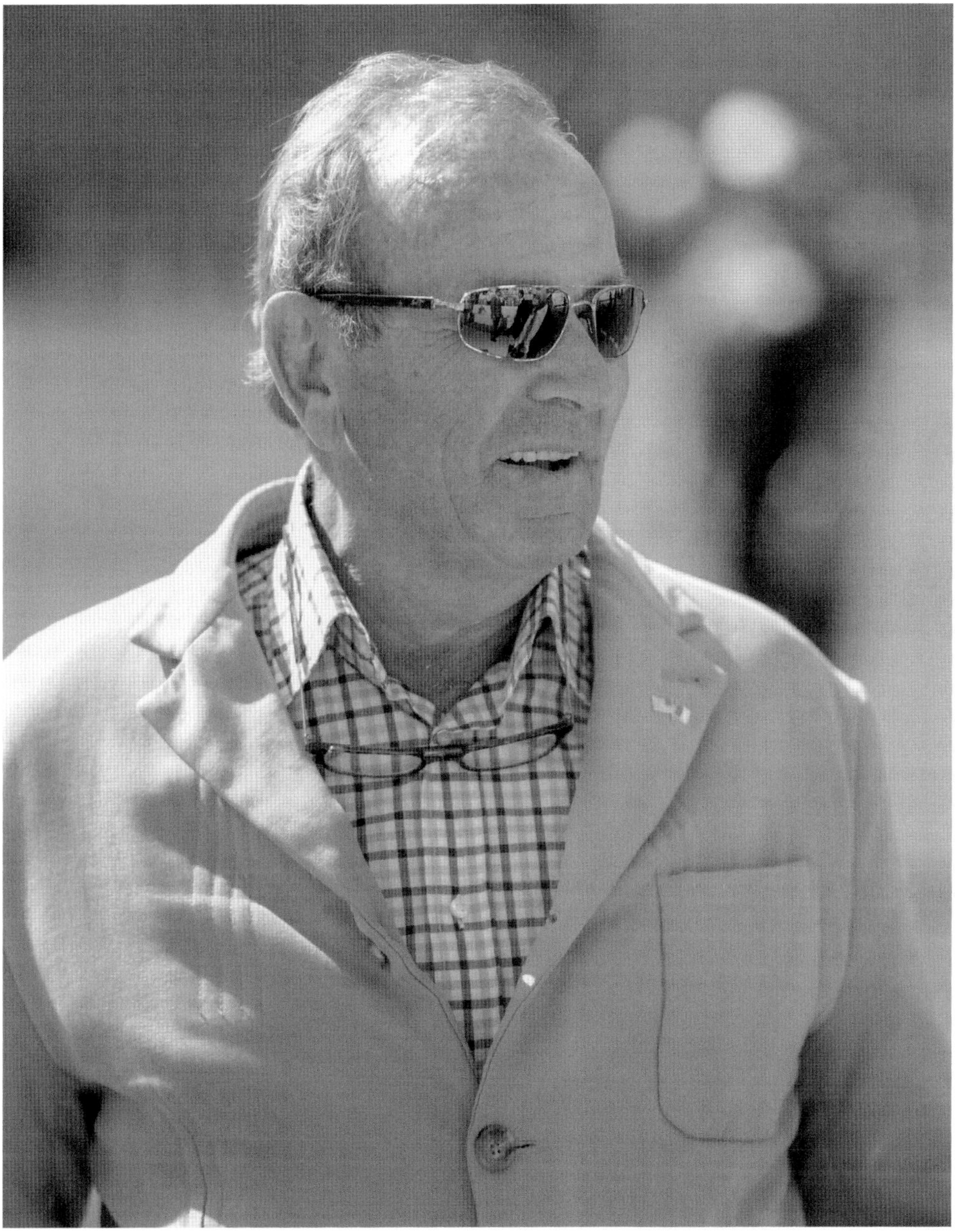

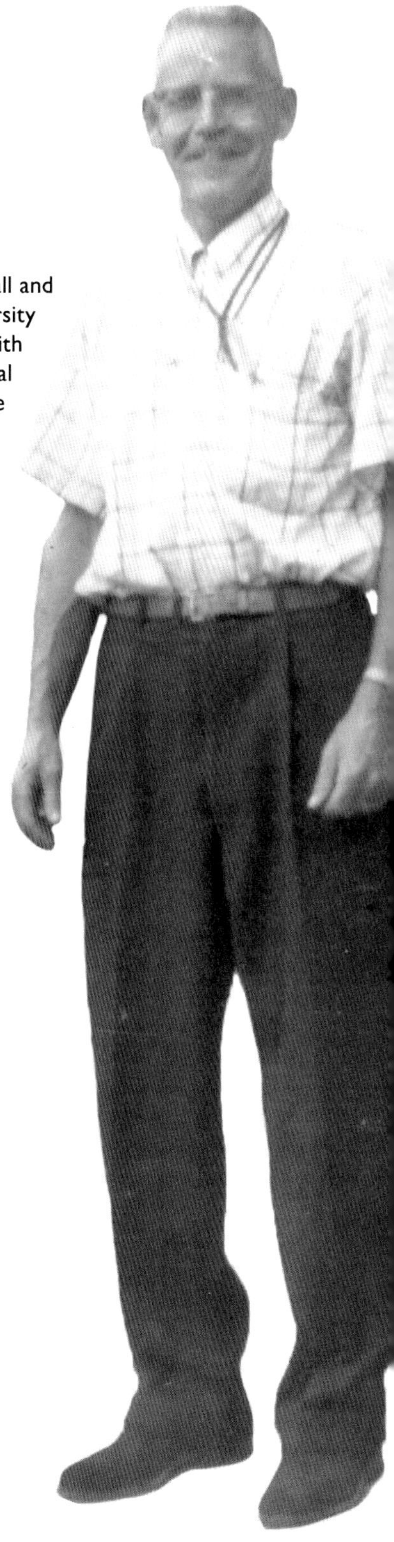

Cecil F. Smith

Cecil Smith excelled in baseball, basketball, and especially football and track. It was only natural that, upon graduation from the University of Wisconsin, he would coach the sports he loved. "Smitty" Smith came to Prairie du Chien High School in 1930 to teach physical education and coach baseball, football, and basketball, which he did until he entered the US Army. Retiring as a lieutenant colonel, Smith returned to Prairie du Chien, resuming all his coaching duties until his health forced him to discontinue coaching in 1954. His interest in track remained, and he started an interscholastic cross-country program in 1960.

When Smitty arrived in Prairie du Chien, he saw that children of all ages could benefit from a summer recreation program, so he convinced the city to established a department of recreation and sponsor a variety of summer sports. In 1989, the field on which Smitty had once coached high school baseball and football teams, now used for the summer recreation program, was named Cecil F. Smith Field. That year, he was inducted into the Wisconsin Football Coaches Association Hall of Fame. (Courtesy Prairie du Chien Historical Society.)

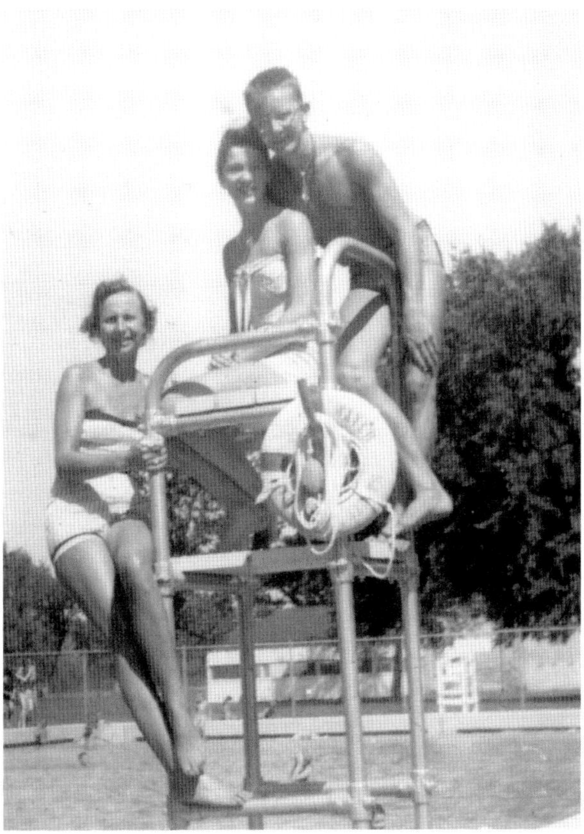

Barbetta M. Cardin Koecke Bloyer

Like all children who lived by the Mississippi River, Barbetta Bloyer learned to swim at an early age. She became the head lifeguard at the municipal pool and taught water safety for 13 years. Cecil Smith suggested to the lifeguards that perhaps they could organize a synchronized-swim team. Bloyer led the team, selecting the music and designing the routines. Their first public performance was on August 29, 1956. She is seen here at left with Janet Gremore and George Kahler. (Courtesy George and Janet Kahler.)

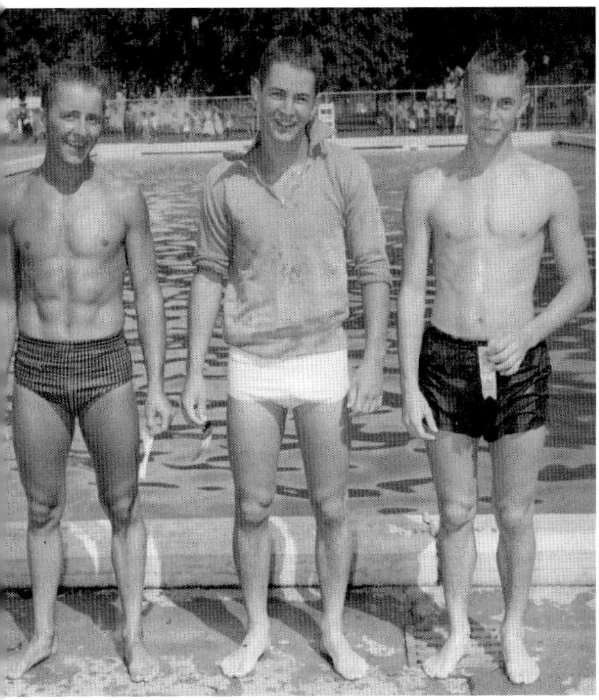

George Kahler, Chuck Smith, Don Heal

Beginning in 1937, *The Courier Press* sponsored annual swim meets, in which any resident, grades kindergarten and older, could enter. With Cecil Smith as recreation director, another component, in addition to synchronized swimming, was added to the program: diving exhibitions. George Kahler (left), one of the lifeguards, was also an excellent diver. George and Ronnie "Hot Rod" Kramer put together a program of "piggy-back" diving, with Dick Elliot and Don Heal (right) as clown divers. (Courtesy George and Janet Kahler.)

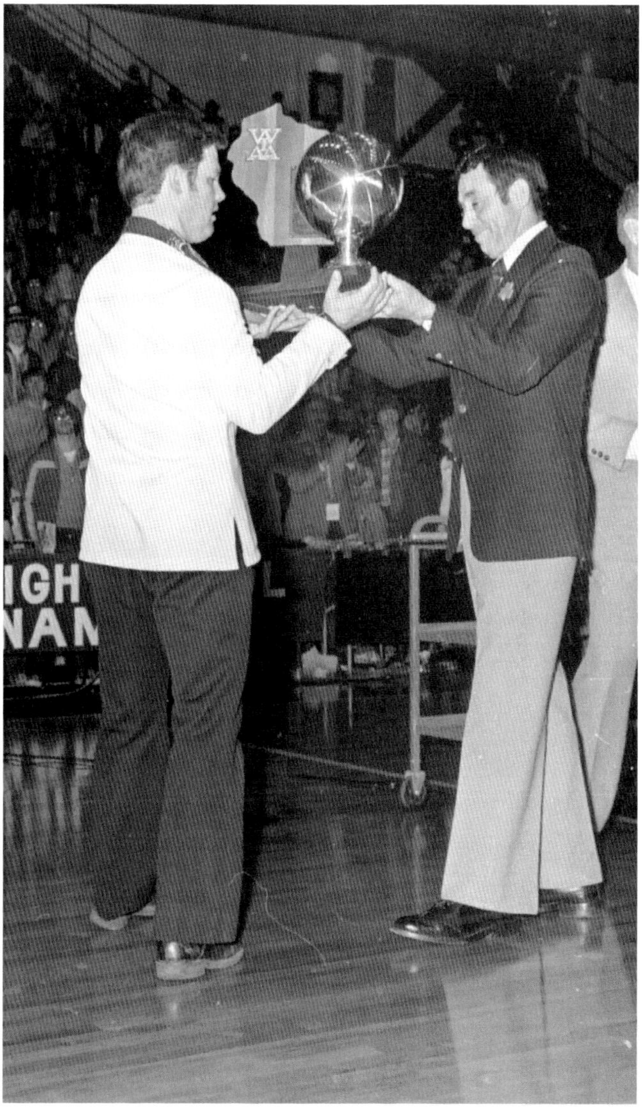

John C. Mulrooney

It is impossible to talk about track and field at Prairie du Chien High School without mentioning Jack Mulrooney (right). The program Mulrooney built in the 1950s has produced four state titles and countless conference championships. The outdoor sports stadium at Prairie du Chien High School bears his name. Mulrooney's crowning achievement is the Prairie Relays, begun in 1954. The event, an invitational meet for schools throughout the Southwest Athletic Conference, consisted of only track relay events. The relays continue to this day.

Mulrooney came to Prairie du Chien in 1949 to teach civics, geography, and physical education. He coached track, football, and basketball for the next 10 years. After leaving Prairie du Chien, he returned one year later to be assistant principal. When B.A. Kennedy retired in 1962, Mulrooney became superintendent of schools for the Prairie du Chien School District and held that position until he retired in 1991. He continues to volunteer as a relay judge at the state track meet.

In 1996, Jack Mulrooney was inducted into the Wisconsin Cross Country Coaches Association Hall of Fame. (Courtesy the Mulrooney family.)

Mulrooney Children

Jack and Glee Mulrooney (seated at center) had five children, and each of them followed in their father's footsteps. Patrick (standing at left) ran track at UW–La Crosse and was a high school track coach for 33 years. In 1980, he organized the first Turkey Trot for Prairie du Chien. The Mulrooney children attend the annual race when they can, and Jack has always been the official starter each year.

Michael (standing at right) also became a high school cross-country and distance-running coach, having two Division I teams. In 2004, he was inducted into the Wisconsin Cross Country Coaches Association Hall of Fame.

Ann (seated at right) was on the track team throughout high school, winning the mile race at the state championships in 1973, 1974, and 1975. In 1976, she won both the mile and the 880 meters to lead the Prairie du Chien girls' team to its second straight Class B state title and helped the Blackhawks win their first state cross-country championship. For her achievements, Ann was honored by inclusion in *Sports Illustrated*'s "Faces in the Crowd" in the July 26, 1976, issue. In 1990, she was inducted into the Wisconsin Track Coaches Association Hall of Fame.

Mary Beth (seated at left) won the 440-yard dash in Class B at the state track meet in 1977 and was state track-and-field champion. (Courtesy the Mulrooney family.)

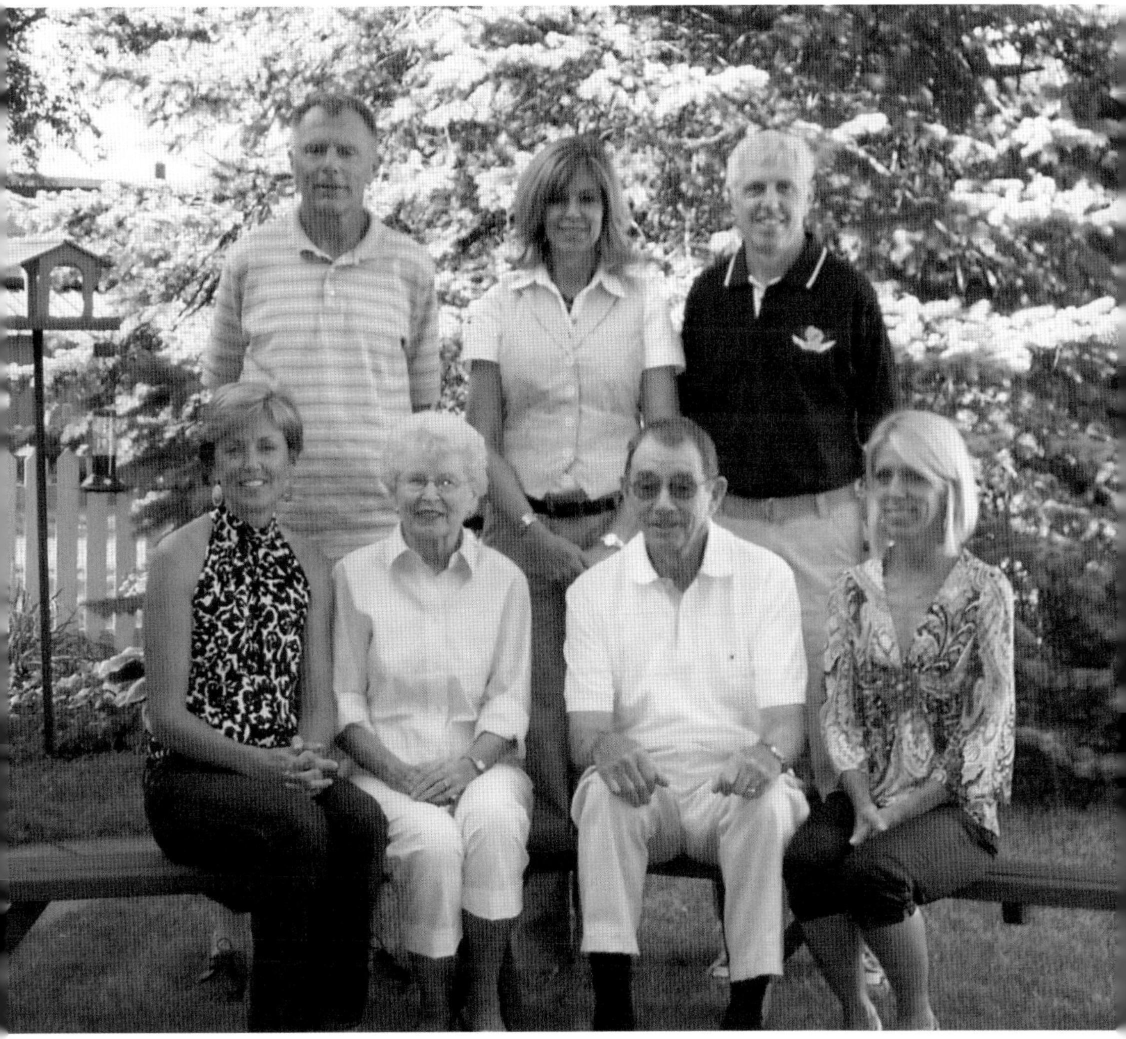

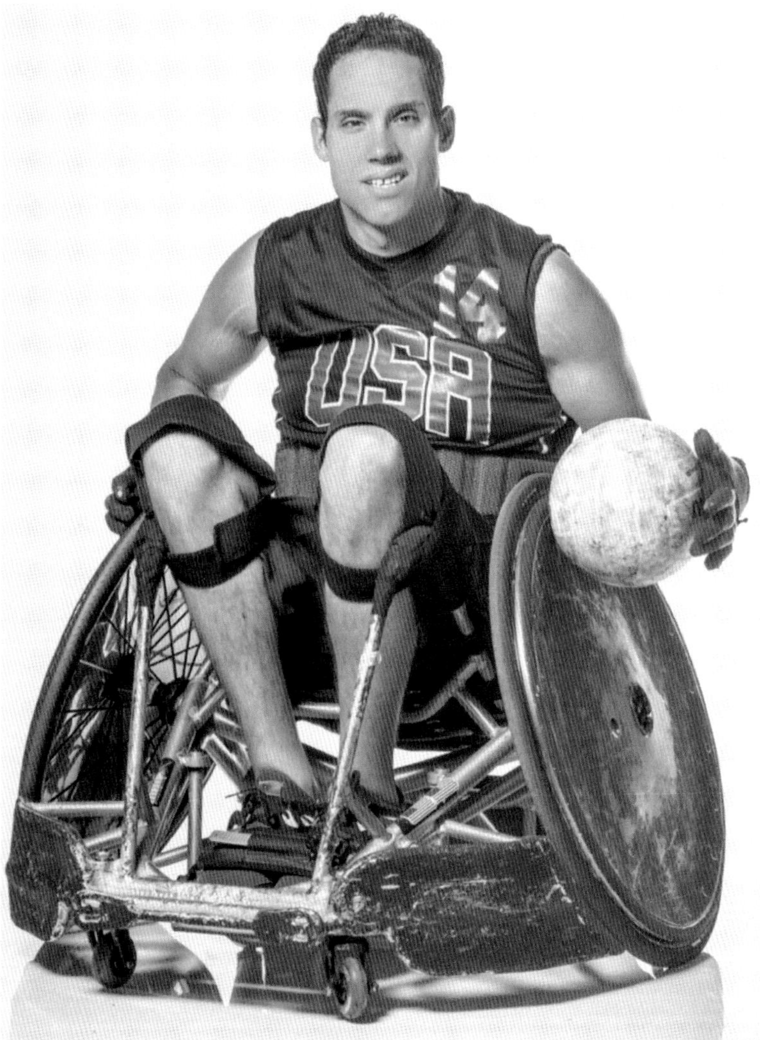

Joe Delagrave

Joe Delagrave and his family moved to Prairie du Chien when Joe was in middle school. He showed the athletic ability that would make him a great football and basketball player in high school. Known and well liked by the entire student body, Delagrave was elected to the student council and had the lead in the fall school musical. In 2003, he earned a football scholarship as a tight end. The summer after his freshman year, he came home. On July 10, he was on the Mississippi River with friends when the boat struck the river bottom. Joe was thrown forward, breaking two vertebrae in his neck. He would never walk again.

A year later, Delagrave returned to college and wanted to be active in sports. He checked out what could be played from a wheelchair and came upon wheelchair rugby. Giving the sport a try, it intrigued him, so he practiced with a club and went to a camp. Then he saw a webcast of the US Paralympic Team playing the gold medal match in Beijing in 2008. He made the decision: this was what he wanted to do.

Delagrave and April, his wife, made a huge change in their lives. They moved to Phoenix so Joe could play for the Phoenix Fusion, hoping to gain a berth on the 2010 US Paralympic Team. He tried out, made the team, and went to London. The team beat Japan to win a bronze medal. (Courtesy Loren Worthington.)

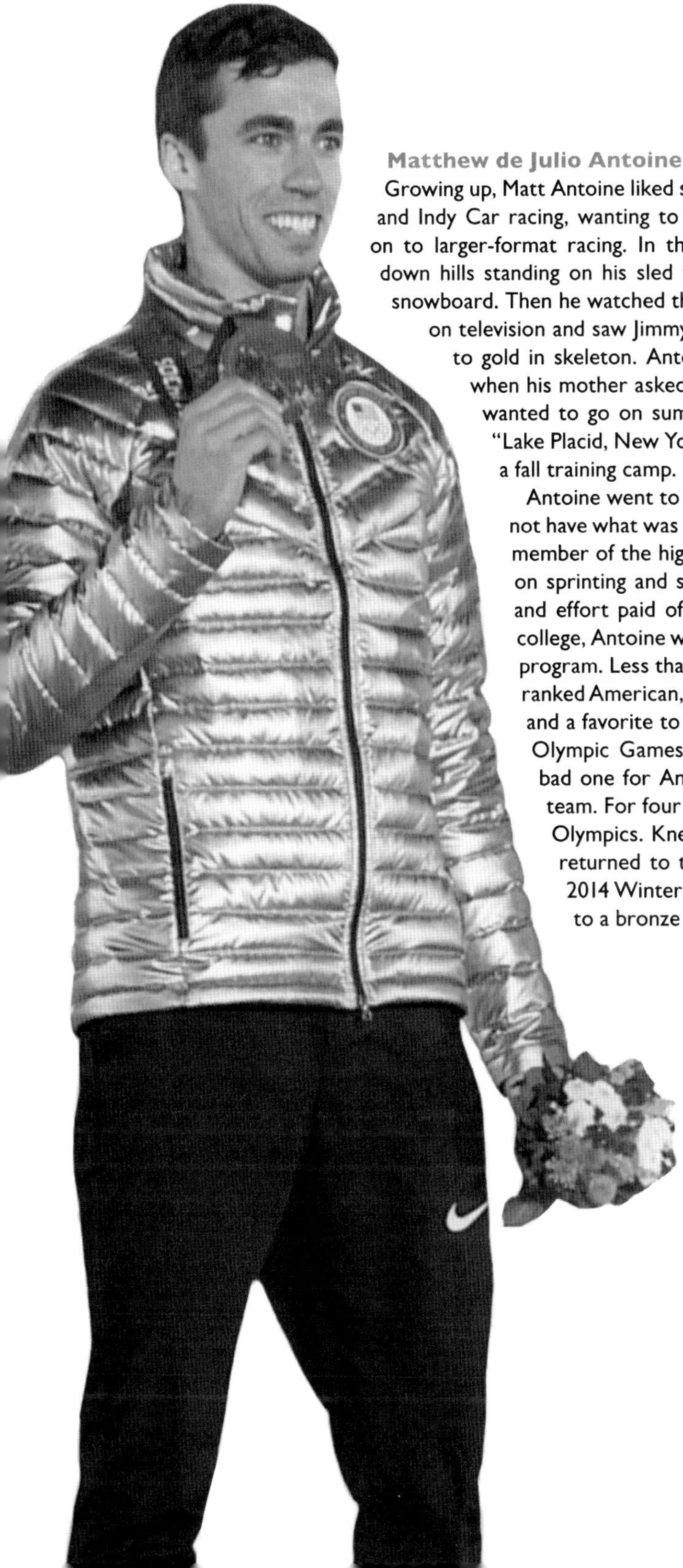

Matthew de Julio Antoine
Growing up, Matt Antoine liked speed. He watched Formula One and Indy Car racing, wanting to race go-karts and maybe move on to larger-format racing. In the winter, he went from sliding down hills standing on his sled to mastering the half-pipe on a snowboard. Then he watched the 2002 Winter Olympic Games on television and saw Jimmy Shea of the United States slide to gold in skeleton. Antoine researched the sport, and, when his mother asked where he and his brother Nick wanted to go on summer vacation, Matt responded, "Lake Placid, New York." Tryouts were being held for a fall training camp.

Antoine went to the camp, only to be told he did not have what was needed to be a skeleton slider. A member of the high school track team, he focused on sprinting and starting skills. His determination and effort paid off. In 2003, his first semester of college, Antoine was accepted into the US skeleton program. Less than six years later, he was the top-ranked American, Intercontinental Cup Champion, and a favorite to win a medal at the 2010 Winter Olympic Games. The 2009–2010 season was a bad one for Antoine, and he did not make the team. For four years, he focused on making the Olympics. Knee surgery did not deter him; he returned to the number-one ranking. At the 2014 Winter Games in Sochi, Russia, Matt slid to a bronze medal. (Author's collection).

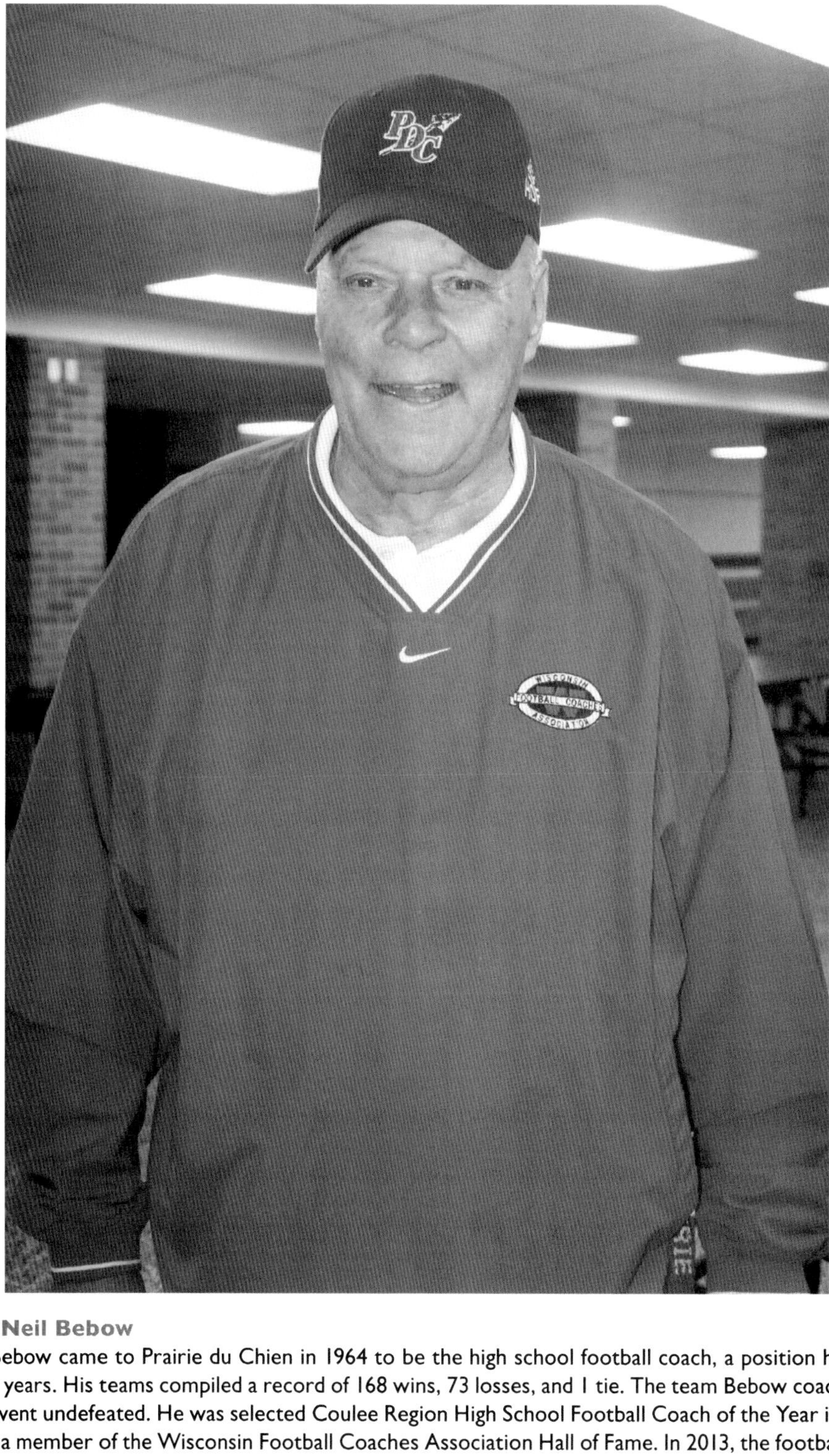

Paul Neil Bebow

Paul Bebow came to Prairie du Chien in 1964 to be the high school football coach, a position he held for 27 years. His teams compiled a record of 168 wins, 73 losses, and 1 tie. The team Bebow coached in 1971 went undefeated. He was selected Coulee Region High School Football Coach of the Year in 1998 and is a member of the Wisconsin Football Coaches Association Hall of Fame. In 2013, the football field in Mulrooney Stadium was named Paul Bebow Field. (Author's collection).

CHAPTER FIVE

Part of the River and Heritage

Shadows of the past silently moving through the crevices of my mind, like the mists of the river on a cool morning. I stand in the peace this place provides. Here where it started. My past. My history. My heritage.

—Jeff Lessard, 2014

For hundreds of years, the Mississippi River brought people to Prairie du Chien. Many of the visitors and settlers left a permanent physical structure, a reminder of their presence on the prairie, be it a mound, a fortification, a commercial building, a home, or letters and objects. In the 19th century, people romantically viewed the reminders of the past as ruins or relics, with the assumption they would disappear in the wake of American progress. In the 20th century, some residents realized that the history of the many cultures and people who spent all or part of their lives at Prairie du Chien had an importance and needed to be recorded, preserved, and shared. Special funding brought writers, artists, and museum curators into the community, and they recorded the rich culture and history of the river and heritage of past residents and worked to share it not only with their neighbors, but with visitors and the nation. Due to their dedication, part of the past has been retained in buildings, art, music, and stories.

When the French opted to make their homes at Prairie du Chien, they chose to live not on the mainland, but on a large island surrounded by the Mississippi River. When Prairie du Chien incorporated as a city in 1872, the island became the Fourth Ward. The people who made a living from the river preferred to live in the Fourth Ward, even though the river periodically lapped at their doorsteps. Among people living in the ward and along North Main Street, the cultural heritage of the river and their ancestors continued within their families. Into the 20th century, many spoke the language, sang the songs, told the stories, and made a living from the river, adapting to the innovations of progress but never losing the basis of their heritage. The power of the Mississippi River inundated the ward several times, especially in 1965, when the river rose to a record 25.4 feet. Most of the residents returned to the Fourth Ward, repairing their homes. A few raised their houses so that they would be above flood level. After extreme flooding in 1969, 1978, and 1980 forced residents from their homes and damaged structures, the City of Prairie du Chien was approached with a program created by the US Corps of Engineers and the Department of Housing and Urban Development. By 1990, all of the residents of the Fourth Ward had been relocated. Though the ward is gone, there is a greater appreciation of the French Canadian culture once dominant at Prairie du Chien and a way of life that is part of the river. Contemporary writers, archivists, and filmmakers are making sure that the traditions of life on the river are preserved.

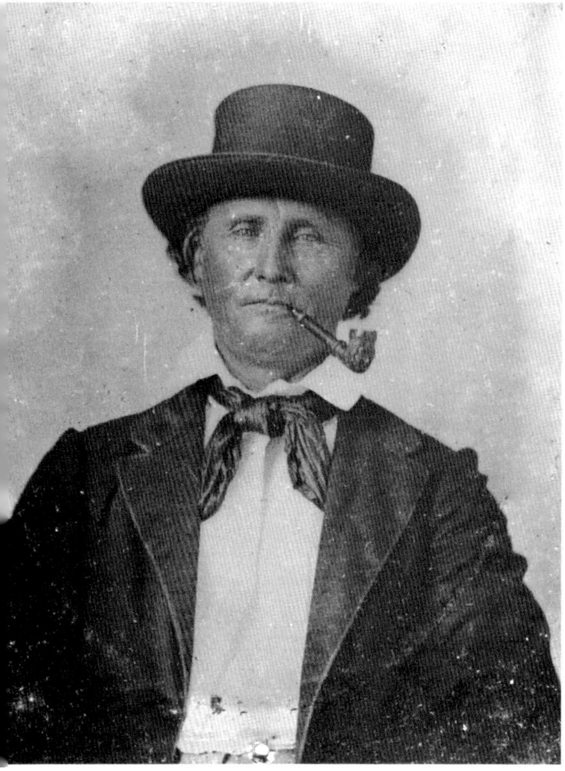

Julian Carriere
Julian Carriere left Quebec, engaged to work in the Missouri River fur trade. After his marriage to Leocadie Lessard, the couple settled at Prairie du Chien. They farmed on the bluffs east of "Frenchtown." (Courtesy Prairie du Chien Historical Society.)

Albert Coryer
As Albert Coryer grew up, he listened to the stories his grandfather Julian told of the fur trade and the remembrances his grandmother and parents had of living in "Frenchtown." In his unique style of writing, Albert recorded these stories, which are some of the best recollections of ordinary life in early Prairie du Chien. (Courtesy Prairie du Chien Historical Society.)

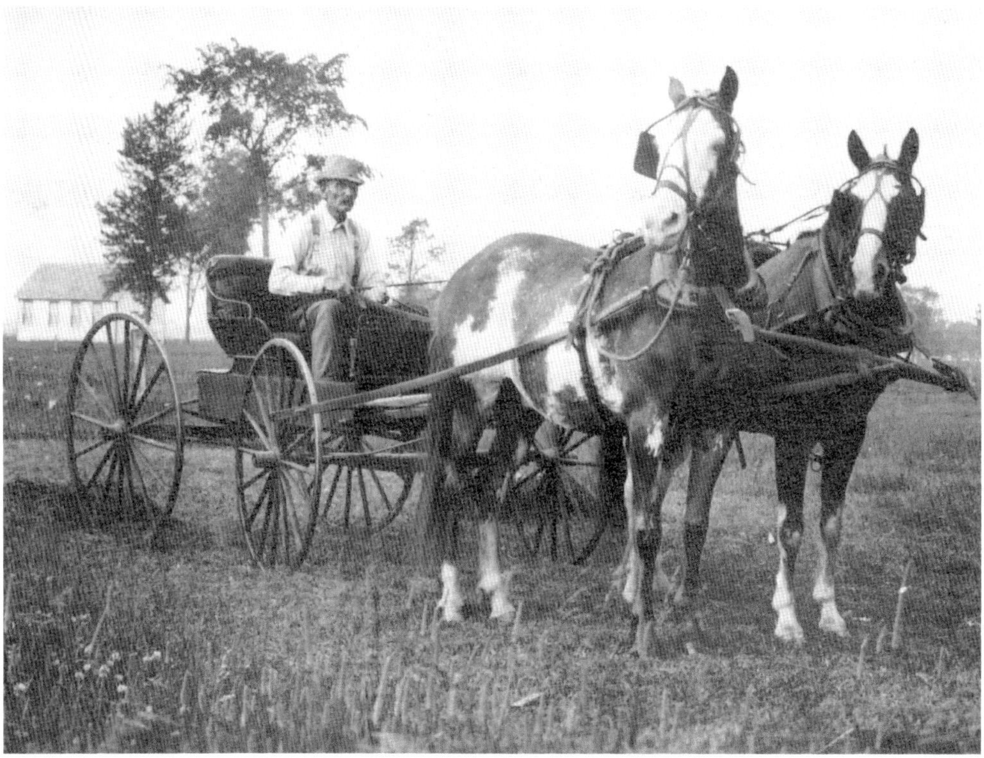

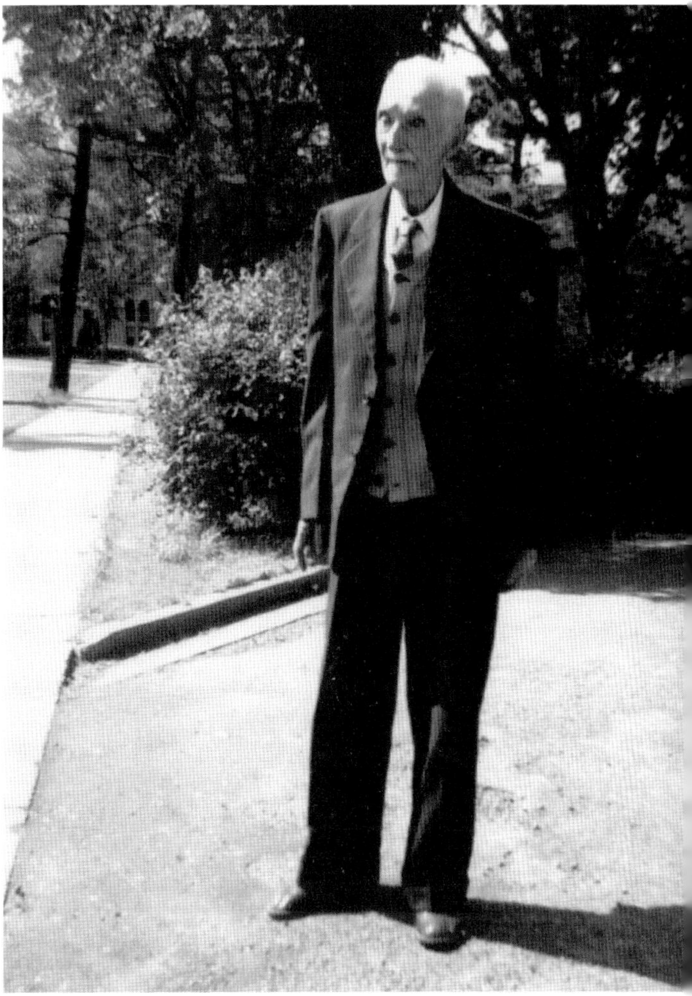

Reuben Valley
Reuben Valley was only one year old when his parents and family left their small village along the St. Lawrence River in Quebec to come to Prairie du Chien. They were part of the migration of French-speaking people to Wisconsin beginning in the mid-1830s. The children grew up listening to the adults sing songs and tell stories of their voyageur heritage.

Mary Agnes Starr, a Wisconsin folklorist, came to Prairie du Chien several times, recording French Canadian voyageur songs sung by Reuben "Urbain" Valley and Virginia LaBonne Valley. "The Old Voyageur," was 99 years old and blind when he sang "A la claire fontaine." The recordings of Reuben Valley are preserved at the Library of Congress. (Author's collection.)

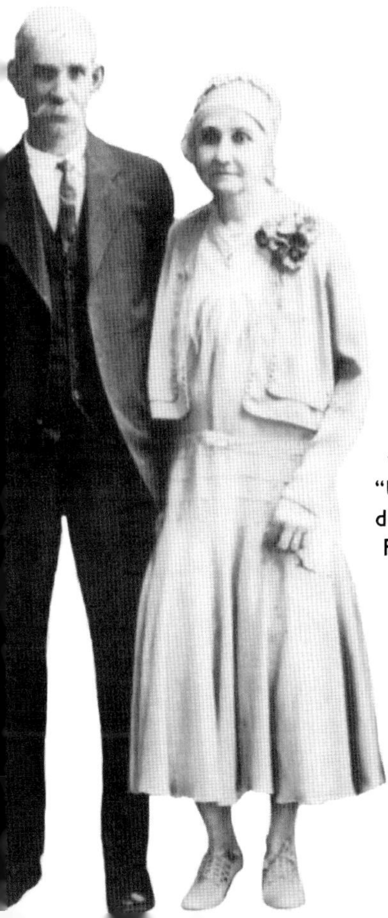

John Fernette
Generations of Fernette men were skilled carpenters. While working on homes and buildings, the Mississippi River influenced "Uncle Jack" (pictured with Mary Cota Fernette). He built boats during the day and rested in the evening, playing his fiddle and singing French Canadian songs. His son was a carpenter, and his grandson Robert repaired boats. When the floodwaters of 1965 swirled into their house and boat shop, the three Fernette families moved onto houseboats, where they lived until the waters receded. Uncle Jack's great-grandson carries on the family name and tradition with Bob's Marine Service. (Courtesy the Fernette family.)

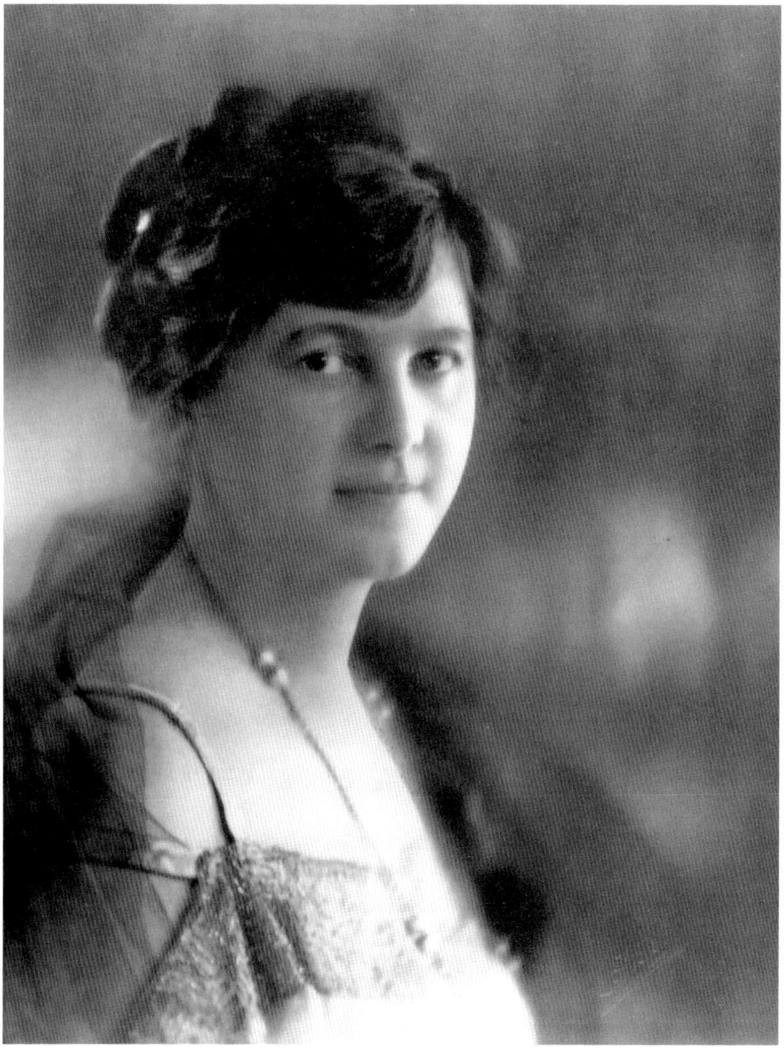

Laura Case Sherry

As the daughter of the owner of the Case Company, Laura Case grew up in comfortable surroundings. Unlike many women of her time, Laura went to college, studying theater in Chicago and New York. She returned to Prairie du Chien and, in 1902, married Edward P. Sherry.

Edward and Laura moved to Milwaukee. Retaining her love of the theater, Laura was the founding spirit of the Wisconsin Players. The group produced many plays, most of which were written by Wisconsin men and women. Zona Gale wrote her first play, *The Neighbors,* for the organization in 1914. Laura Sherry, Zona Gale, and the others were part of the "Wisconsin Idea" at a time when Midwestern writers were rebelling and writing about American life.

Sherry never forgot the people of French-Canadian heritage and their stories that were so much a part of Prairie du Chien when she was a child. Recalling those days, she compiled a volume of poetry, *Old Prairie du Chien.* It was published in a limited edition in 1931, for which Zona Gale wrote the introduction. Laura Sherry had, in Gale's words, caught "the elusive" in her poems. Some of the pieces, like "Jean Lessar's Wife" and "My Horse, She's Called It Charlemagne," were written in a French-Canadian patois. Other poems, like "A Ravine Town" and "Across the Prairie and Over the Hills," captured the natural spirit to be found in the land. (Courtesy Wisconsin Historical Society.)

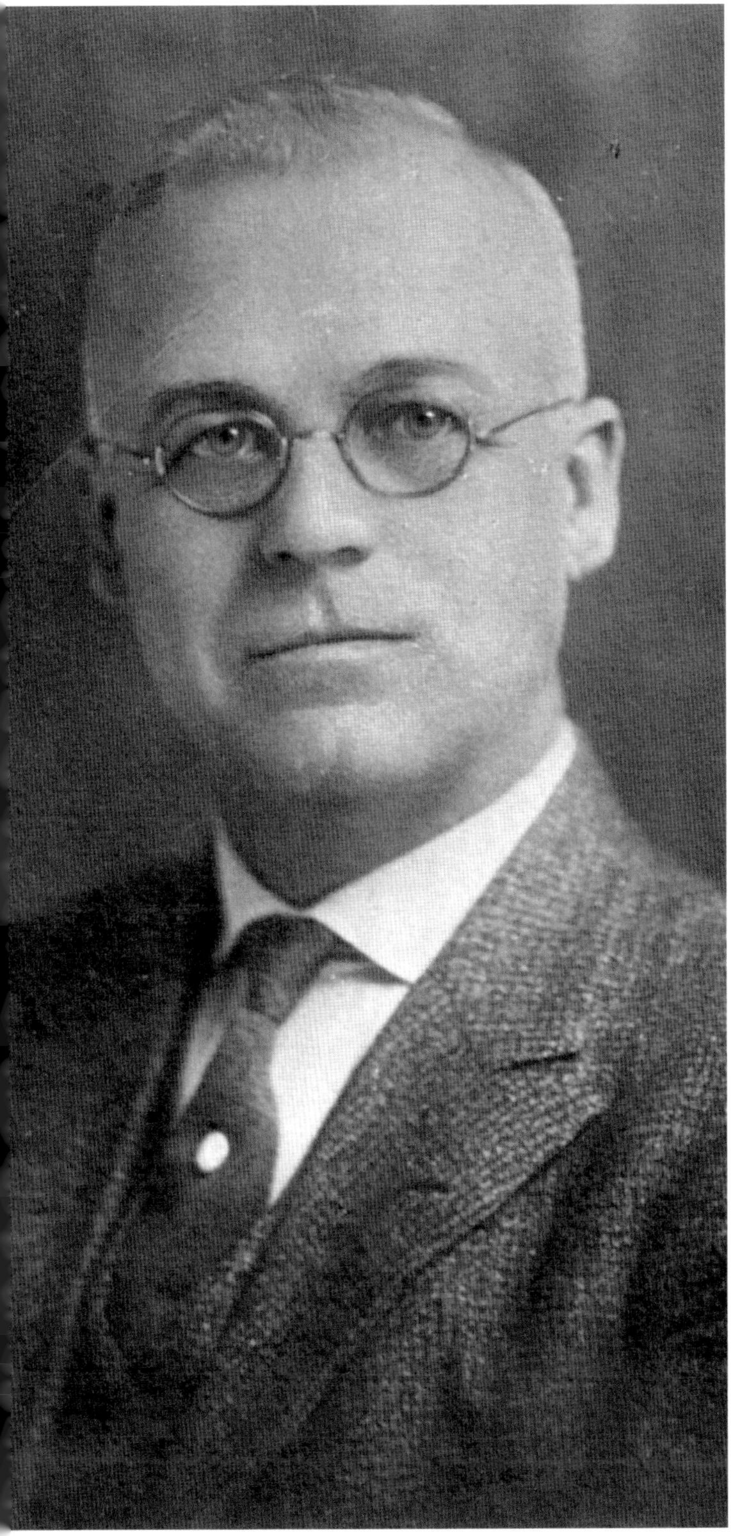

John H. Peacock
John Peacock grew up in Prairie du Chien at a time when clamming on the Upper Mississippi River between Lansing and Muscatine, Iowa, was a major industry. The fishermen harvested tons of clams each summer for their shells, which were sold to button factories. Though occupied as a barber, Peacock had heard stories of the freshwater pearls the fishermen sometimes found in the clams.

By 1899, Peacock began to spend more time following leads on pearls. He would purchase pearls, selling them to one of the registered pearl buyers from Europe or India who stayed at the hotels in Prairie du Chien. Not only did he make astute purchases, he learned the skill of peeling the layers from freshwater pearls to improve their quality or color. For more than 30 years, he dealt in pearls and was well known throughout the area. (Courtesy Prairie du Chien Historical Society, Martner Collection.)

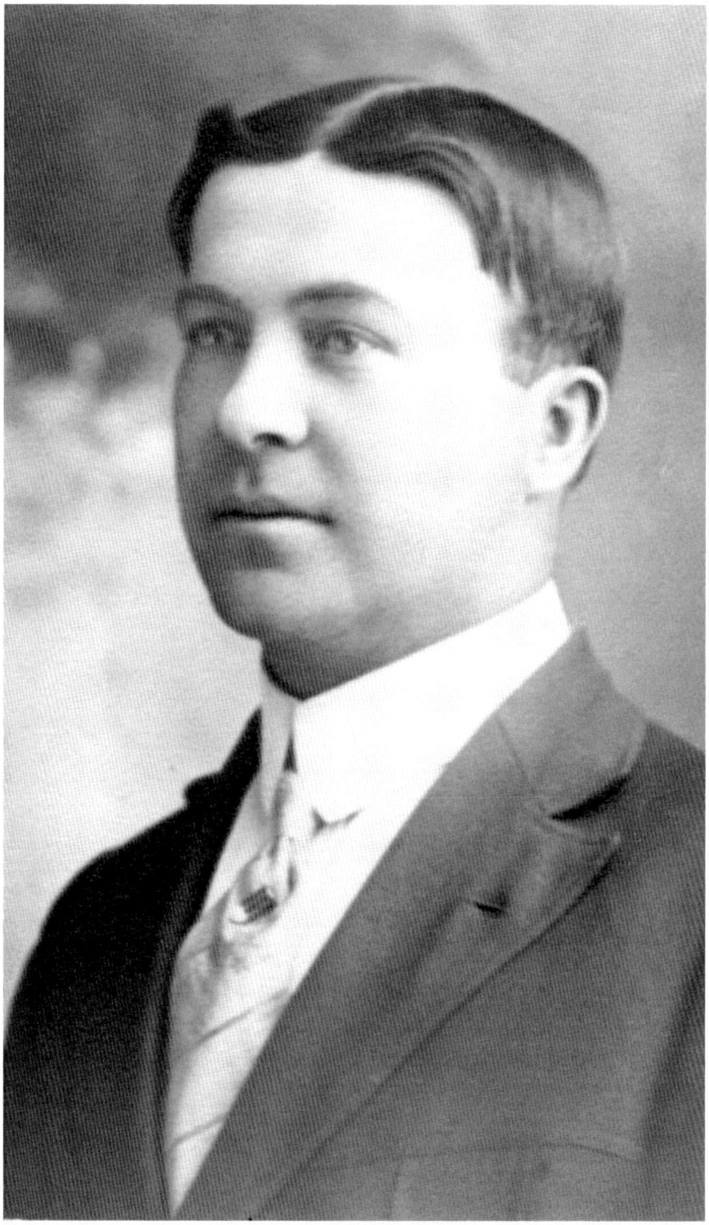

Michael J. Suhrada

Being mayor of the City of Prairie du Chien was not a full-time position. So, like his predecessors and the mayors who would follow, Michael Suhrada had a profession outside of his civic duties. He was a jeweler and watchmaker, owning his own store, from which he also purchased and sold Mississippi pearls.

Suhrada had an avocation as well. An avid duck hunter, he learned to carve and paint decoys. He was one of several men in the 1930s living in Prairie du Chien who made decoys that today are collected because of the skill displayed in their carving and their detailed painting. Peter LaRoque and Theron Dodd were his contemporaries. Suhrada was the most prolific carver in the 1920s and 1930s and taught the skill to Joe and Pep Marousek, who owned the bakery next to Suhrada's jewelry store. (Courtesy City of Prairie du Chien.)

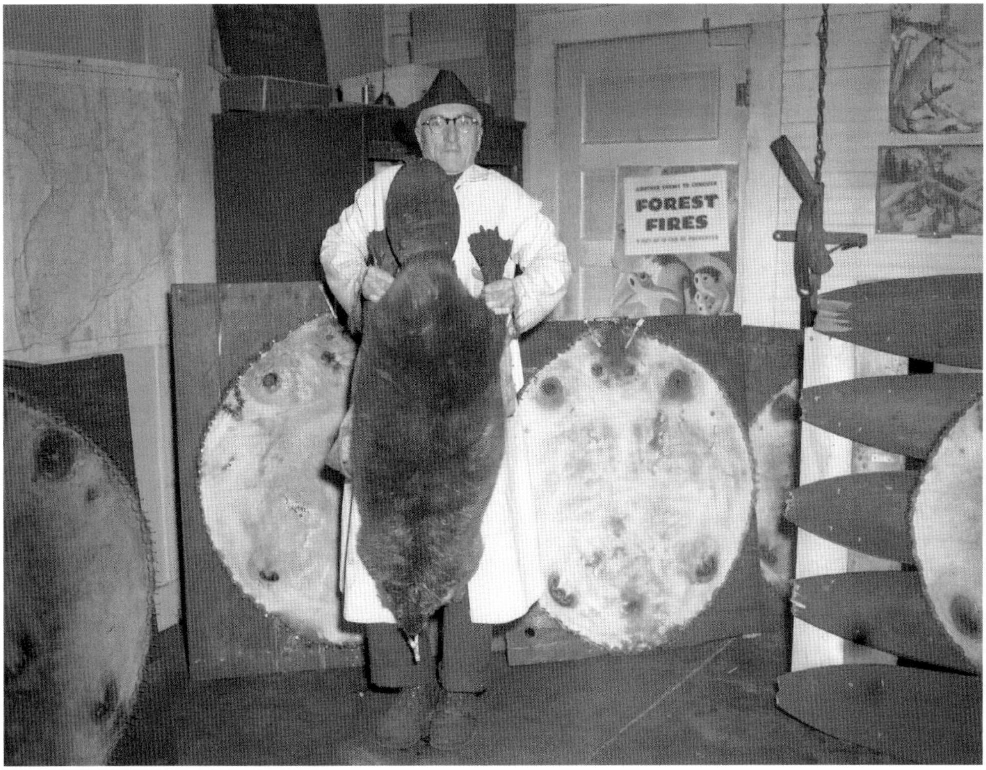

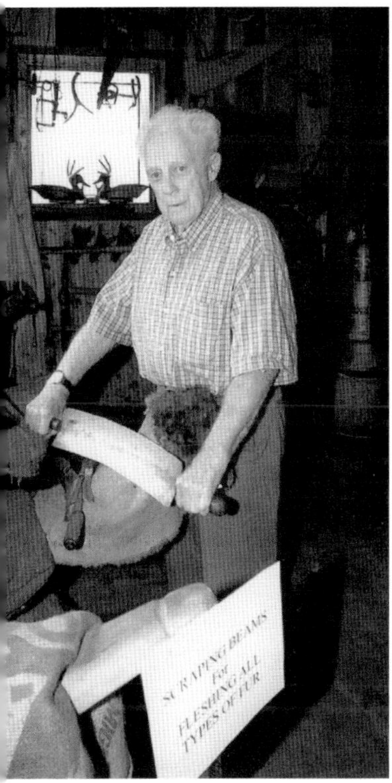

Zernard Deyeorl Brown
Working for his father, who advertised that T.J. Brown is "the largest receiver of furs in the west," Z.D. Brown came to Prairie du Chien in the 1930s as a buyer of raw furs. He opened his own business, The Alaska-Canadian Fur Trading Company, and became known throughout the Midwest for the quality of furs he bought and sold. (Courtesy Prairie du Chien Historical Society, Peckham Collection.)

Lavern Steiner
At the age of 16, Lavern Steiner started to work for Z.D. Brown, learning the art of processing raw furs and the skill of buying and selling. When Brown retired, "Lefty" bought the business, including the unique building that housed the fur company. Any spare time Steiner found outside of his carpentry work and raising a family, he dedicated to working with furs. Into the 21st century, Steiner continued buying and selling furs, a tradition begun by the Indians and the fur traders. The business dwindled as the declining price for furs did not justify the work involved, but Steiner still comes to the company store to tend flowers and share stories. (Courtesy William F. Howe.)

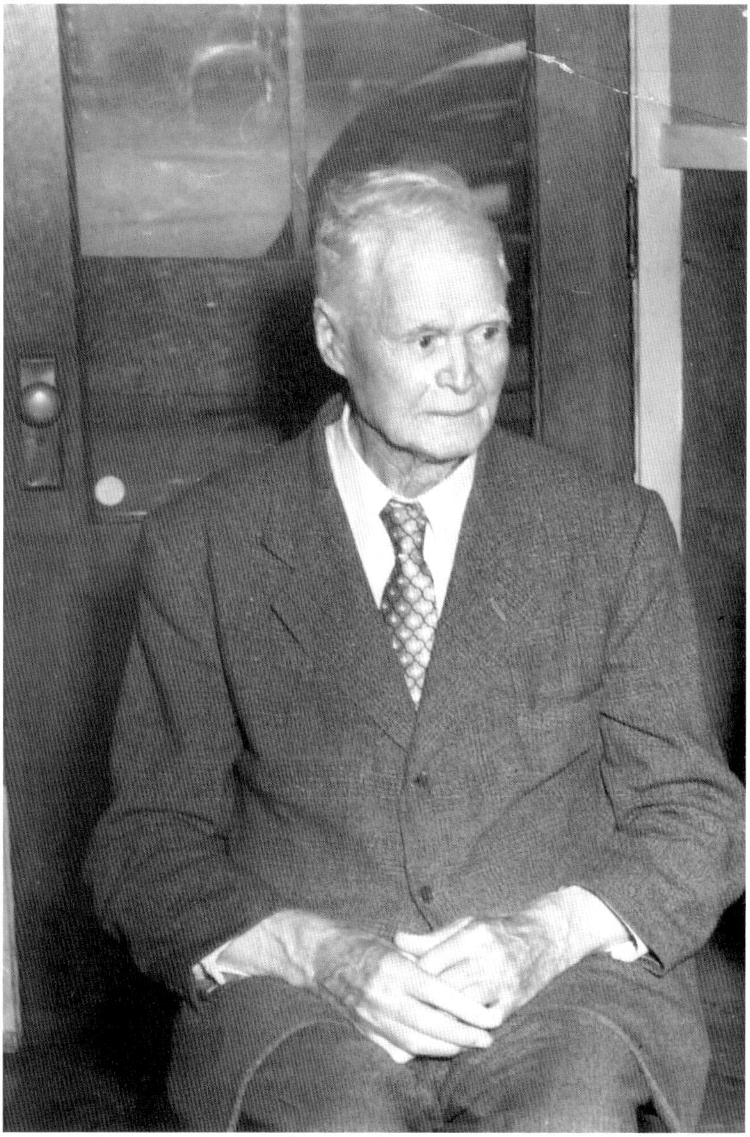

Dr. Peter Lawrence Scanlan

A member of the American Expeditionary Force, Dr. Peter Scanlan set up a private medical practice in Prairie du Chien after World War I. The history of the area fascinated Dr. Scanlan, and he began to conduct research, traveling to St. Louis and Washington, DC, to study documents untouched since being placed in storage 100 years before. His daughter Marian helped him with the translation of letters written in French. The wealth of information he compiled was published in 1937 as *Prairie du Chien: French, British, American*. Echoing this book, Marian wrote a pamphlet on the history of Prairie du Chien for schoolchildren. Dr. Scanlan continued to write monographs and articles detailing the events and personalities contained in his book. Scanlan, along with Cal Peters, J. Alvin Druyor, and Drs. Satter and Farrell, founded the Dr. William Beaumont Foundation, the purpose of which was to raise funds for the restoration of the Fort Crawford Hospital. He was working on a second book about Prairie du Chien at the time of his death. *Prairie du Chien: French, British, American* still stands as the most definitive work on Wisconsin's second-oldest community. (Courtesy Prairie du Chien Historical Society.)

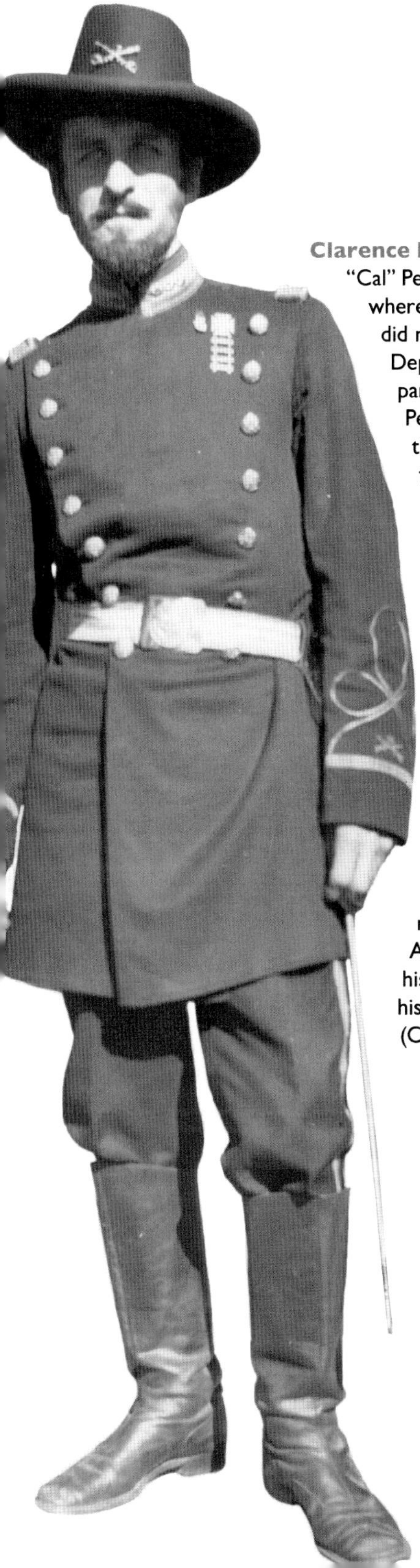

Clarence Nicholas Peters

"Cal" Peters had just finished instruction at the Chicago Art Institute, where he had met and married Helen Marie Hall. Their future did not look good; no one could afford to hire artists during the Depression. Then, Congress passed the Federal Art Project as part of the Works Progress Administration in August 1935. Peters found employment as one of several WPA artists at the Stout Institute in Menominee, Wisconsin. In 1936, again funded by the WPA, Peters painted a mural of Truax Field in Madison, Wisconsin. His biggest commission came when he was retained as part of the large WPA grant given to the City of Prairie du Chien for the creation of Dousman Park. From 1936 to 1948, Peters researched the history of Prairie du Chien. Using what he learned, he designed and fabricated 10 minutely detailed dioramas and painted 11 murals. As the curator of the Museum Prairie du Chien, he placed these works, in conjunction with exhibits of objects, in such a manner as to illuminate the history of the community from the time of the mastodon hunters to the coming of the railroad. Helen Peters wrote the guide to the museum and her husband's art. In 1949, Cal Peters left Prairie du Chien to become the curator of history at the Los Angeles County Museum. While out West, he created other murals, paintings, and dioramas, some of which are now part of the collection of the Postal History Foundation. All of his work is carefully researched and represents actual historical events. Here, Peters is pictured in costume for a historical pageant that was held as part of Villa Louis Days. (Courtesy Prairie du Chien Historical Society.)

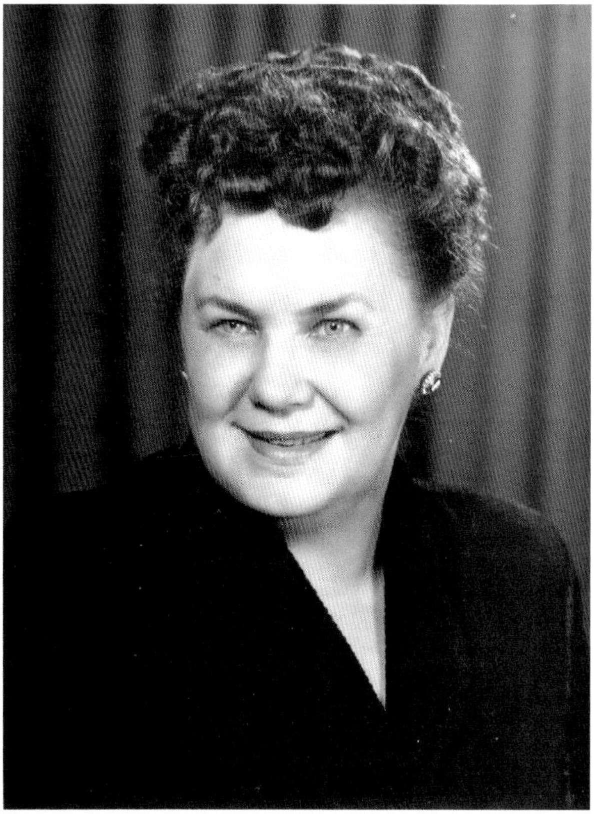

Florence Craig Bittner
Bittner had a love of the river, history, and Indian culture, possibly sparked by a family trip on the Missouri and Mississippi Rivers in 1919. When the City of Prairie du Chien began restoring the Villa Louis, a curator was needed to direct the site and work with Cal Peters. Florence was hired for the position. With a kind and jovial personality, she was beloved by her staff, and the public responded to her hearty welcome. She became a longtime friend of Virginia Dousman Bigelow. When the State Historical Society of Wisconsin took over the Villa Louis, Bittner continued as curator and hostess for the Dousman home. (Courtesy the Bittner family.)

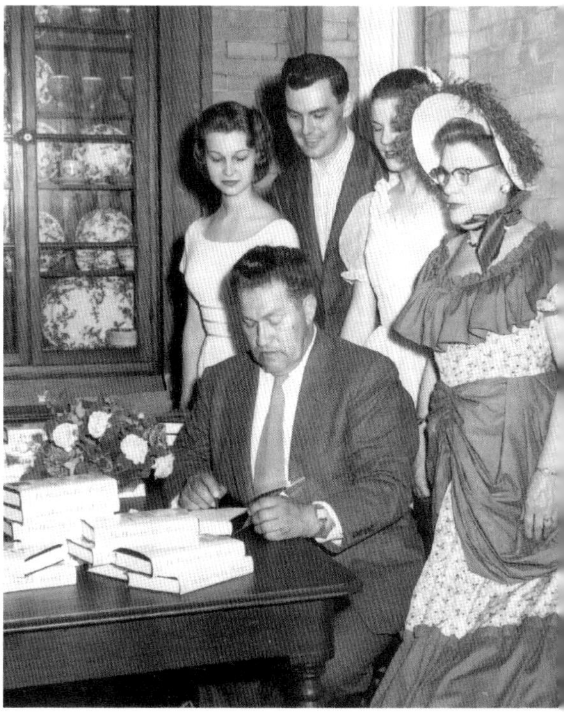

August Derleth
Many of August Derleth's books had as their central character the Wisconsin River Valley and historical personages of southwestern Wisconsin. In 1940, Derleth wrote *Bright Journey*, a novel about the arrival of Hercules Dousman to Prairie du Chien and the fur trade. He followed this book 18 years later with *The House on the Mound.* Derleth made the story of Prohibition and the Villa Louis the plot in the children's book *The House by the River.* Each summer, into the mid-1960s, Derleth visited the Villa Louis to preside over a day selling and autographing his books. (Courtesy Prairie du Chien Historical Society, Howe Collection.)

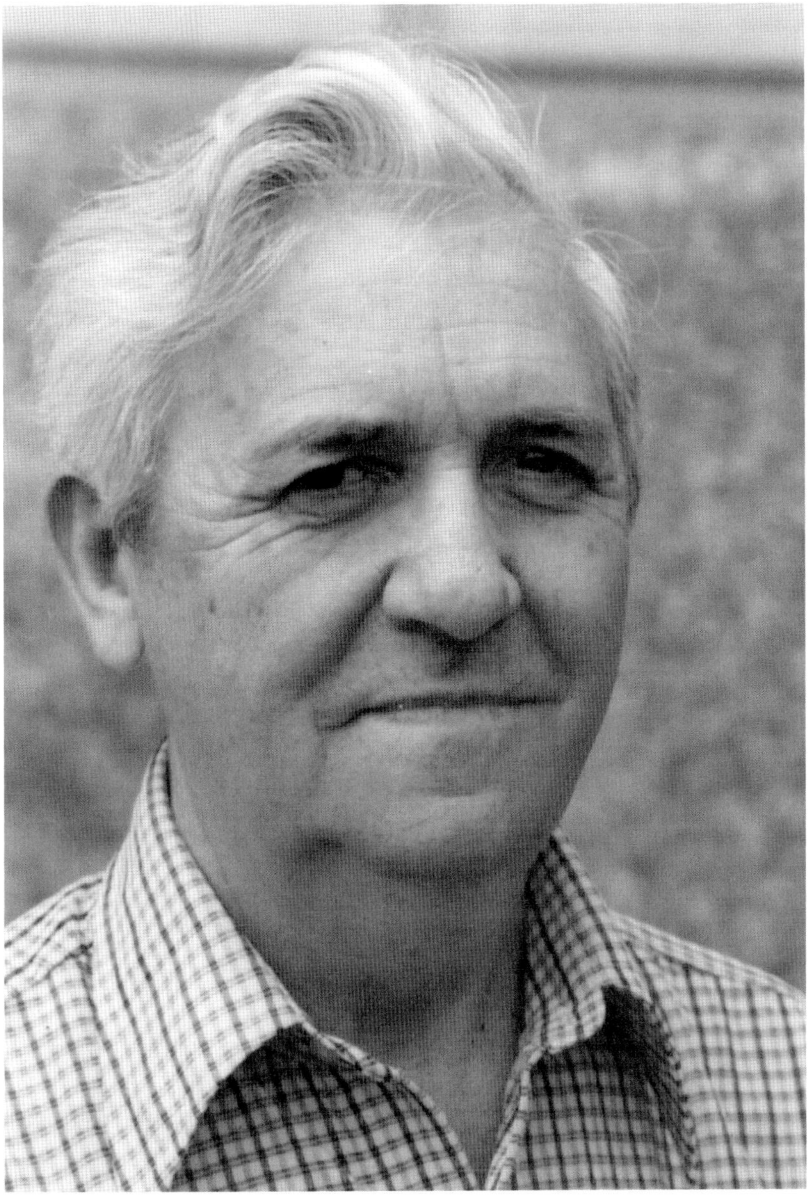

Griffith H. Williams

"Griff" Williams worked for the Farm Supply Co-op in Wautoma, Wisconsin. When the co-op opened a new office in Prairie du Chien in 1949, Williams interviewed for and received the job. Traveling the county to visit farmers, he chatted with the men, and they opened up to the newcomer, telling stories about growing up in Crawford County prior to World War II. Selling insurance, Williams met even more people with interesting stories to relate. He believed these reminiscences should be recorded before they were lost. In 1971, he received a small grant from the National Endowment for the Humanities for an oral-history program. Williams interviewed 23 men and 7 women, recording stories and memories of events in their lives. He was the consulting historian for the creation and dedication of the Cornelius Family Park and the 1980 opening of the Prairie du Chien Regional Tourist Information Center. (Courtesy the Williams family.)

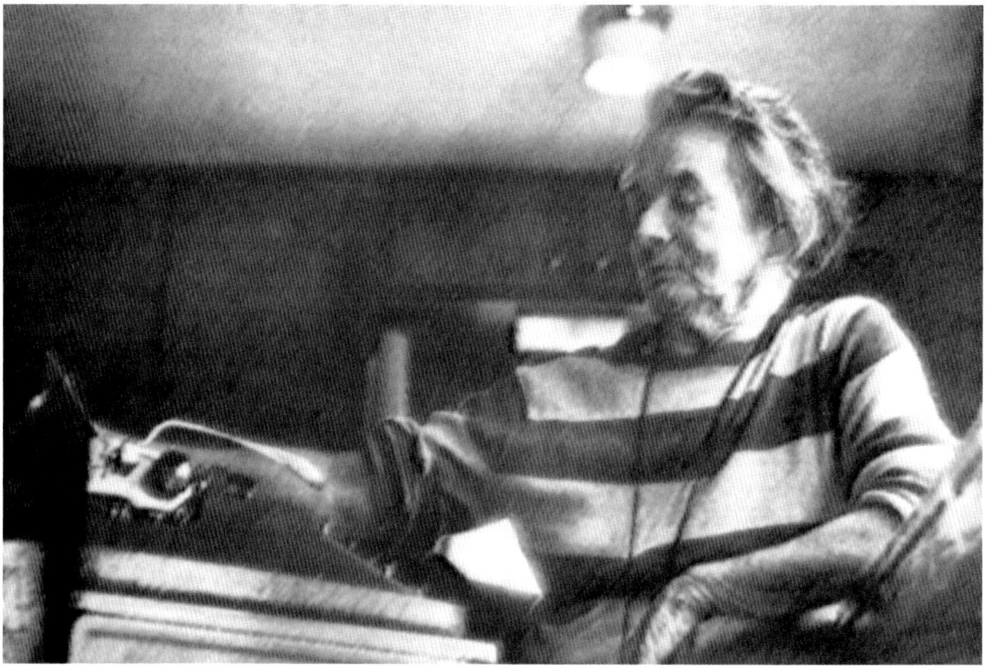

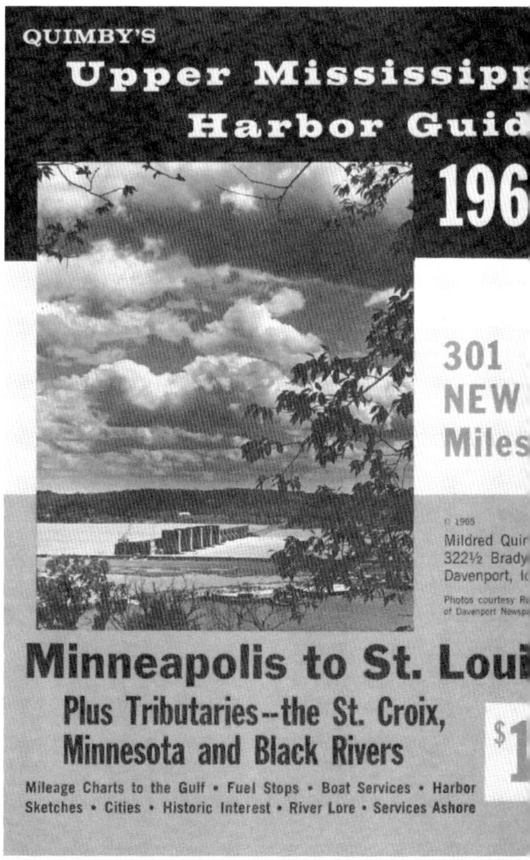

Mildred Quimby

A comment typical of those who knew Mildred Quimby says, "One look at her and you knew Quimby hung close to the river. A character in every sense of the word, a river rat to be sure. The old Mississippi will never be quite the same after Quimby's death." Mildred Quimby worked for major newspapers, but she had fallen in love with rivers as a child while on canoe trips. She returned to Wisconsin, settling across from Prairie du Chien and the Mississippi River. For 21 years, she traveled up and down the river, collecting information for *Quimby's Upper Mississippi Harbor Guide*. The guide began as a personal notebook full of notations on harbor locations, facilities for boaters, and mileages. She then published her records in mimeograph form. Quimby traveled the Mississippi River in her 16-foot boat. What she could not cover by water, she did from her white Dodge Omni. A mutt she picked up on one of her trips always traveled with her. Boaters found her guide to be more accurate and complete than publications produced by the Army Corps of Engineers. Per Quimby's request, upon her death in 1983, her ashes were cast into the Mississippi River at Prairie du Chien. (Above, courtesy *Quimby's Cruising Guide*; right, courtesy Prairie du Chien Historical Society.)

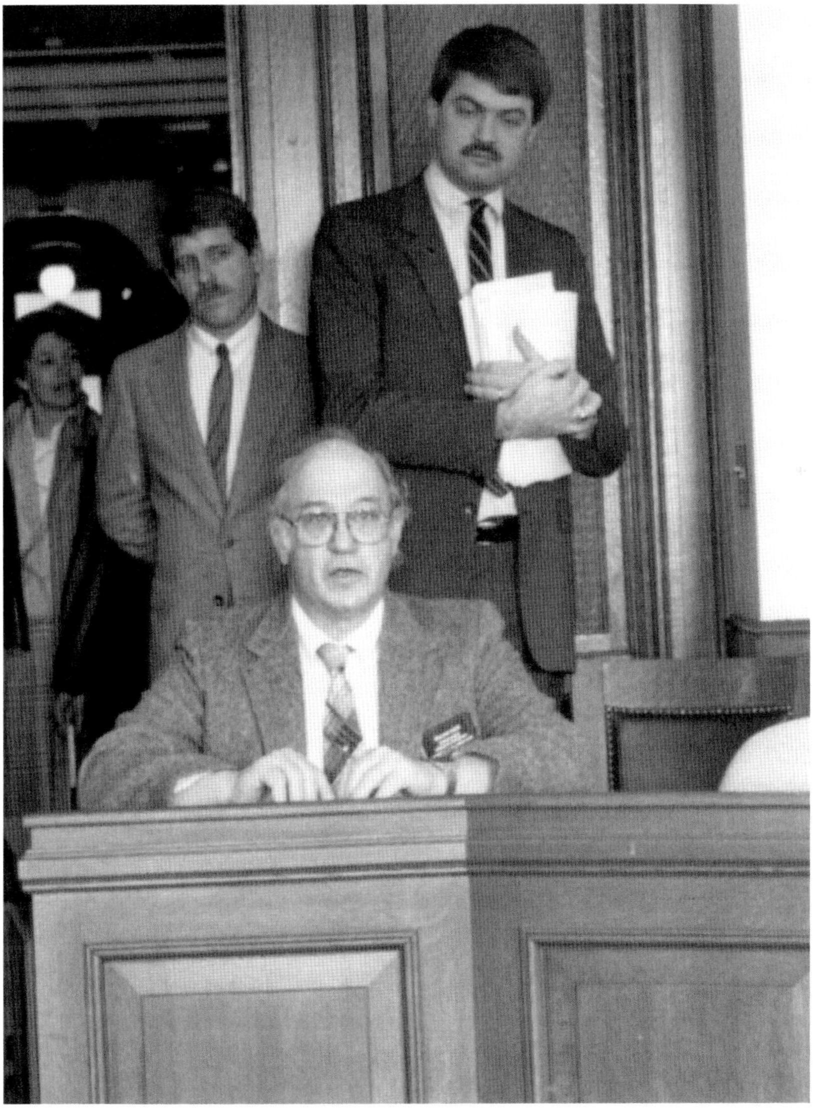

William F. Howe

From an early age, like his father and grandfather, Bill Howe was drawn to the Mississippi River. He has boated, fished, and swam the river in the summer, hunted ducks in the fall, and skated the sloughs in the winter. He knows the flow of every backwater and the location of each wing dam. Howe's knowledge of and passion for the Mississippi River have not gone unnoticed. In 1953, he was appointed to the Wisconsin Conservation Congress, and is now the longest active member. Governor Dreyfus made Howe a member of the Wisconsin-Minnesota Boundary Area Commission. He was appointed by the Wisconsin Department of Natural Resources to the citizen advisory committee for the Lower Wisconsin Riverway Project, and is active on other commissions pertaining to the Mississippi. Because of his knowledge of the waterway and its wildlife, Howe has testified in Washington, DC, and in Madison on environmental and management issues. With the death of his father, Lyman Howe, in 1949, Bill Howe became editor of *The Courier*. He still boats and fishes the Mississippi River, but, when he reached his late 80s, his children forbade him from conducting his solitary skating of the sloughs. (Courtesy Prairie du Chien Historical Society, Howe Collection.)

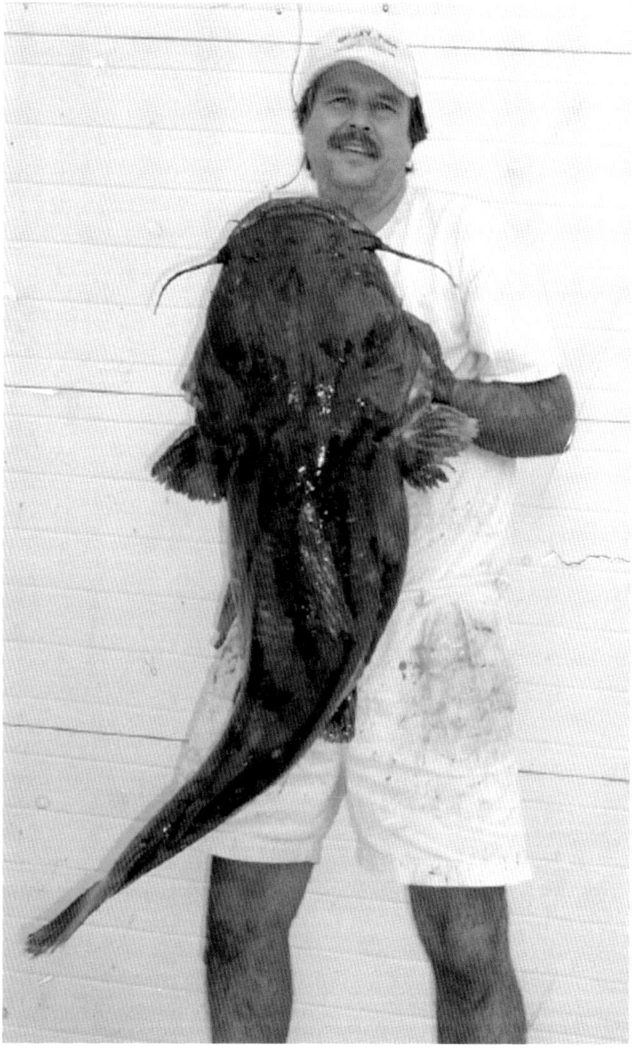

Michael J. Valley

There were about 75 full-time commercial fishermen on the Upper Mississippi River 40 years ago. Now, it is down to a mere handful, one of whom is Mike Valley. His grandfather Carl and his father, Dallas, were commercial fishermen. When not on the river fishing, Carl and Dallas both carved duck decoys and prowled the wooded areas of Crawford County, hunting morel mushrooms. Many a time, Mike tagged along.

Mike Valley opened his own fish shop four years after graduating from high school, and today, over 25 years later, it is an institution in Prairie du Chien. Each morning, Valley and one or two others are on the Mississippi River in hopes of netting a good catch. With few markets for fresh fish, Valley brings his catch home and smokes the fish in a shed behind his shop. He sells not only smoked and pickled fish, but turtle meat and frog legs. He makes some of the fish and turtle meat into bologna, summer sausage, and jerky. Like his grandfather and father, Valley carves and accurately paints decoys. He has expanded from ducks to geese, fish, and amphibians, including a 126-inch muskie, on display outside his market. His knowledge of the Mississippi River, the life within it, and the lore of the men and women who found existence from the river is extensive. He has produced a video explaining how to smoke fish the old-fashioned way, with hickory wood, and he was featured on *American River Renegades.* (Courtesy Mike Valley.)

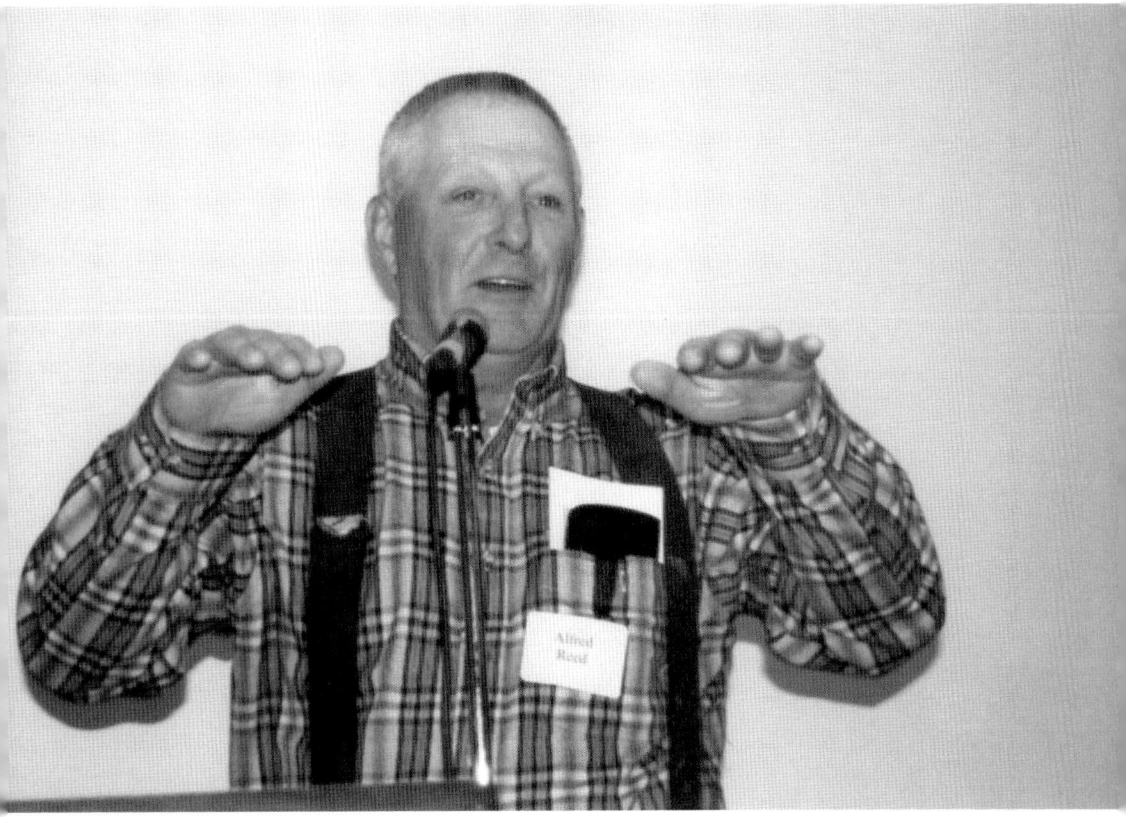

Alfred E. Reed
The descendant of a scout for the US Army stationed at Fort Crawford, Al Reed grew up close to where his ancestor had served. Living in the Fourth Ward, Reed spent much of his free time on the river, exploring the many islands, where he found remains of the first Indian cultures of the Upper Mississippi River. An avocational archaeologist, his knowledge of the islands and the artifacts he cataloged was so extensive that archaeologists from the University of Wisconsin system consulted him any time they came to Prairie du Chien. A newly located mound group was named for Reed and listed in the National Register of Historic Places. In 1998, the Mississippi Valley Archaeological Center at the University of Wisconsin–LaCrosse presented Reed with the Regional Archaeologist Award. Reed donated his collection to the Mississippi Valley Archaeological Center. (Courtesy Mississippi Valley Archaeology Center.)

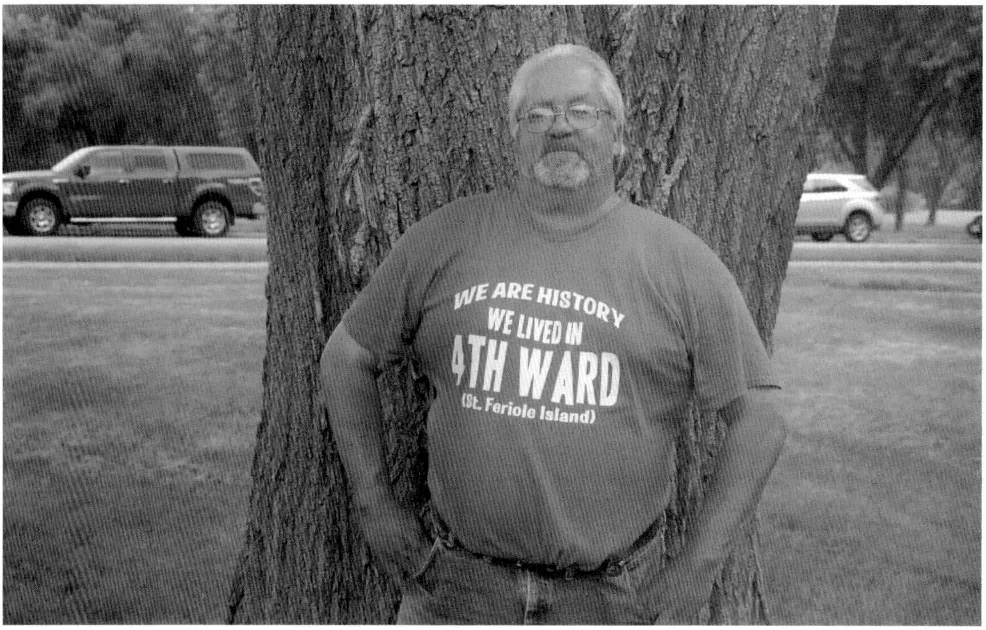

Jeff Lessard

Homes of five generations of the Lessard family stood within "a stone's throw" of one another south of Blackhawk Avenue in the Fourth Ward. All are now gone; the family and neighbors relocated in the 1970s and 1980s. Jeff Lessard regularly writes about growing up in the Fourth Ward on Facebook. Many of his stories have been published in *Big River* magazine. His stories are a poetic blend of interaction with and the beauty of nature, the neighborhood of the Fourth Ward, and adventures on the river and island. His stories are happy memories of growing up, yet there is a poignant melancholy. He writes, "The stories these lots now empty tell." To Lessard, the Fourth Ward is "part of my very being." (Author's collection.)

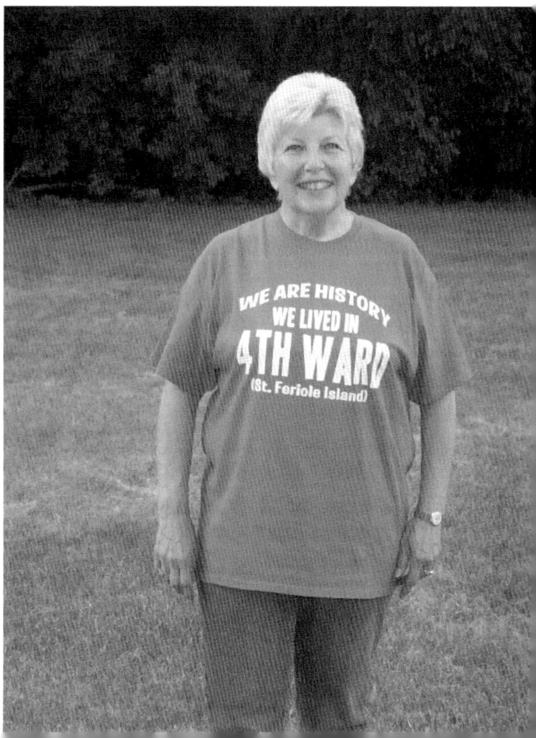

Bette Valley Beneker

As families and houses began to be moved out of the Fourth Ward, Bette Beneker's mother, Mary Valley, drew a map and started to write down the locations of the houses and who had lived in them. Beneker believed that the work her mother had done from memory needed to be continued. Using printed sources and the memories of older residents, Beneker has compiled an extensive record of the 250-plus homes that were once in the Fourth Ward and has listed the occupants of those homes as far back as possible. The "neighborhood" is preserved by her and Jeff Lessard. (Author's collection).

CHAPTER SIX

Promoters and Entrepreneurs

*He provided good leadership and was always positive about Prairie du Chien. . . .
He was the best promoter of Prairie du Chien.*

—Gary Koch, 2001

The first person to promote Prairie du Chien was Rev. Alfred E. Brunson. In 1857, he published the pamphlet *Prairie du Chien. Its Present Position and Future Prospects* in response to inquiries as to why one should settle or invest in Prairie du Chien. He cited commercial benefits of the community, including the desirable position on the river between Dubuque and St. Paul, the docking facilities for steamboats, and the arrival of the Milwaukee & Mississippi Railroad connecting the Great Lakes with the Mississippi River. As the community grew, there were employment opportunities for skilled and unskilled workers and their families. Listing churches, schools, mills, lumberyards and brickyards, and quarries as assets, Brunson bragged that Prairie du Chien was "exceeded by no place west or north of Chicago."

By the mid-1880s, C.W. Butterfield realized that Prairie du Chien's attraction lay in the river and bluffs. It was a place ideal for "the tourist and summer traveler." For the sportsman, the hills and coulees offered deer, rabbits, and fowl in "unlimited quantities," and the Mississippi River and its tributaries teemed with innumerable fish. Geologists could find fossils and preserved strata of rock in the 400 feet of exposed bluffs. And the summits of the bluffs afforded the most magnificent views of the Mississippi and Wisconsin Rivers.

In 1915, several professionals and businessmen formed the Commercial Club of Prairie du Chien, forerunner of the chamber of commerce. While the chamber worked to improve the quality of life for Prairie du Chien and to attract commercial firms, by the 1930s, its members realized that recreation was the biggest industry in Prairie du Chien. Individuals created products for tourism, established weekend events, and formed groups that had as their goal enticing people to come and enjoy the beauty of nature and history found at Prairie du Chien.

Always thinking, men and women took their knowledge and skills and used their abilities to benefit a society greater than Prairie du Chien. Some established businesses. Others invented products or maintained long-valued goods and skills. And others carried the name and pride of the community to the national level.

Each in their own way promoted Prairie du Chien as a community in which to spend some time, whether a weekend or longer.

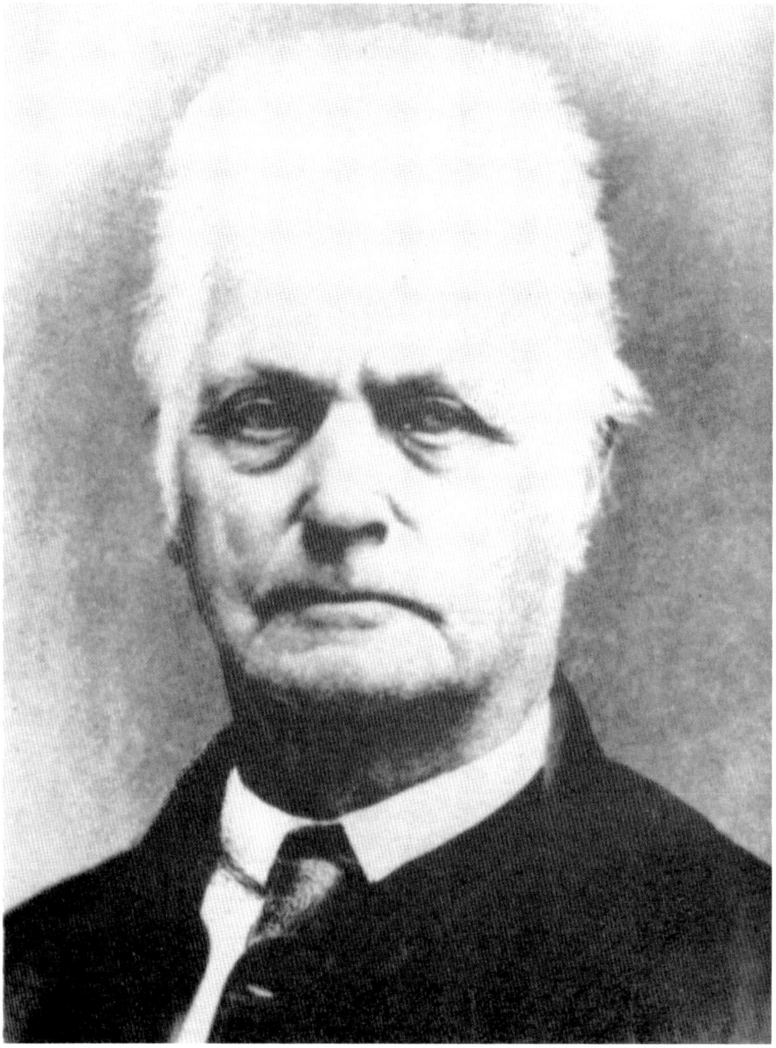

Rev. Alfred E. Brunson

Alfred Brunson arrived in Prairie du Chien the year before Wisconsin became a territory. A Methodist minister, he came to work among the Ojibwe. While he wished to convert them to Christianity, Brunson felt it very important that the Indians learn to read and write English so they would be able to conduct business to their advantage. After a couple of years, Brunson's health failed. Sporadically ministering to the Methodist community in Prairie du Chien, Brunson participated in the many opportunities the frontier offered. He turned to reading law and was elected to the territorial legislature in 1840. Then, two years later, he received a commission as subagent to the La Pointe Indian Agency on Lake Superior. In 1850, he returned to the ministry. When the Civil War began, he volunteered his services as chaplain. Though 68, he was assigned to the 31st Regiment, Wisconsin Volunteers.

Throughout all his exploits, he wrote about the area in which he lived and of his work among the Indians. He was a correspondent to several newspapers; in 1857, with the arrival of the railroad at Prairie du Chien, he wrote for the *Milwaukee Sentinel*. In *Prairie du Chien: Its Present Location and Future Prospects*, Brunson envisioned the expansion of the small community into a major metropolis. He also authored the two-volume *A Western Pioneer: Or Incidents in the Life and Times of Rev. Alfred Brunson Related by Himself.* (Author's collection.)

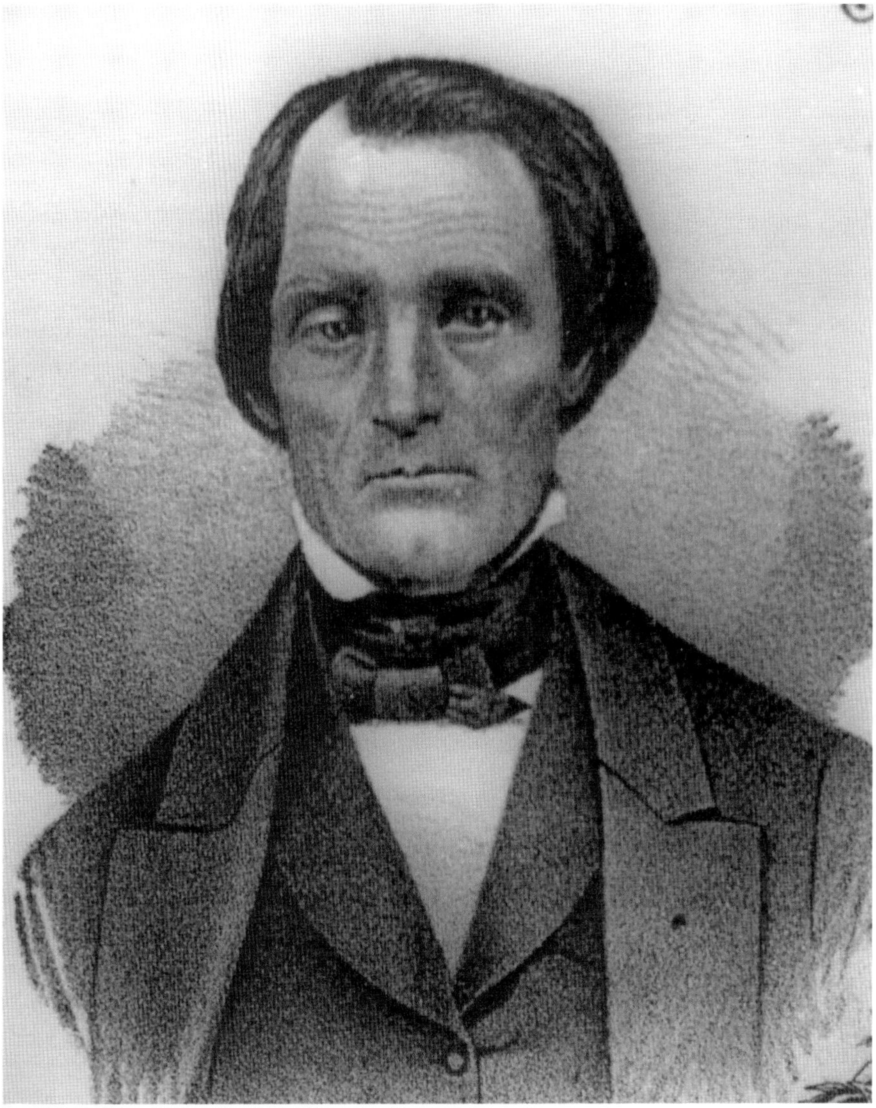

Alexander MacGregor
Adventuresome, like his ancestors who had left Scotland, Alexander MacGregor left upstate New York for Chicago. Arriving in Prairie du Chien in 1835, he saw a need for a ferry to cross the Mississippi River. MacGregor bought part of the Giard Tract in Iowa, naming it "The Ferry Property." He organized a horse ferry, carrying passengers and wagons from the steamboat landing on the south end of Prairie du Chien across the Mississippi River to his landing in Iowa. MacGregor initiated the only means for people, horses, and then automobiles to cross the river until 1932, when a bridge opened. He lived in Prairie du Chien, but then, in 1847, moved his family to what he now called McGregor's Landing. He died there in 1858. He and his last infant were buried in their family cemetery atop the bluff behind the MacGregor home. A longstanding legal feud Alexander had with his brother James over land was settled a year after his death. Ann MacGregor was unhappy with the outcome, so she moved the bodies of her husband and infant son to the family plot in the Evergreen Cemetery in Prairie du Chien. So, despite the fact that McGregor, Iowa, bears Alexander's name, all six Alexander MacGregor family members rest in Prairie du Chien. (Courtesy McGregor Historical Society.)

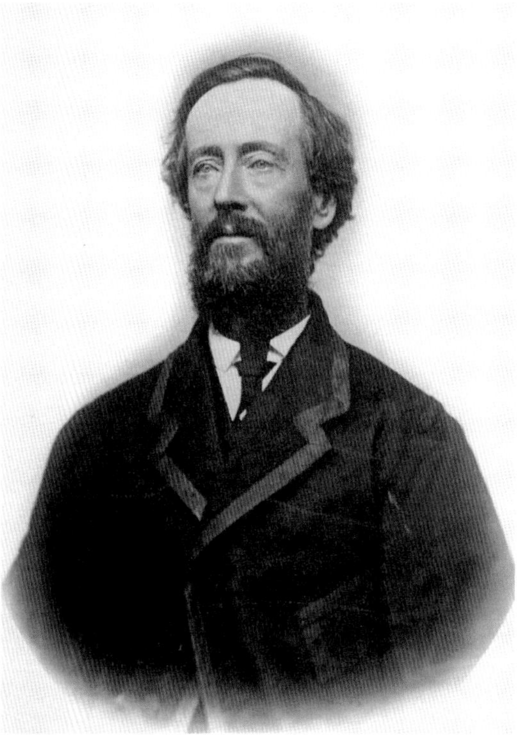

Bernard Walter Marie Brisbois

As the son of Michel Brisbois, B.W. Brisbois built a large stone building for his trading business. But the Indians with whom he had traded were on reservations, so he shifted inventory and operated a general store. Perceptive to the changes occurring, B.W. purchased shares in steamboats and stock in the Milwaukee & Mississippi Railroad. He even speculated with John Lawler in the American Petroleum and Mining Company, in the belief that there was oil to be found in the land around Prairie du Chien. Interviewed three years before his death, B.W. recalled in detail the personality and character of the early residents of Prairie du Chien. (Courtesy Villa Louis Historic Site, Wisconsin Historical Society.)

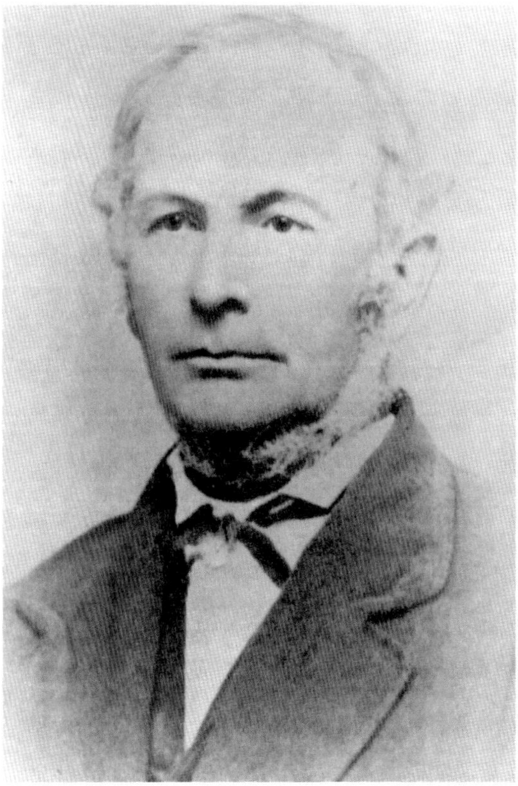

Ira B. Brunson

Like his father, Rev. Alfred Brunson, Ira Brunson involved himself in many occupations. He served in the Wisconsin Territorial Legislature, was appointed postmaster in 1840, and, over the years, held several Crawford County offices, including surveyor, sheriff, register of deeds, clerk of circuit court, and judge of probate court. In 1849, he surveyed the Town of St. Paul in Minnesota Territory. His two most lasting impressions are the survey of the Prairie du Chien Union Plat and the many artesian wells he drilled that still flow. (Courtesy Crawford County Circuit Court.)

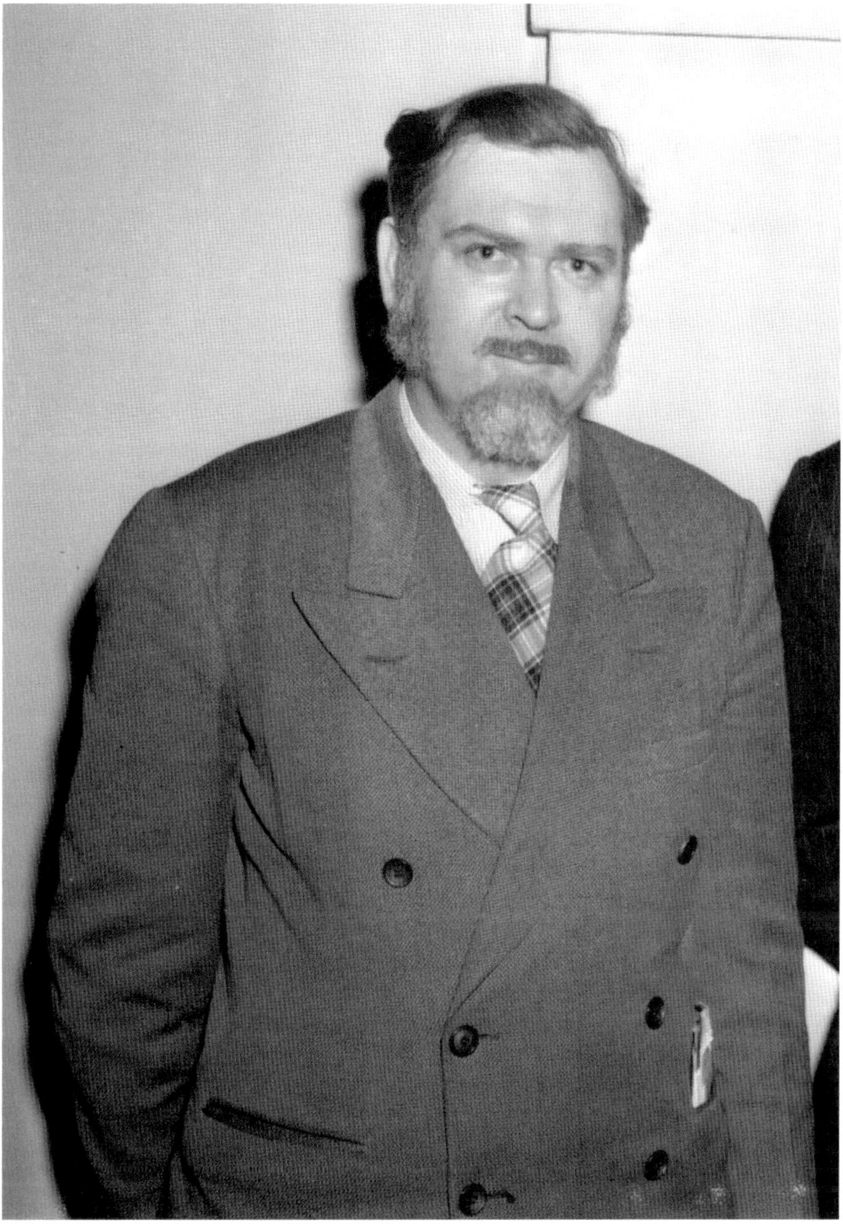

James Alvin Dru'yor

J. Alvin Dru'yor came to Prairie du Chien in 1935 to publish the *Crawford County Press*, then founding the Travel Mats business. People were traveling the country by automobile, and he produced Travel Mats, advertising placemats distributed to restaurants and coffee shops. A mat delineated a local section of highway with "recommended" tourist and commercial stops. Small versions of the mats were bound into books covering an entire highway. Dru'yor's business promoted tourism, and by 1965, it was the second-largest travel recommending organization in the United States. Besides being president of the Prairie du Chien Chamber of Commerce, J. Alvin Dru'yor was appointed to the Mississippi River Parkway Commission. He was chairman of the committee that in 1958 made the pilot's wheel the official emblem of the Great River Road. (Courtesy Wisconsin Historical Society.)

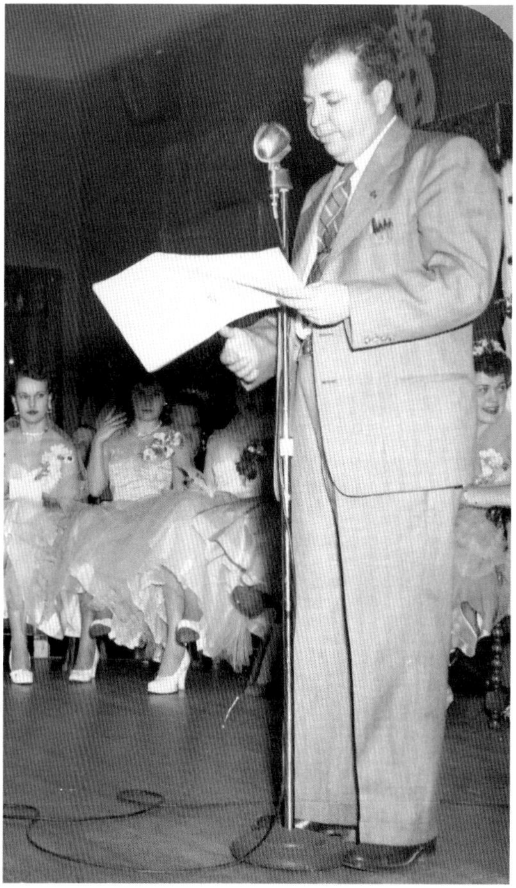

Niles D. Day

Niles "Buck" Day (left, and second from right below) believed that he and his family should be involved in the community, and they were. Buck Day was owner and publisher of *The Prairie Spy*, and he, his wife, Norma, and their children made sure the paper was written, typed, printed, and distributed every week. In 1951, as an active member of the VFW post, he organized the first Ice Fisheree to raise money, then served as chairman for 14 years. As Christmas 1952 drew near, Day heard of some families who needed a helping hand, and of others for whom Christmas would not come for their children. Day talked to some merchants, and thus was born Operation Santa Claus. For 12 years, *The Prairie Spy* spearheaded the program. The VFW met in the old stone schoolhouse, and Day thought this would make a perfect youth center. With support from students, The Stop-n-Bop was born. Buck and Norma and the youth center are gone, but the two other community events continue. The chamber of commerce sponsors the Ice Fisheree on Gremore Lake, and Operation Santa Claus endures through the work of the Jaycees. Pictured below is the 1953 Ice Fisheree Committee. (Both, courtesy the Day family.)

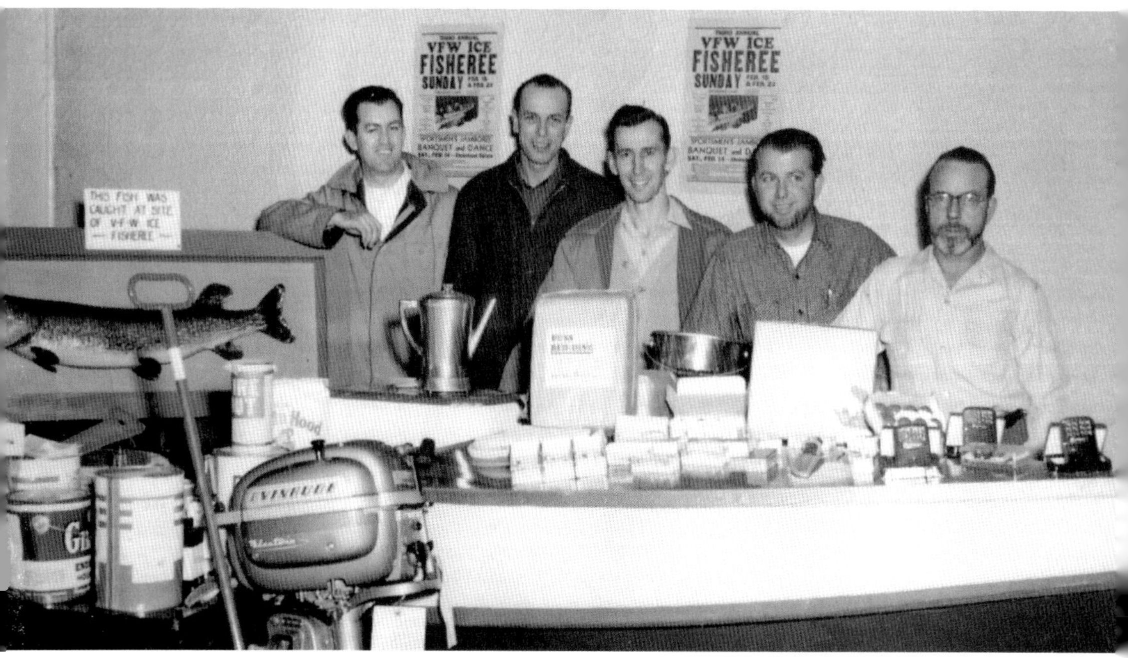

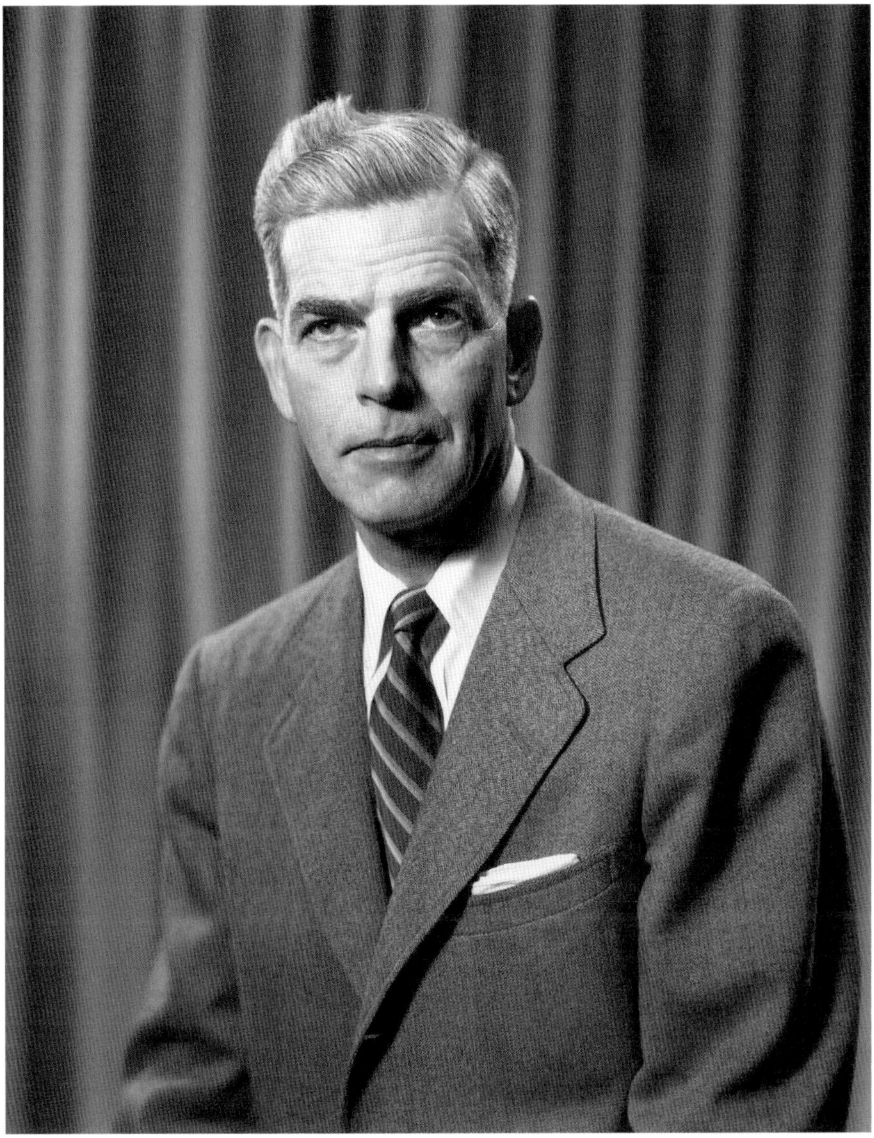

Martinus J. Dyrud

Marty Dyrud was a chemical engineer, working for a company that also owned Burgess Cellulose. That connection, and the fact that Prairie du Chien was the hometown of his wife, Blanche Paris, drew the couple back. Marty opened Dyrud Laboratories, but the history of Prairie du Chien and Wisconsin became his prime interest. In 1943, he helped found the Dr. William Beaumont Foundation and was elected its president. In the mid-1950s, he aired a series of "History Chats" on WPRE radio. His topics ranged widely across the history of Prairie du Chien and its vicinity, and the show revealed much about how the media produced history programs for a popular audience in the middle of the 20th century. Dyrud's avocation brought him an appointment to the board of curators of the State Historical Society of Wisconsin. He was an organizing member of the Historic Sites Foundation in 1960, which, for many years, operated Circus World Museum in Baraboo, Wisconsin. It was a fitting connection, for, as a young boy growing up in Baraboo, Marty's neighbors were the family of Albert Ringling, owner of Ringling Brothers Circus. (Courtesy Prairie du Chien Historical Society, Peckham Collection.)

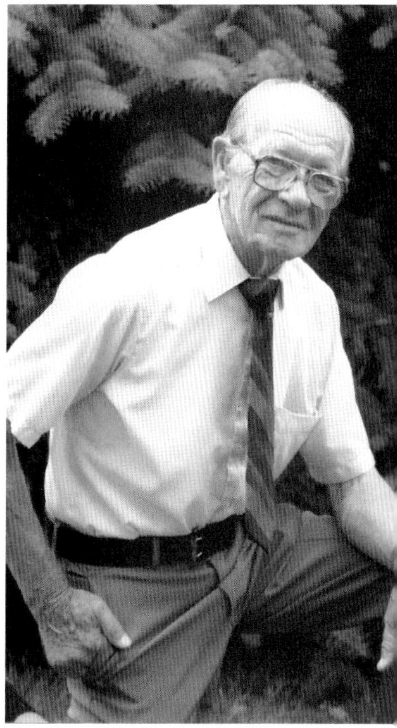

Arthur J. Frydenlund

A barber by trade, Art Frydenlund and his wife, Elaine, opened the Brisbois Motel, surrounded by bluffs brilliant in autumn colors. Art remarked that many people in the Midwest did not have the opportunity to see such magnificence, and that therefore, "We ought to get the word out." Thus began 50 years of promoting the natural beauty and history of the area. Frydenlund served as director of Wisconsin Innkeepers, president of Blackhawk Country, director of Hidden Valleys, and a member of the chamber of commerce and the Industrial Development Corporation, helping bring 3M to Prairie du Chien. He was appointed to the state tourism committee and served on the county board. In his spare time, Frydenlund enjoyed archery, built a ski jump, and tinkered in his workshop. He holds several patents, including improvements for accuracy in archery; barbering equipment; and a miter guide for portable saws, a prototype of the miter saw. In 1984, he was honored as a "longtime pioneer in the promotion of tourism and industry in southwest Wisconsin and northeastern Iowa." Frydenlund is pictured below with his miter guide invention. (Right, courtesy the Frydenlund family; below, courtesy Prairie du Chien Historical Society, Peckham Collection.)

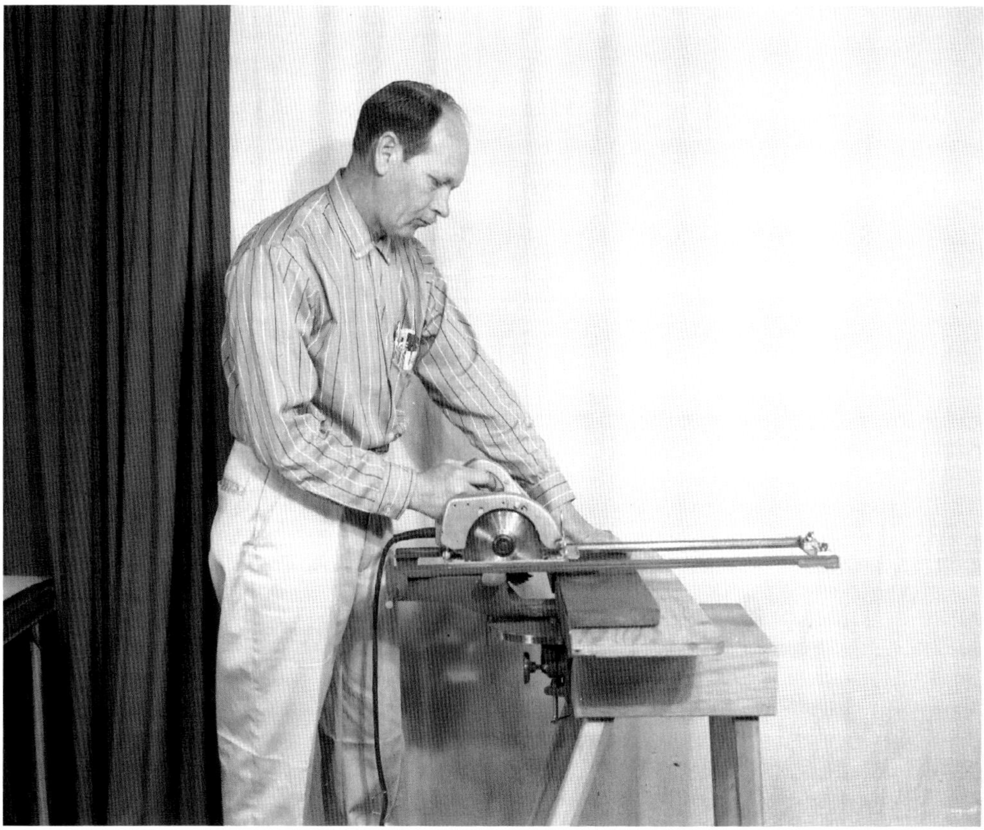

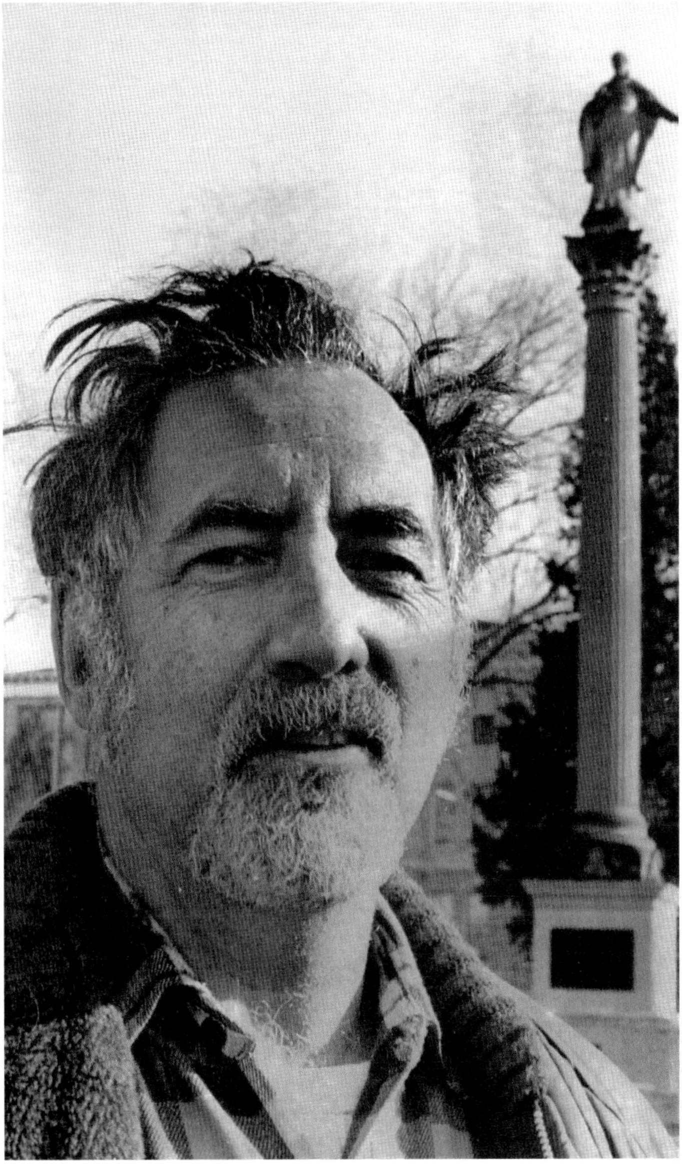

David Meyer

Dave Meyer could be seen every day at the post office, chomping on a cigar, always with a story and a laugh. Owner of Meyer Brothers Salvage, Meyer described himself as a former junk dealer turned "scrap consultant." Always involved in the community, he was elected president of the Kiwanis Club and president of the chamber of commerce. While president of the chamber, Dave helped organize The Great Fire Engine Race of America, held for the first time on Memorial Day weekend in 1971. The 52-mile race wound its way throughout Crawford County. Meyer said he would follow the classic fire truck in his wrecker to "pick up the pieces." The following year, he convinced Charles Kuralt to come to Prairie du Chien and film the race for *On the Road*. In 1973, Gov. Patrick Lucey appointed Meyer chairman of the 26-member Wisconsin Committee for the Marquette-Jolliet Tercentenary, to coordinate the reenactment of Marquette and Jolliet's 2,900-mile canoe trip. (Courtesy Prairie du Chien Historical Society.)

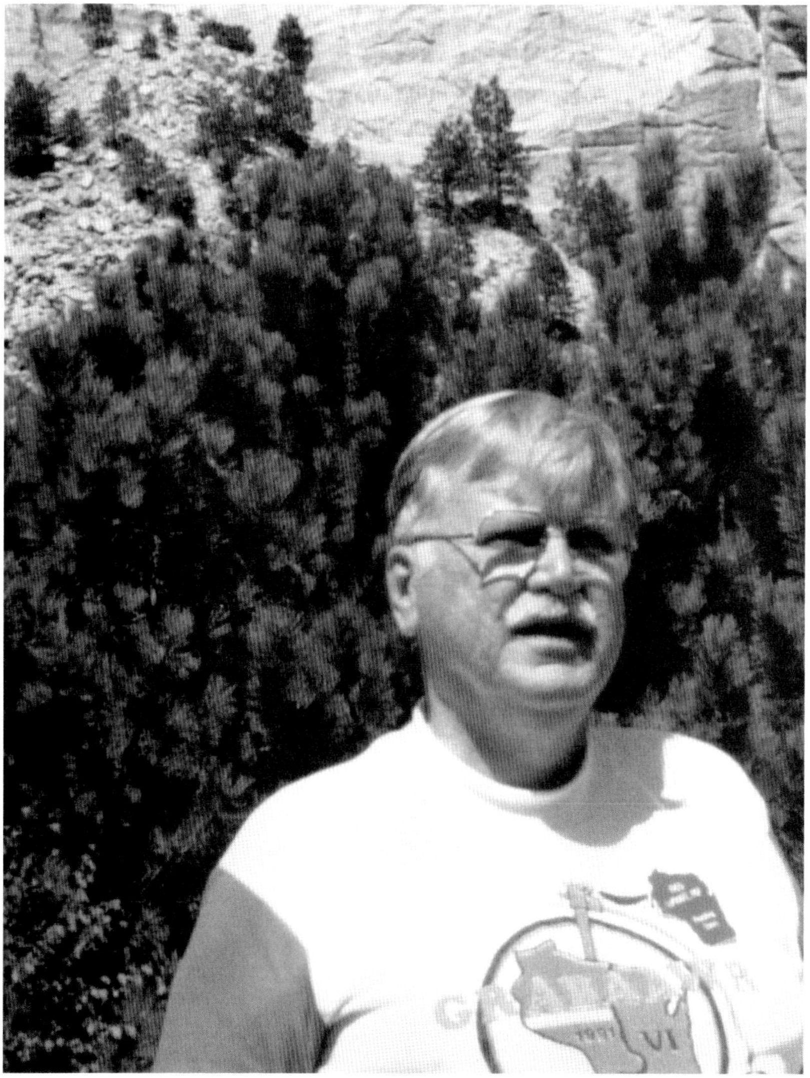

Charles Frederick La Pointe

An educator, musician, and songwriter, Fred LaPointe taught at Prairie du Chien and Wauzeka, but always promoted Prairie du Chien, where his ancestors had settled in the late 1700s.

When the position as executive secretary/director of the Prairie du Chien Chamber of Commerce opened in 1976, Fred redirected his energy and focus and threw all his abilities into promoting the community and its French heritage. For almost 30 years, he worked ceaselessly. He provided the initial information and contact to bring the ships *Delta Queen* and *Mississippi Queen* to Prairie du Chien and maintained relations to ensure the boats docked year after year. He organized The Year of the French in 1985, a yearlong venture to celebrate the 300th anniversary of French presence on the prairie with Fort St. Nicolas. He was the constant presence behind the Prairie du Chien Committee for the Performing Arts and supervised various tours. The State of Wisconsin Division of Tourism and the department of transportation gave special recognition to La Pointe for all he did to promote Wisconsin.

After his death, the chamber of commerce established the C.F. LaPointe Award, an honor that is given annually for service to the community. It is the most prestigious and longstanding award the chamber bestows on its members. (Courtesy the LaPointe family.)

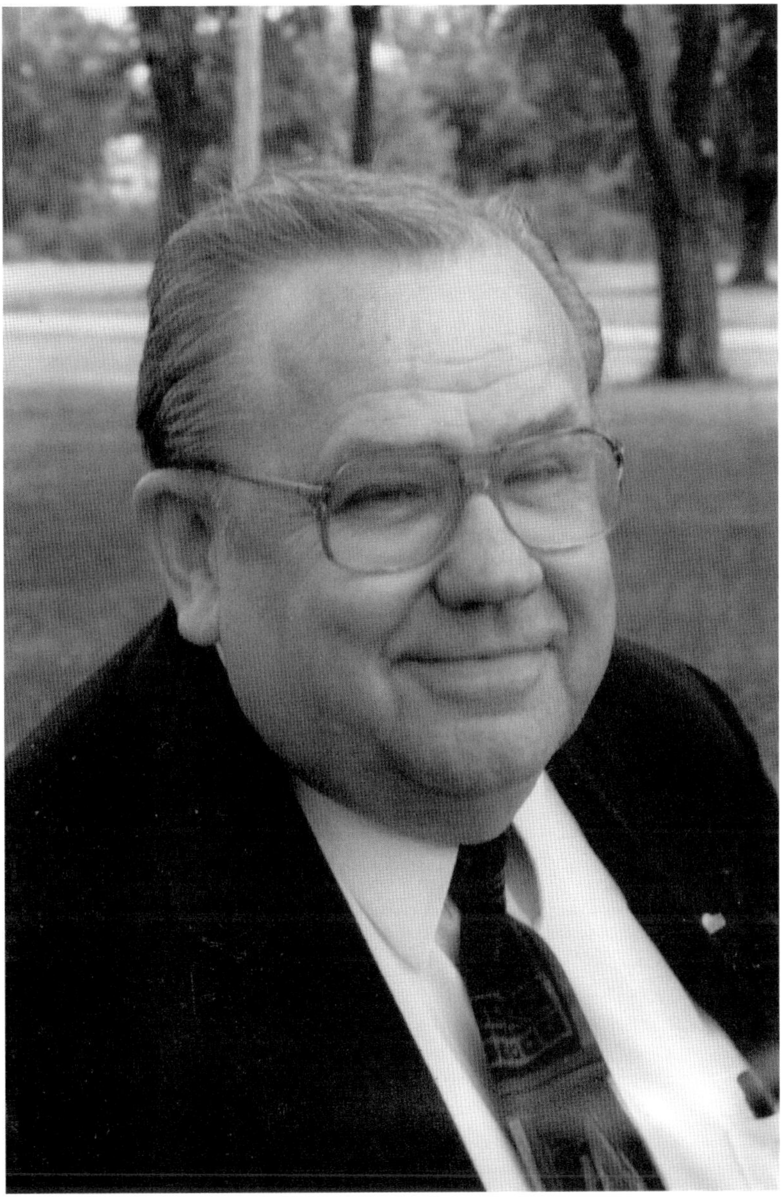

James R. Bittner

Prairie du Chien was always Jim Bittner's home; he never thought of living anywhere else. Always upbeat, he participated wherever he was wanted, from acting as referee at the daily competitive kickball games held in his front yard, to being the emcee at the annual Scout-o-Rama. When the Eagles Club began its annual Eagles Heart and Cancer Telethon in 1975, Bittner was a natural to introduce the guests and urge donations. He and Al Craig had entertained many audiences for years with their skits. Though there were some good performers on the telethon, none made people laugh like Bittner and Craig did. Elected mayor in 1980, Bittner constantly promoted Prairie du Chien for the 12 years he was in office. He helped form the Prairie du Chien Historical Society in 1996 to save the Fort Crawford Hospital, serving as president. The historical society recognized Bittner as its first citizen laureate. (Courtesy the Bittner family.)

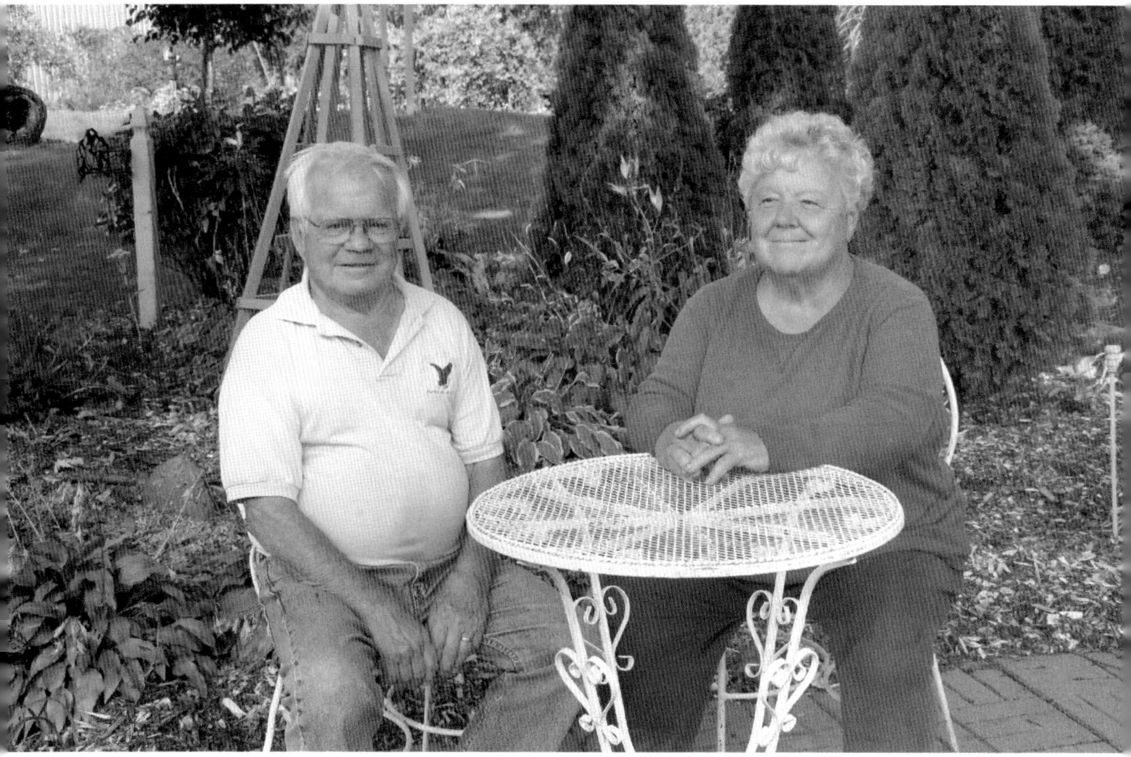

Thomas Nelson and Catherine Nelson

Though Tom Nelson retired from teaching in 2004, saying he could not keep up with the students, his energy is boundless. He is constantly hatching ideas to promote Prairie du Chien and improve the visual impact of the community. He comes up with an idea, implements it, and has the ability to enthuse others so that they will help him.

For years, Nelson has directed the beatification of St. Feriole Island, the former Fourth Ward. He has personally laid thousands of brick pavers along the waterfront and planted varieties of deciduous trees and evergreens, each tree designated for a person from Prairie du Chien. He came up with the idea to create the Trail of Presidents. According to Nelson, every person has a story, and every tree has a story, and this project mated a person with a tree. Before the project was begun, all the trees had been purchased and were dedicated on Arbor Day 2014.

In the winter, Nelson cannot work on the island, but he keeps busy. When Jim Bittner could no longer be the master of ceremonies for the annual Eagles Heart and Cancer Telethon, Nelson stepped right in. He still keeps the program lively with his costumes and nonstop patter and jokes.

Cathie Nelson can also be found on St. Feriole Island. Her project is the Memorial Gardens, a multiblock area landscaped with plantings, walkways, and niches, each piece of foliage designed and planted in memory of a loved one. In 2005, Roy George contacted Tom and Cathie Nelson about establishing a garden on the island. They enlisted the help of Donna Teynor and had an architect design the layout. Each section was adopted in memory of a loved one. The Memorial Gardens is maintained by the person or organization that adopted it, with Cathie and Donna overseeing the work.

Tom credits Cathie for the impetus behind what has become an annual community New Year's Eve celebration. In 2000, Tom, Cathie, and two other couples were bored with that holiday's activities. Tom related that they had seen a peach drop in Georgia and, to laughs, suggested that maybe they should drop a carp. And Carp Fest was born. This crazy idea draws over 1,000 people each year. They brave the cold to gather at bonfires, listen to music, kiss "Lucky" the carp, and watch him being slowly "dropped" by a crane. (Author's collection.)

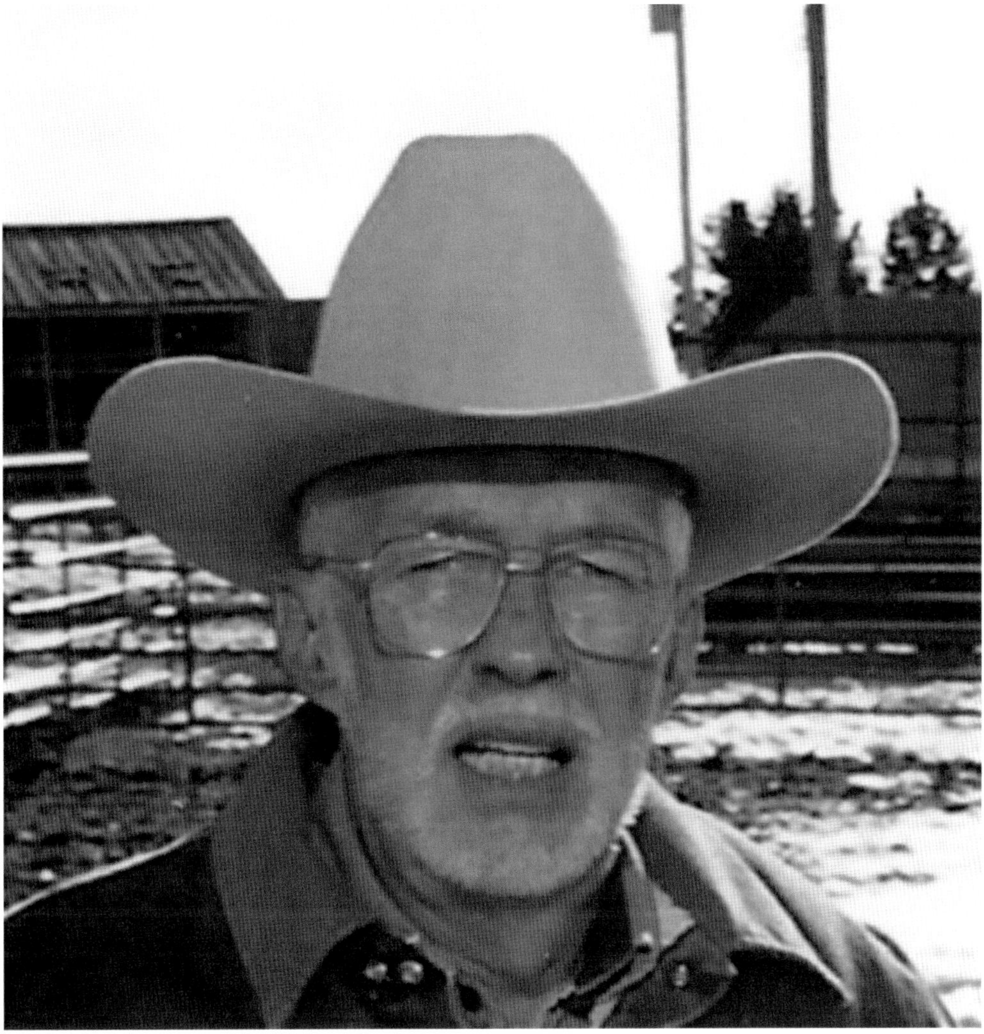

Jimmy J. White
When Jim White married JoAnne Cech, he was a retail sales manager for Speed Queen. A friend persuaded him to install coin-operated washers at a mobile home court. He did, and then he installed a few more. Then, JoAnne and he purchased 60 more machines at $100 each, and the rest, as they say, is history. When Jim and JoAnne returned to Prairie du Chien in 1971, Jim began distributing coin-operated machines full time. He focused on rural areas, made sure the machines were maintained, and thereby kept costs down. At the age of 48, Jim White retired, turning the business over to his son, Jay. Working summers helping his uncle run pony rides had instilled in White a love of horses. He resumed riding, and then decided to see the world or horseback. Returning home, White kept thinking that the community needed a place to enjoy horses, a children's ranch. To acquire funds to purchase land, buy horses, and equip a horse for children, Jim and JoAnne operated a raffle. In 1994, The Children's Ranch became a reality. Operated as a nonprofit organization by volunteers, the 470-acre ranch offers various equestrian activities, events, and social gatherings. It is a place where young people and horses interact. (Courtesy *The Courier Press.*)

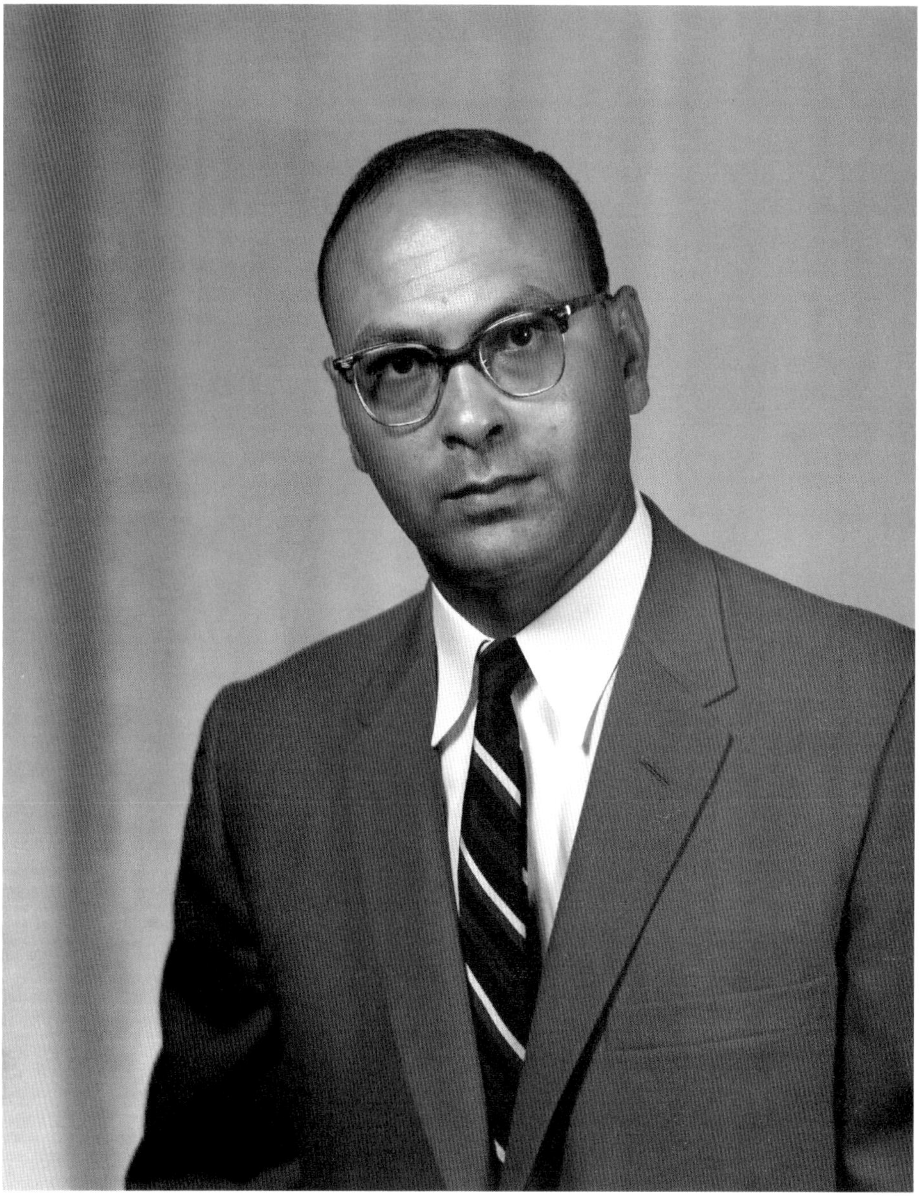

Mahmoud M. Shihata

Receiving a doctorate in soil chemistry from the University of Wisconsin, Moe Shihata returned to Egypt with his wife, Mary. They both taught, he at the University of Alexandria. As Mary was from Wisconsin, they returned, settling at Prairie du Chien. A soil chemist for Growmark Inc., Moe Shihata was always testing different ideas. He helped develop Eeesy Grow, a revolutionary idea in fertilizer. It was a five-year, slow-release product contained in individual packets that were planted with trees. With the process patented, Shihata started S&D Products. He purchased a small farm to begin a test plot to determine how the fertilizer affected the growth of apple trees. Moe, Mary, and their children planted a few trees. From a test plot, the farm grew into an orchard that offers 18 varieties of apples for both wholesale and retail sale. Moe and Mary's son David runs Shihata's Orchard, which he calls "a hobby out of control." (Courtesy Prairie du Chien Historical Society, Peckham Collection.)

CHAPTER SEVEN

Neighbors

I want to think I made a difference, as you get to know everyone in a small town.

—Norb Aschom, 2011

Prairie du Chien has always been a community of neighborhoods. The first French-speaking residents established three villages on the prairie. The Main Village was on the island, the Village of St. Friol was across the slough on the mainland, and the Upper Village was farther north. When Americans came to Prairie du Chien, they chose land on the south end of the prairie, which they called "Lower Town," as it was below Fort Crawford. The new commercial district that started just before the Civil War on Bluff Street (Blackhawk Avenue) became "Upper Town." When the City of Prairie du Chien incorporated in 1872, four wards formed the municipality. The old Main Village was now the Fourth Ward, and Lower Town became the First Ward. Bluff Street divided the Second from the Third Wards. People called the old Upper Village, north of the city, Frenchtown. Each of the wards and Frenchtown was a small community, with a firehouse, a school, a small grocery store, and neighborhood tavern. Even as modernization brought changes to Prairie du Chien, residents into the 21st century call areas of the community the Fourth Ward, Lowertown, and Frenchtown. These were parts of town in which the people were not residents, but neighbors.

To a child, neighbors are the lady at the grocery store who helps find the items that mom sent them to buy, or the couple at the dime store who weighs out a quarter pound of candy because that is all the money the child has. Neighbors are the families who allow their yard, basement, or corral to be the neighborhood gathering place. To adults, neighbors are the doctors who make house calls when one is too sick to go to the clinic. Neighbors are the bankers who know residents and consider their reputation instead of credit reports when advancing funds. Neighbors are lawyers who take a phone call at home on a Sunday night.

Neighbors are the local photographers who record the momentous events in a person's life. Neighbors are the media people who make sure that a local event is announced so that all who wish can participate.

To everyone, neighbors are the people who go out of their way, often volunteering time, to be kind and helpful, to make sure the community has what it needs. They ask nothing in return. Over the years, Prairie du Chien has had many neighbors like this and, thankfully, still does. Some are remembered, and some have been forgotten over time. Everyone in this book is a neighbor, and many others, which space does not allow for here, are also worthy of recognition. Through all of their efforts, individual and combined, these people have made Prairie du Chien a better place to live, a community about which all can be proud to say, "This is my home town."

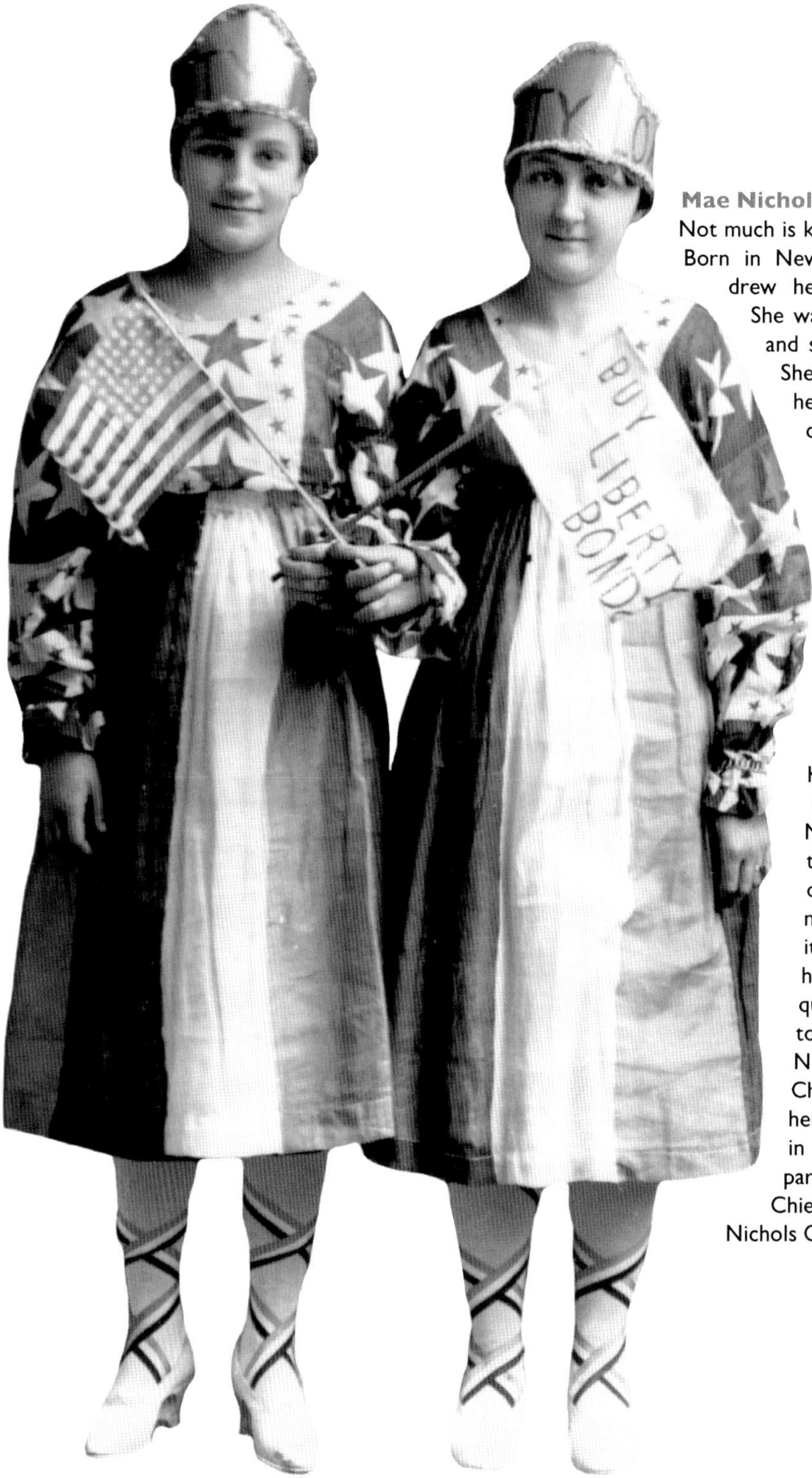

Mae Nichols

Not much is known about Mae Nichols. Born in New York State, something drew her to Prairie du Chien. She was remembered as "short and stocky and had dark hair. She always had stains on her fingers." Those stains came from developing solutions, as Nichols was a photographer. By 1906, she had opened a studio, offering "Artistic Photography." She recorded many bridal couples and their attendants and took natural, relaxed portraits of children and adults. She developed Kodak film for others. No ordinary photographer, Nichols was a member of the Women's Federation of Photographers and mounted exhibitions of its members' works in her studio. Then, just as quietly as she had come to the community, Mae Nichols left Prairie du Chien. This photograph of hers shows unidentified girls in the 1918 Fourth of July parade. (Courtesy Prairie du Chien Historical Society, Mae Nichols Collection.)

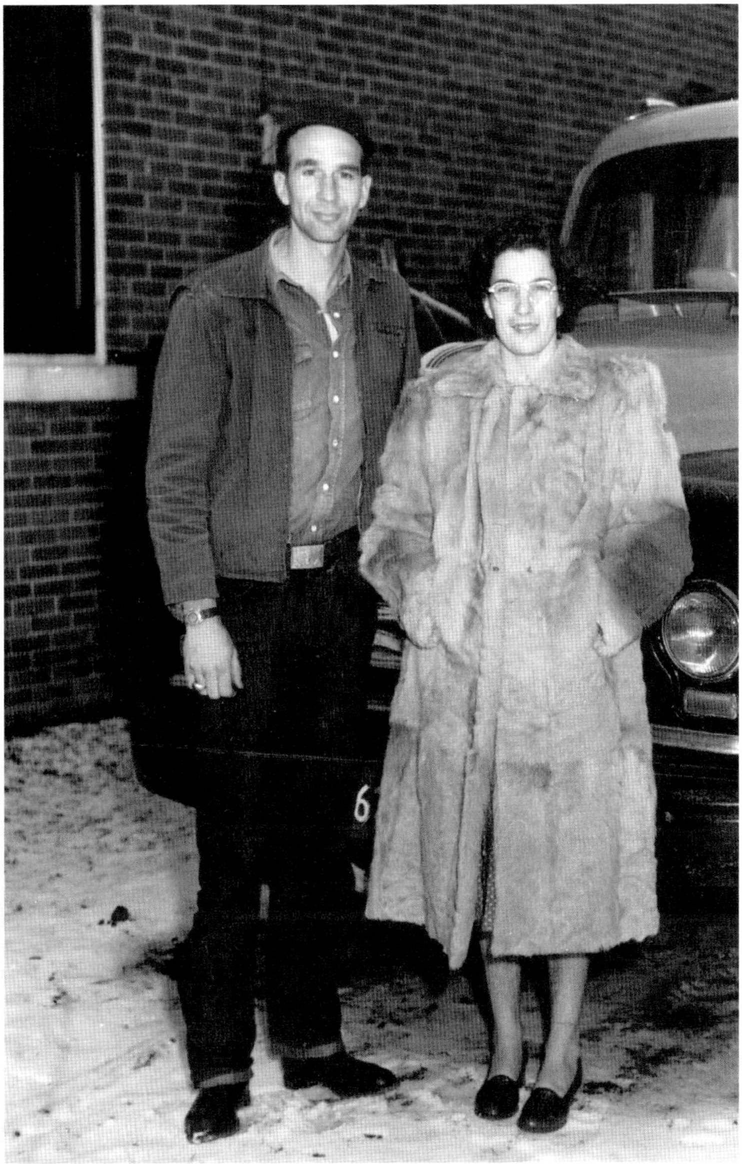

Daniel S. and Hazel Boom

A farmer and owner of Boom Brokerage trucking firm, Daniel Boom was an avid outdoorsman who loved horses. While living in Eastman, Dan helped organize the Blackhawk Saddle Club, which led to annual horse shows in that community. When he and Hazel moved to Prairie du Chien, they built the first horse arena in Crawford County. Dan loved children; he always had gum for them and patiently taught them birdcalls. The arena was always open for anyone to use, and Dan obligingly trucked ponies and horses to area trail rides. When Daniel LaRiviere donated his farm to the City of Prairie du Chien, Dan Boom helped develop the LaRiviere Horse Park.

Hazel Boom opened their house to children and any horse riders. She also worked full time at the Wisconsin Telephone Company office in Prairie du Chien. She and her coworkers handled a switchboard, asking "Number, please?" for many years. Prairie du Chien was one of the last communities to have dial telephone service. (Courtesy Prairie du Chien Historical Society, Howe Collection.)

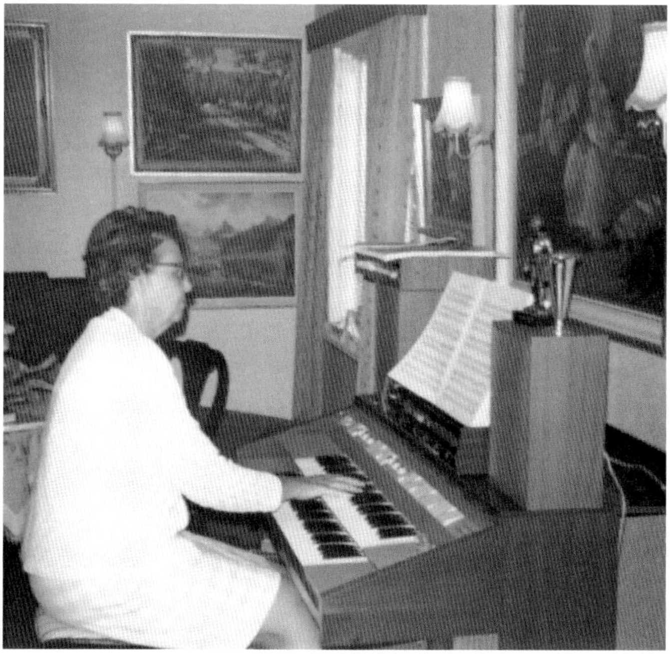

Theresa M. Powers

Music was a part of so many lives. Bands and singing societies were part of communities and fraternal organizations. At family gatherings, at least one person brought an instrument, and soon, all were singing and clapping to favorite tunes. Growing up, Theresa Powers was surrounded by music, and music remained a part of her life for 101 years. "Tres" taught in various communities, and when she married Reuben Powers, they settled in Prairie du Chien. Though Tres had no children, she and Reuben's home was always filled with the voices and music of children. Tres and Reuben opened Powers' Accordion Studio in their home. While they taught piano, organ, and guitar, the accordion was the popular instrument. Tres's students performed recitals in her home and on stage; in gratitude and affection, they present her with their student pictures year after year. (Both, courtesy the Powers family.)

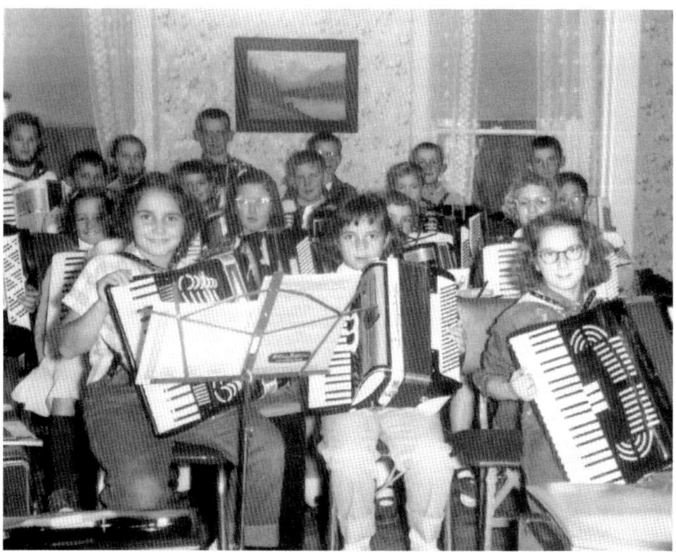

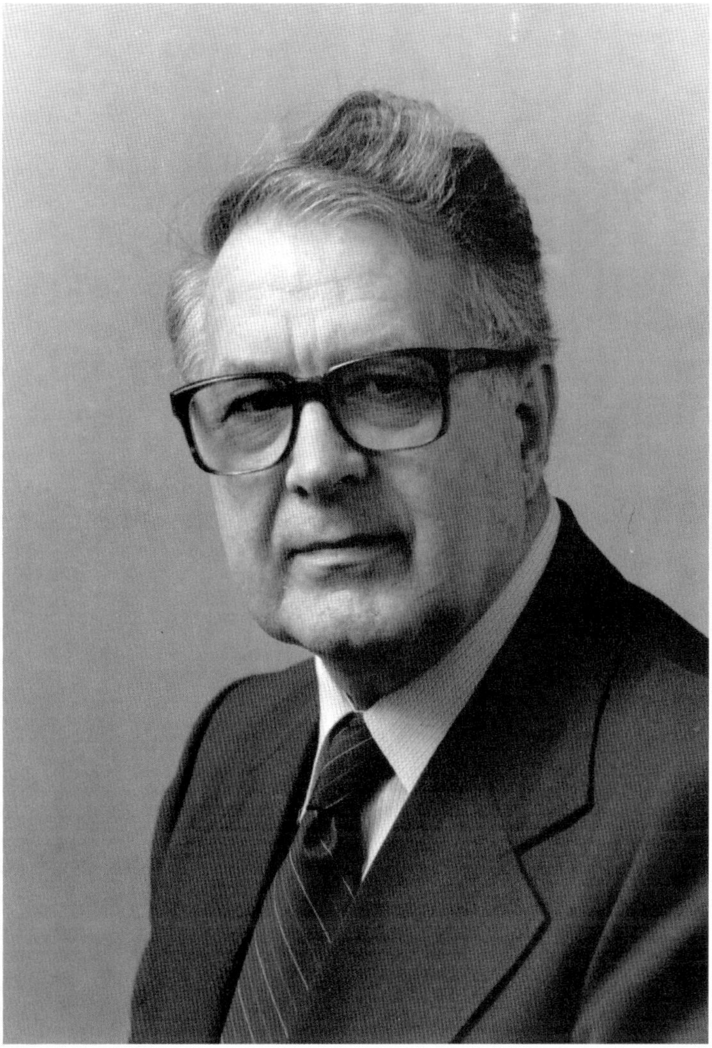

Gordon L. Peckham
When the United States declared war on Germany, Peckham enlisted in the Army. Having an artistic eye, he was deployed as an aerial reconnaissance photographer in the European theater.

Returning home, Peckham settled in Prairie du Chien, marrying Marjorie Kieser. He set up a photography studio. For the next 30 years, he photographed hundreds of area residents as they graduated from high school and got married. In the mid-1950s, he thought he should document the community, and so he photographically recorded building after building along Blackhawk Avenue and throughout the city.

Across the street from his home stood the new Fort Crawford Medical Museum. Retiring from photography, Peckham was the museum's curator, using his artistic talent to design and install exhibits. His ability to create exhibits on early medical history drew the attention of others, and he moved to Springfield, Illinois, to be one of the five founders of the Pearson Museum at the State Illinois University School of Medicine. But Prairie du Chien beckoned, and he and his family returned. He indulged in his hobby, painting scenes of the Mississippi River at Prairie du Chien and the rolling lands of the Wisconsin River Valley. His extensive archive of negatives was preserved by his family and given to the Prairie du Chien Historical Society. (Courtesy Prairie du Chien Historical Society, Peckham Collection.)

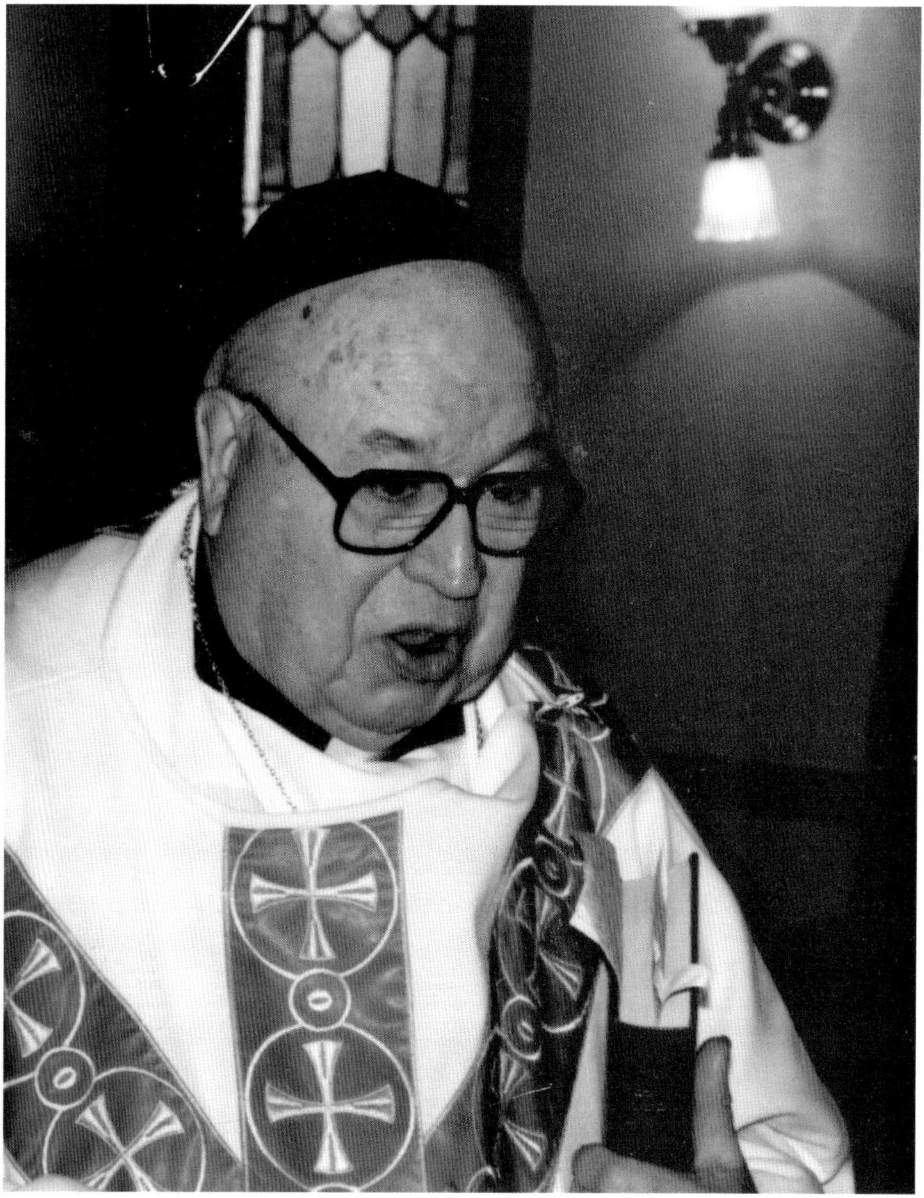

Rev. E. Raymond Sims

From the age of six, Raymond Sims wanted to be a preacher. He would preach to children in the schoolyard, and they would listen in rapt attention. In 1965, Raymond Sims was ordained an Episcopal priest and, four years later, came to Prairie du Chien, where he remained for the rest of his life. Beside Prairie du Chien, Father Sims had parishes in five other communities. Father Sims studied all faiths and was truly an ecumenical man. He organized the Prairie du Chien Ministerial Association, a monthly gathering of priests and ministers of all faiths, and was the impetus for the radio program *Words to Live By*. Father Sims involved himself in the welfare of the community, being active in the Kiwanis Club and Salvation Army. He became chairman of the Crawford County Human Services Board. Sims retired in 1990 to spend more time with his garden of tulips, and then came out of retirement to minister to Holy Trinity Episcopal Church. (Courtesy the Finn family.)

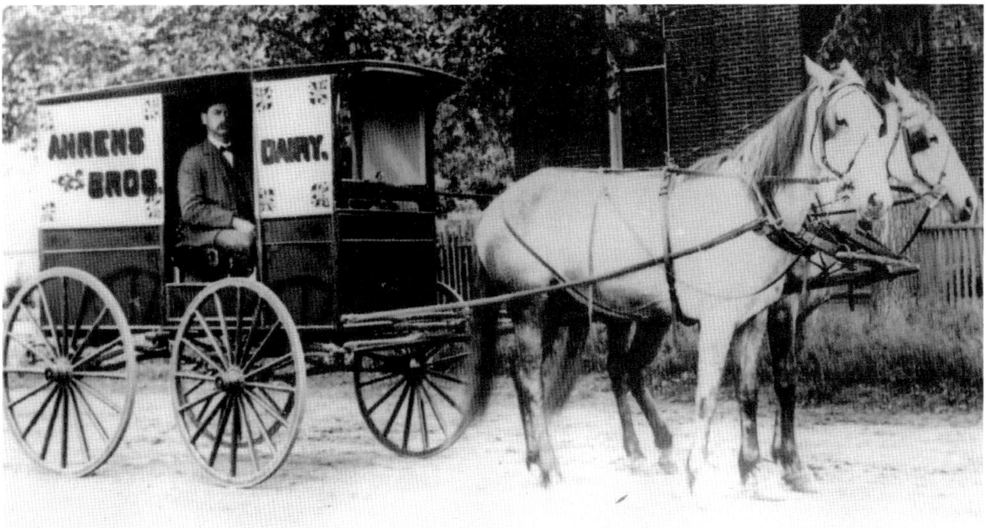

Frederick Ahrens Family

Frederick Ahrens Sr. migrated from Germany, coming to Prairie du Chien in 1868. He began a dairy farm, furnishing milk, cream, and eggs to steamboat and rafting crews and delivering to residents within the community. His wagon was filled with milk cans, and he would charge by the dipper. His sons Frank and Fred Jr. (above) took over the dairy, and, in time, Frank bought out Fred. Frank, with the help of his five sons, began bottling milk, and in 1946, with the requirement that milk be pasteurized, installed equipment to update the bottling plant. Frank's son Willard managed the delivery route and, with his smiles and jokes, was a welcome figure at many homes. Ahrens Dairy also supplied milk products to local grocery stores. The herd expanded to 100 Holstein and Guernsey cows, and the Ahrens family pioneered the development of Holsteins. In 1972, a large company bought out the milk route, ending over 100 years of locally produced dairy products. Pictured below are, from left to right, Fred Ahrens Jr., Sara Ahrens Becker, and Frank Ahrens Sr. (Both, courtesy the Ahrens family.)

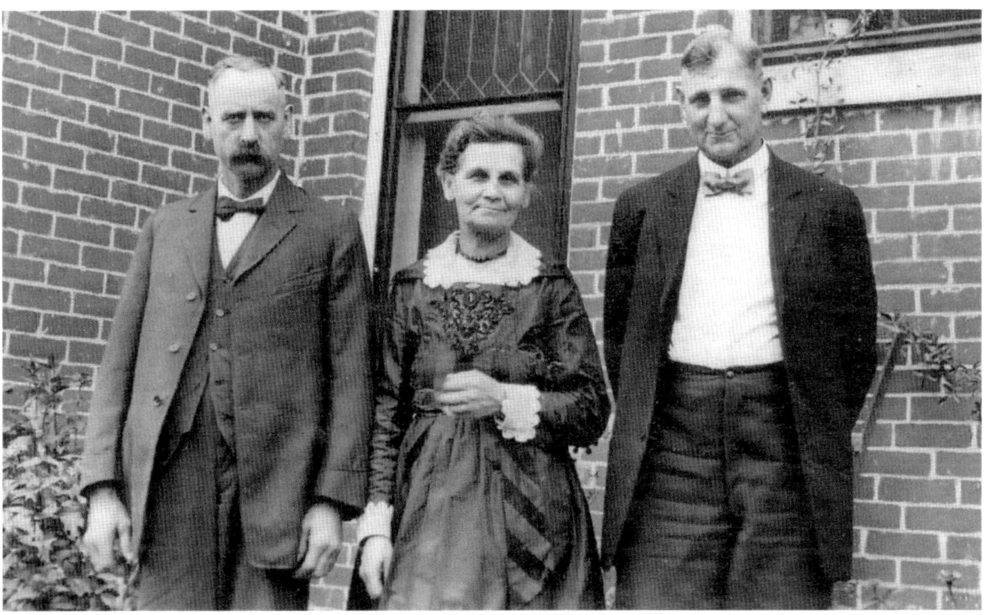

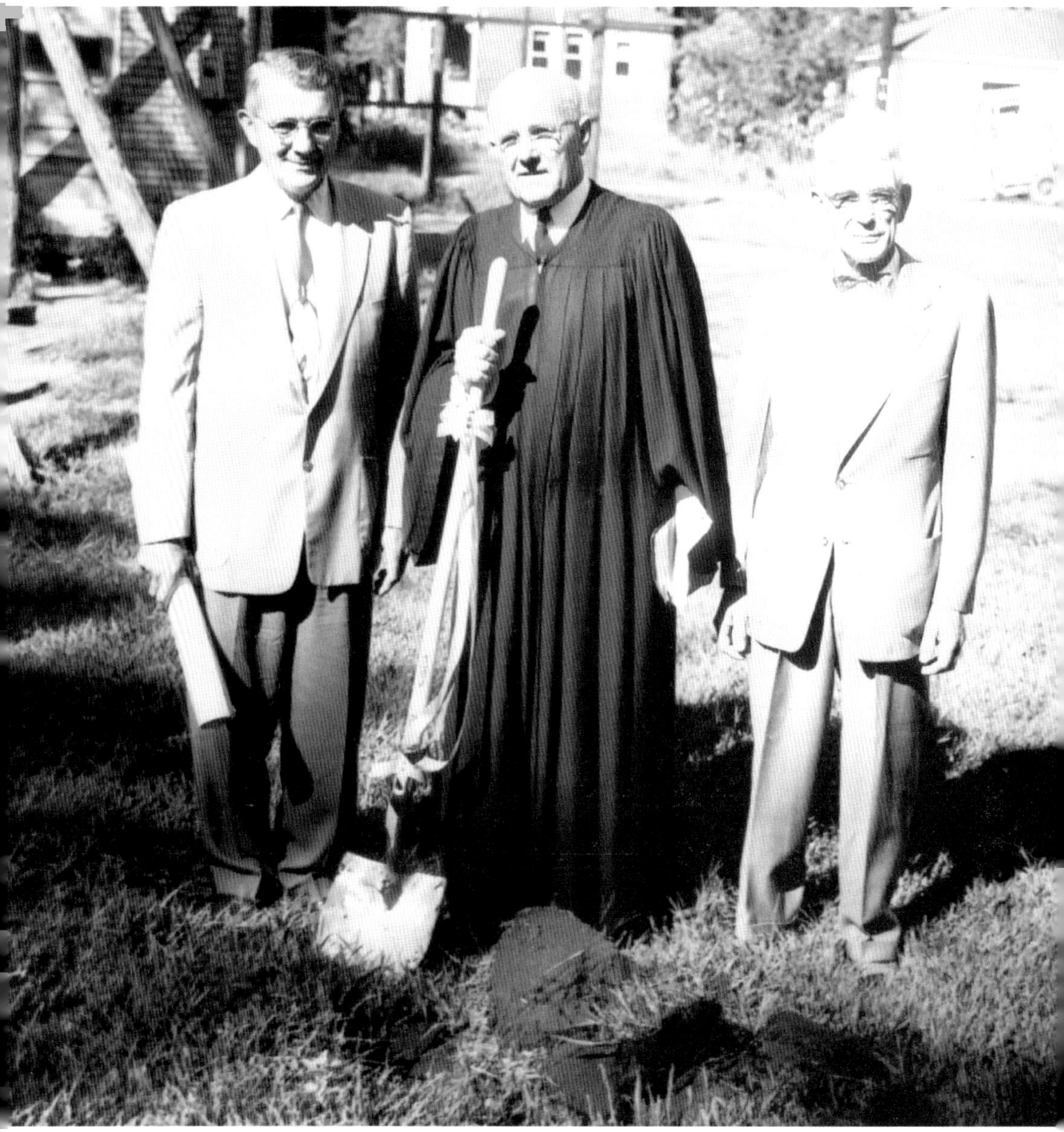

Arthur B. and William C. Steiner

Valentin Steiner arrived in the United States from Bavaria as a skilled stonecutter. His enlistment in the Army brought him to the Midwest. When he mustered out in 1844, he settled in Prairie du Chien. From him, Valentin's sons and grandsons all learned the building trade. Arthur and William Steiner, two of Valentin's grandsons, formed Steiner Brothers Construction. For many years, Art and Bill built and remodeled homes and were general contractors for commercial and religious buildings in Prairie du Chien. As teenagers, Art's and Bill's sons worked for Steiner Brothers Construction. As their fathers retired, each of the sons started their own contracting businesses, as did several grandsons. Steiner Associates of Prairie du Chien carries on the family tradition into the sixth generation.

In this photograph, Art (left) and Bill (right) stand with Rev. Walter Bodamer at the ground breaking for St. Peter's Church. (Courtesy Prairie du Chien Historical Society, Howe Collection.)

Gertrude and Stanley Hamann

Prairie du Chien was too small a community for Woolworth's to open a store. Henry and Gertrude (left) Hamann understood that there was a need for this type of business, so they opened Hamann's Variety Store in 1929. The residents patronized the store, demanding more goods than the rented space could hold. So, in 1939, the Hamanns built their own store a half block east. It held everything from cards to sewing notions, kitchenware to fishing tackle, school supplies to houseplants. In the basement were shelves of toys and the paint and wallpaper department. It was every child's delight to be given a quarter to "go to Hamann's" and buy penny candy and wander among the toys. Stanley (right) and his wife, Leona, took over the business, and then Stanley's son Rick and his wife, Patty, assumed operations. But nothing changed. The same oak counters held merchandise, and the floors creaked as one walked down the long aisles. (Courtesy Prairie du Chien Historical Society, Howe Collection.)

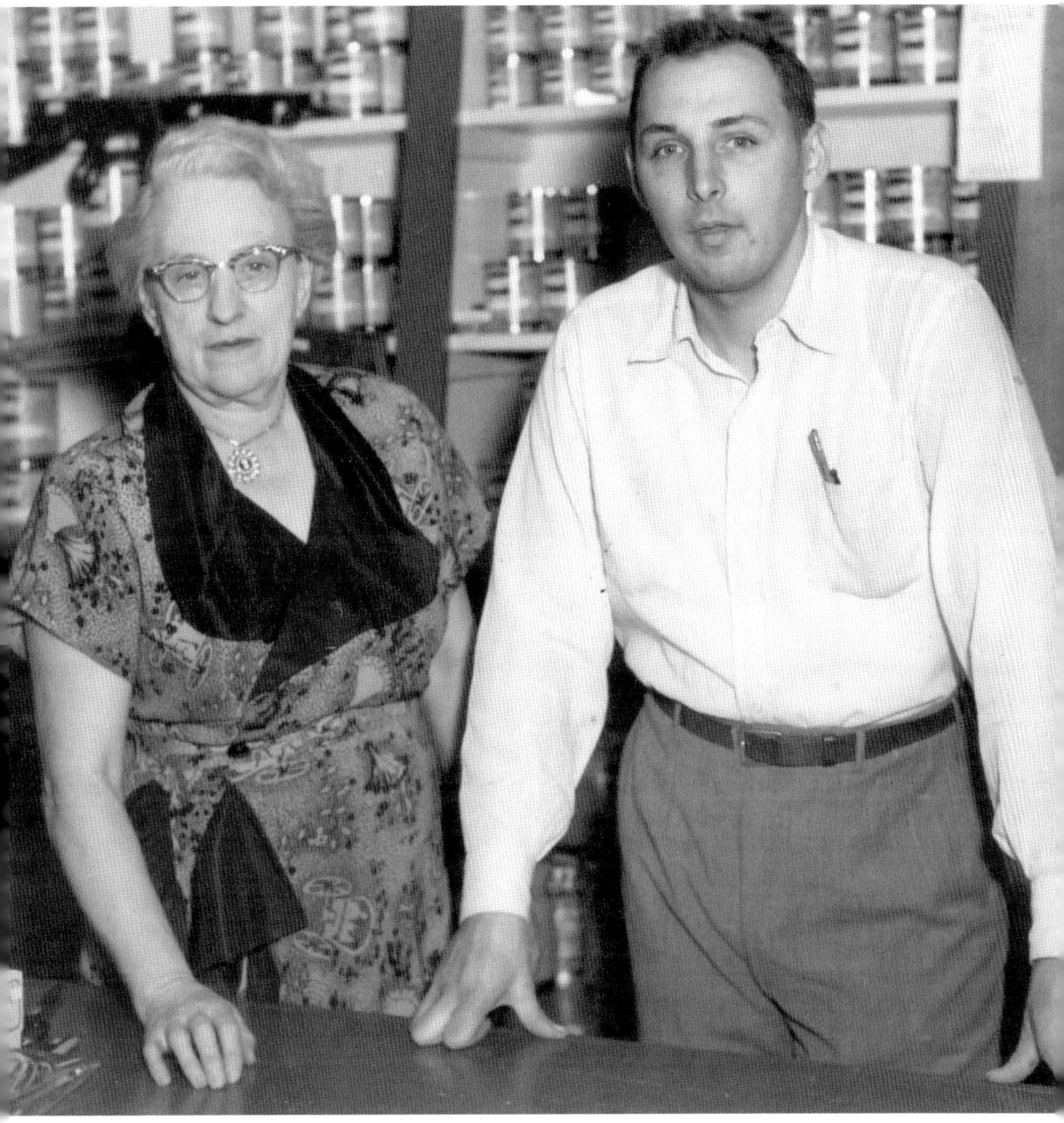

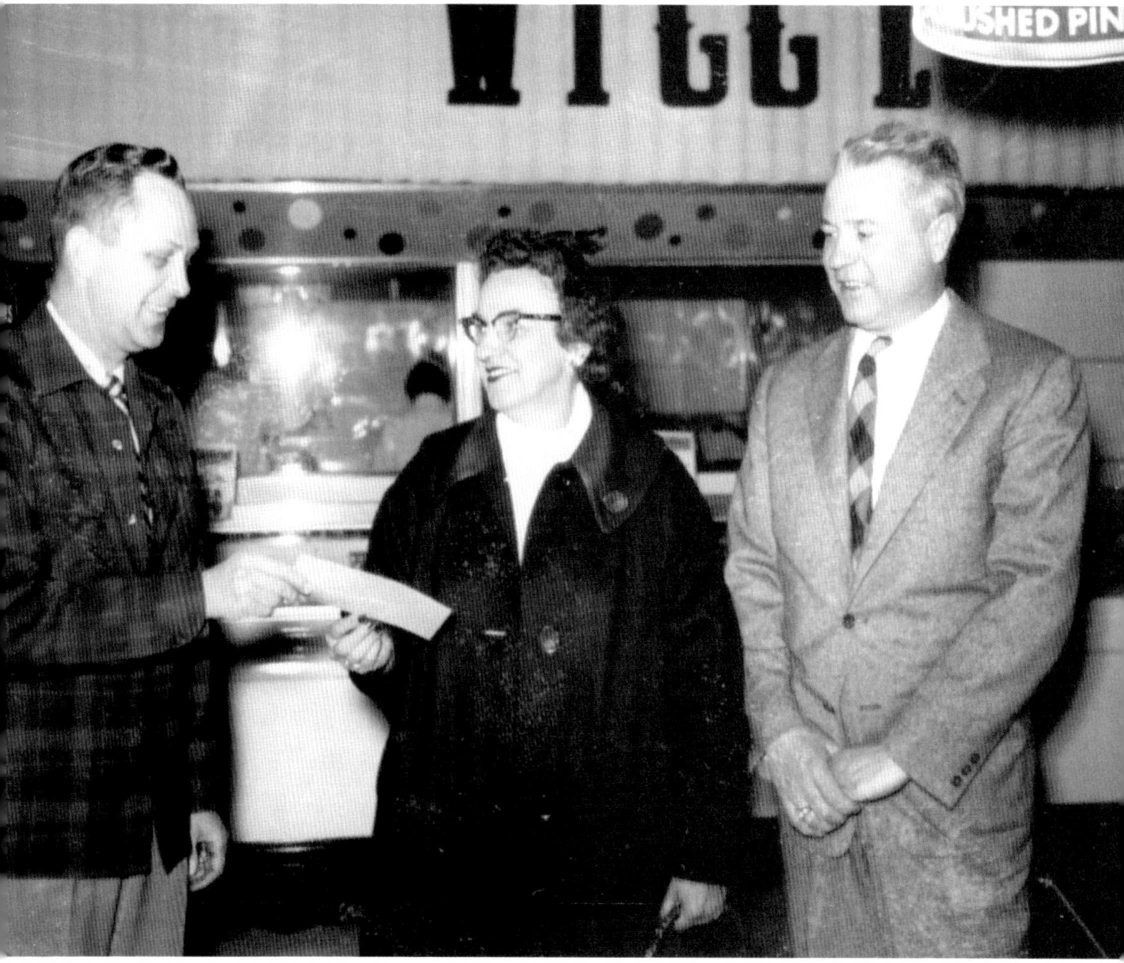

Roy L. George and U. Stuart Asche

Roy George (right) began his grocery career as a salesman for Badger Wholesale, a job he returned to after his service in the Army Air Force. In 1948, he partnered with U. Stuart Asche (left), his brother-in-law, and opened R&S Superette. Renting a very small space did not allow them room to expand; companies in the mid-1950s began to offer a greater selection of foods. George decided they had to go modern. After two years of planning, the Piggly Wiggly opened in 1955 on the edge of town. The new grocery store was large and modern, boasting "motorized check-out" and "magic doors." The Piggly Wiggly built by George and Asche, with Stuart's wife, Beth George Asche, quietly managing finances, was the beginning of Commerce Court, the first shopping center in Prairie du Chien. In 1962, the partnership opened a newer and larger store and began to build structures, bringing more retail and service businesses. Roy George sponsored various promotions, including Mothers' Day breakfasts and visits by Miss Wisconsin and Elsie the Cow. He was very active in local civic organizations and was elected president of the National Piggly Wiggly Operators Association. Many people worked their entire careers for Roy George and Stuart Asche. (Courtesy the George family.)

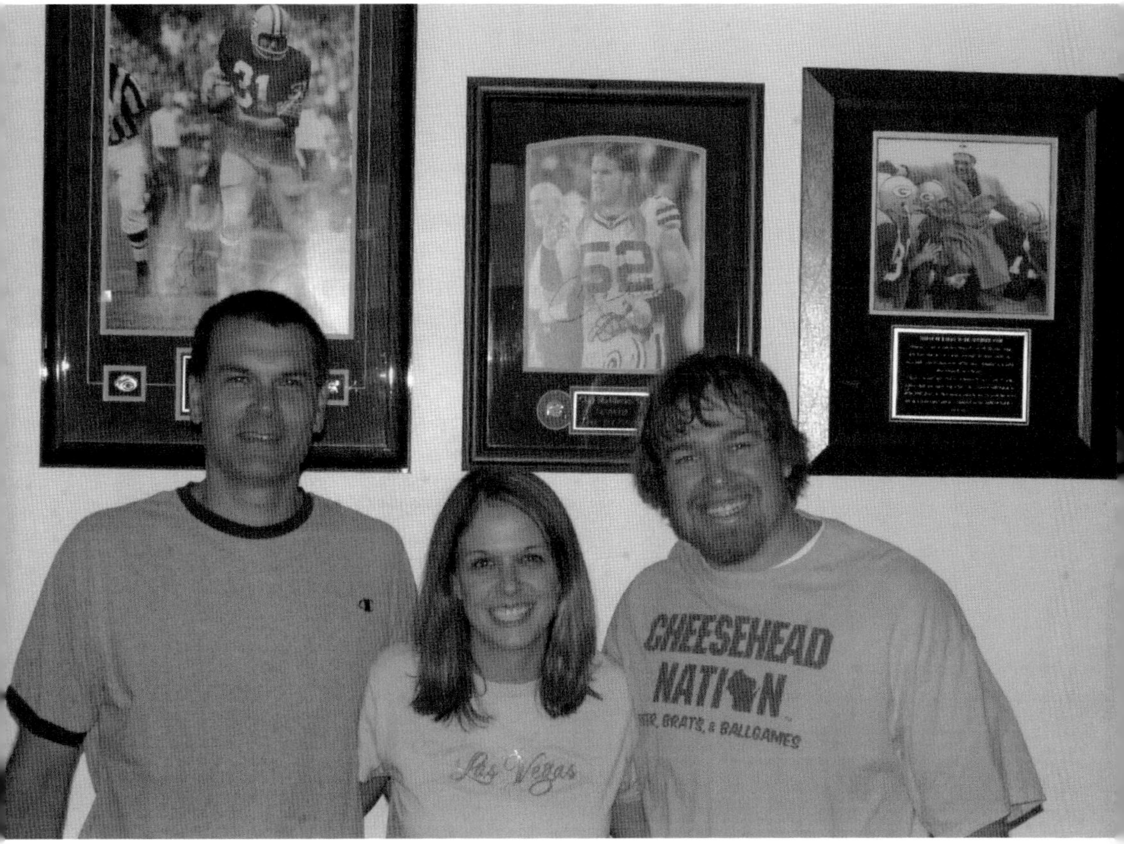

Harold Shulka Family

James "Jim" Panka, a younger son of John Panka, left the family farm to operate a pool hall. With the repeal of Prohibition, Jim eyed the Metropolitan Block his father owned. Brother George was managing the theater, so Jim decided to open a tavern in the part of the building that had been a clothing store. The tavern, Jim's, opened in 1934. A fire two years later damaged the block, but the Panka family rebuilt and upgraded the theater and tavern. Another fire in 1949 was just as destructive, but, six months later, the Metro Theater and Jim's Bar were open, and their patrons returned. Jim passed the bar on to his son, Bill. He in turn sold the bar business to Harold "Fuzz" and Myrna Shulka in the late 1960s. They retained the name Jim's Bar. Except for a few years when the bar belonged to Gary and LaVonne Paulson, it has been owned and operated by members of the Panka and Shulka families. Rich and Karen Shulka have passed the business on to their children Scott (right) and Bridget (center) and their son-in-law Scott Nichols (left). A neighborhood bar, Jim's sponsors a city league softball team and a basketball team. Adorned with Green Bay Packers memorabilia, Jim's is a place where everyone truly knows one another's name. (Courtesy *The Courier Press.*)

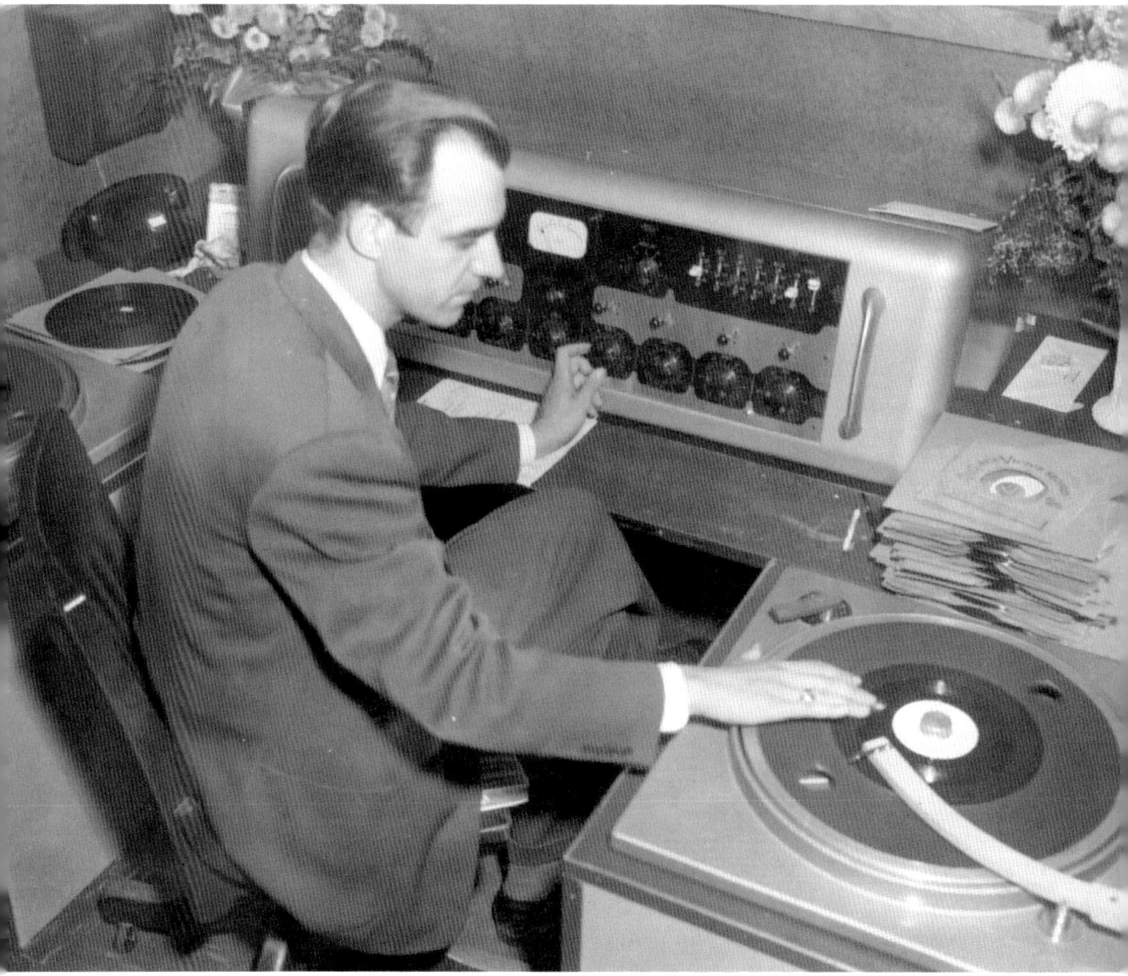

Walter P. Schlaugat Jr.

Walt Schlaugat and his brother learned about ham radios and their operation from their father, and thus was a passion born that directed Walt's entire life. After graduating with an engineering degree and serving as a radio operator in the Marines, he dreamed of starting a radio station. He visited communities throughout Wisconsin without radio stations and selected Prairie du Chien. In 1952, Schlaugat received the call letters for WPRE. With his knowledge, he brought together and built all the components needed for broadcasting. He wanted the radio station to broadcast music in good taste, so he created his own playlists. He told his staff that he wanted a variety of music that would appeal to people throughout the community, and he wanted to hear something new every day.

During the 1965 flood, the station never stopped broadcasting, though the staff had to move to a remote location. The building was refurbished, enlarged, and the station simulcast as FM/AM. Schlaugat was a private person, wishing to remain in the background and keep the station operational, which he did for 45 years until his retirement and sale of the station in 1997. (Courtesy the Schlaugat family.)

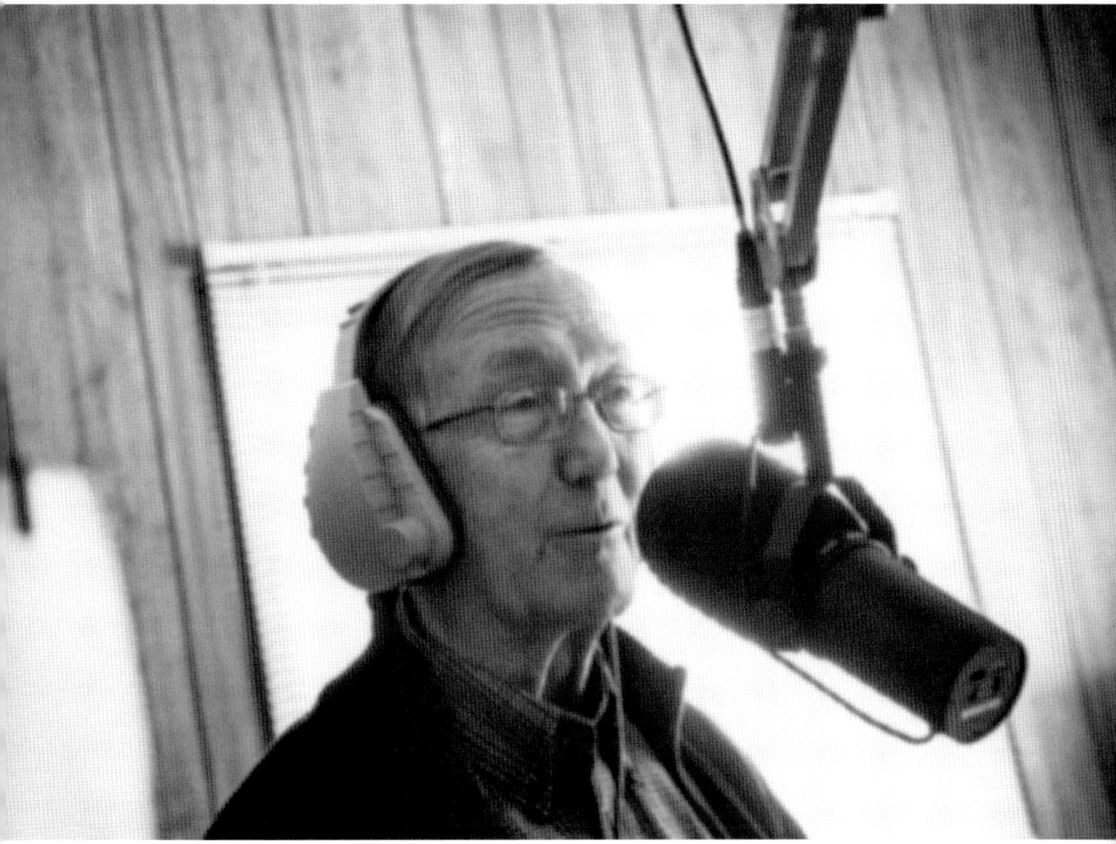

Norbert J. Aschom Jr.

Called "The Voice of Prairie du Chien," Norb Aschom really wanted to be a singer or a broadcaster, so he transferred to Brown Institute of Broadcasting to follow his dream. After only four months at his first job, he received a letter in the spring of 1961 from Walter Schlaugat of WPRE in Prairie du Chien, and the rest is history. For over 50 years, Aschom worked at WPRE-AM and the expansion WQPC-FM. Starting out as a disc jockey, he fulfilled many roles in small-town radio. He read the news, announced births and deaths, called basketball games, and did on-site live interviews. He retired as news director. Everyone enjoyed his banter with Dave Storkson during *People, Places, and Things* and his asking the trivia questions for the *Pronto Pizza Quiz*. Over the years, many nationally known people came to Prairie du Chien. With his soft baritone and pleasing style, Aschom interviewed them all, from Roselyn Carter to Al Gore, and from Paul Harvey to Helen Hayes.

To Norb Aschom, "The most important thing is the local connection." Because of that and his support of education, in 2012, the Prairie du Chien School Board honored him with the Wisconsin Association School District Administrators Child Advocacy Award. The city made March 1, 2013, the day of his retirement after a 52-year radio career, Norb Aschom Day. (Courtesy *The Courier Press.*)

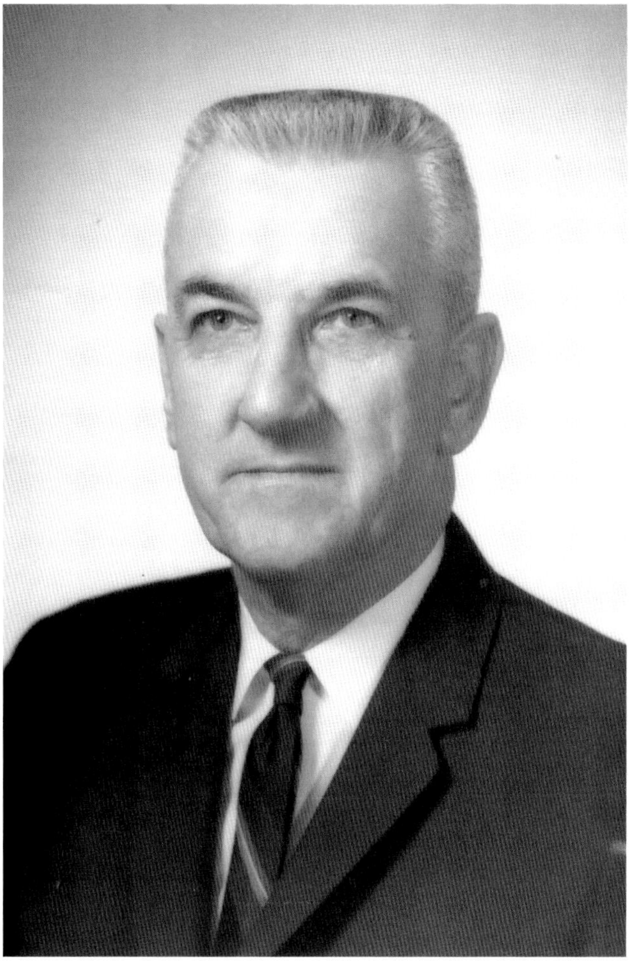

Francis J. Antoine Jr.
After World War II, Frank Antoine returned to Prairie du Chien. He reopened his law office and started a career of service. He had resigned his position as city attorney to enlist, and, after his return to Prairie du Chien, he became city attorney again. In 1948, the Wisconsin Democratic Party nominated Antoine to be its candidate for the Third Congressional District. In October, Pres. Harry Truman stopped in Sparta, Wisconsin, as part of his nationwide Whistle Stop Tour. Antoine had the distinction of introducing the president.

In 1953, Antoine thought it would be beneficial to clients if several lawyers formed a partnership. He contacted a father and son, C.B. and Leary Peterson, and the firm Peterson, Antoine, and Peterson was established. The three men practiced together in a new structure built behind the Antoine home, and each in his own way served the community. Antoine was on the board of directors for Peoples State Bank, while Leary was part of the board of the Prairie City Bank. Leary was appointed counsel for the City of Prairie du Chien and donated his services to St. John's Church. Antoine gave of his expertise to Campion Jesuit High School and St. Gabriel's Church.

Frank Antoine ran for and was elected to the Prairie du Chien School Board, serving as president. To him, though, his highest honor was being selected by his peers to run for president of the Wisconsin Bar Association. In honor of his years of service, Peoples State Bank created the F.J. Antoine Memorial Scholarship.

Peterson, Antoine, and Peterson continues under the direction of Mark and Tom Peterson, Leary's nephew and son. (Courtesy the Antoine family.)

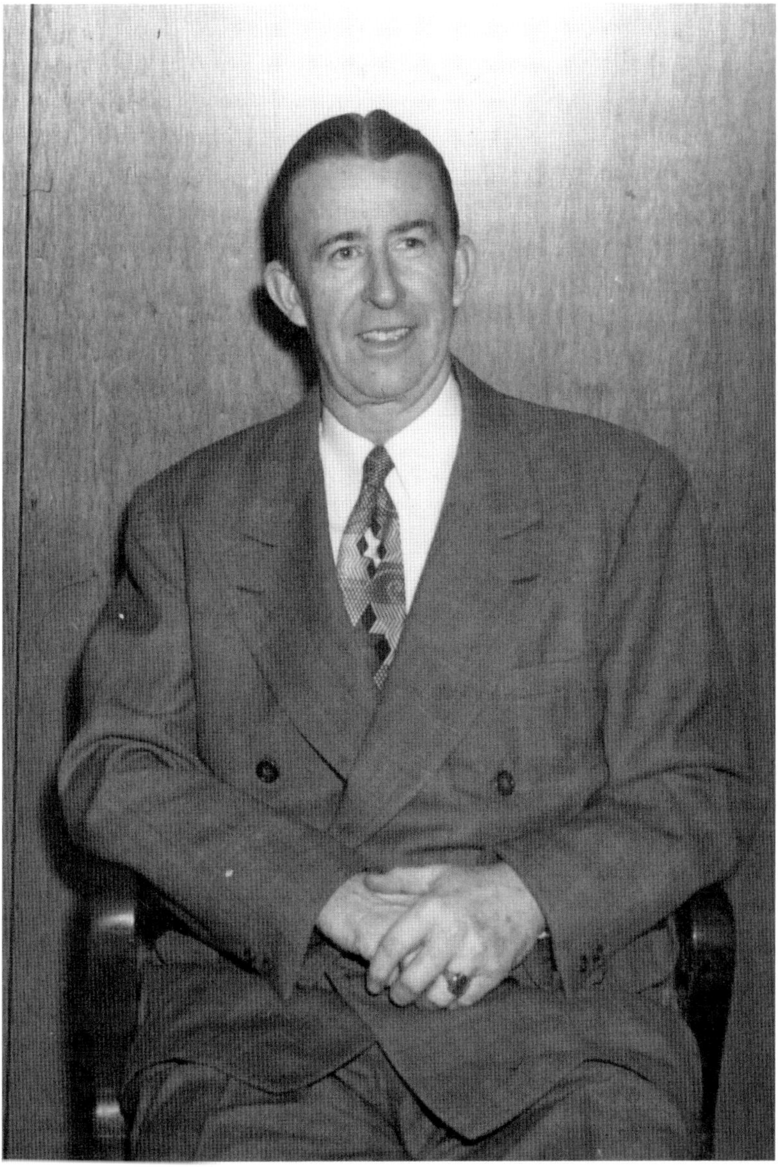

Dr. Thomas Francis Farrell

Born in Seneca, Wisconsin, T.F. Farrell returned from Pennsylvania to his home state to open a medical practice. Working one year in Lancaster, Dr. Farrell established a private practice in Prairie du Chien in 1935 with Dr. John Kane. They purchased a former chiropractic hospital six years later, converting it to a medical hospital and clinic, which they named Beaumont Hospital. When the newly built Prairie du Chien Memorial Hospital opened in 1957, Dr. Farrell closed the Beaumont facility, building the Farrell Clinic across from the new hospital. Dr. Farrell's children were students at the two Catholic high schools in Prairie du Chien, so he provided his services to Campion Jesuit High School and St. Mary's Academy for over 30 years. He served as a charter member of the Campion Board of Regents. Like his father, Dr. Farrell was a member of the board of directors of Peoples State Bank, serving as bank president for 18 years. His son, Tom, continues the family banking tradition, having served as a director of Peoples State Bank for over 30 years. (Courtesy Prairie du Chien Historical Society.)

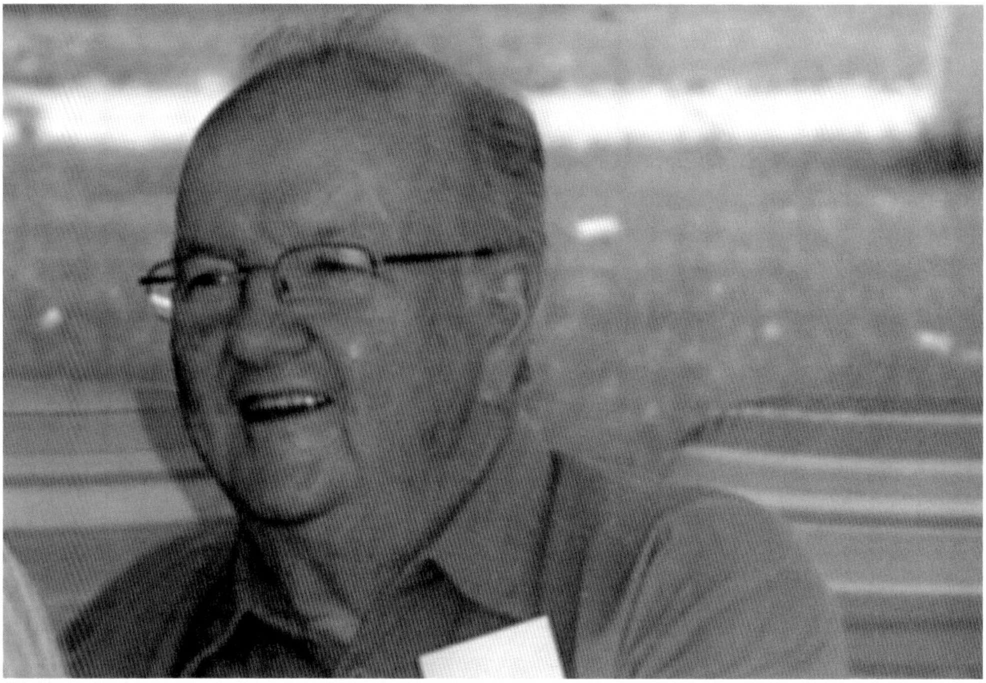

Dr. Michael S. Garrity
Short-staffed at the recently opened Farrell Clinic, "Dr. Mike" Garrity planned to stay for only a year to help his friend Dr. Farrell. That short time turned into 40 years. Upon Dr. Farrell's retirement, Dr. Garrity became president of Farrell Clinic in 1979 and directed the association with Gundersen-Lutheran Clinics, taking leadership roles with Gundersen Lutheran Healthcare. In 1992, Garrity was named Gundersen Lutheran Physician of the Year. Though he retired from practice, he never fully did so, giving time to the American International Health Alliance and serving as a volunteer physician at St. Claire Free Clinic. The Wisconsin State Senate proclaimed June 28, 2009, Dr. Michael S. Garrity Day. (Courtesy William H. Howe.)

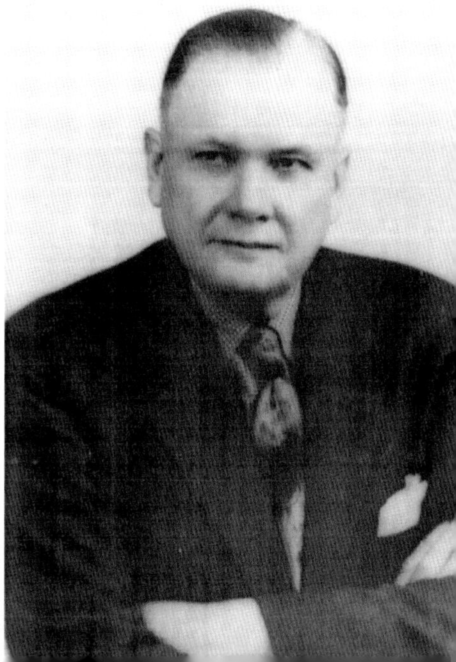

Dr. Olaf Elmer Satter
Dr. O.E. Satter came to Prairie du Chien in 1924 to be the attending surgeon of the Prairie du Chien Sanitarium. Dr. Kane and he changed the facility from a treatment center for rheumatism and lung disorders to a clinic and a hospital. Through the quiet determination and surgical skill of Dr. Satter, the hospital came to be known as a center for surgery and a teaching school for nurses. In 1952, Satter changed its name to General Hospital. When the Prairie du Chien Memorial Hospital opened, Dr. Satter also practiced there, continuing to operate the Prairie du Chien Clinic. (Courtesy the Satter family.)

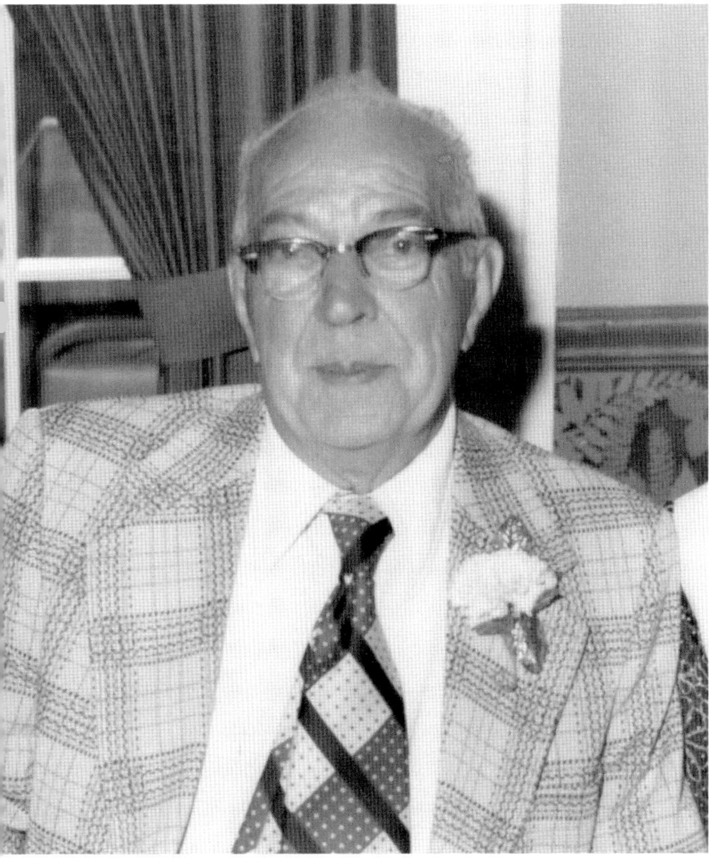

Vincent A. Polodna
When Vince Polodna learned that a committee had formed to investigate the medical needs of the community and decide upon a location for a hospital, he wanted the hospital close to his home. He contacted the committee and said he would donate the land for a new hospital. Everyone was taken by surprise. The hospital was built on the land he and his family donated, and the gift opened the east side of Prairie du Chien to development. Homes started to be built around the hospital and toward the bluffs. A member of the hospital board called the gift "the impetus of development." (Courtesy the Polodna family.)

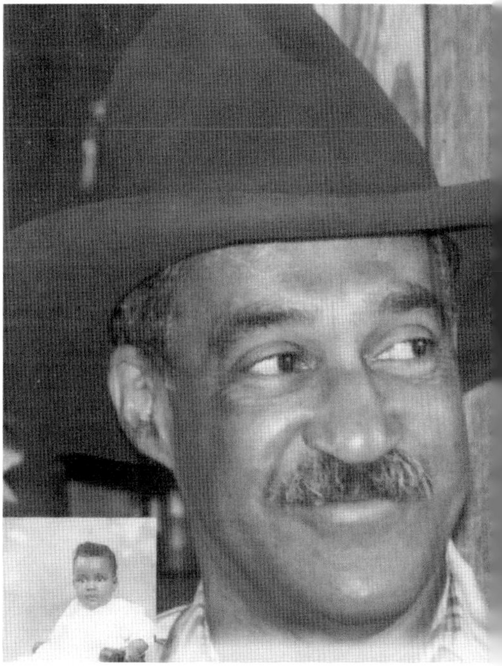

Dr. Clifford C. Smith
Enlisting in the US Army in 1943, Clifford Smith submitted an application to become a pilot. He was accepted and became one of the Tuskegee Airmen.

Smith earned a medical degree and became the first African American resident at the Veterans' Administration Hospital in Iowa City. Dr. Smith brought his family to McGregor, Iowa, where he opened a clinic. Prairie du Chien residents sought him to be their physician because of his skill and compassion. In 1998, Dr. Smith was named National Rural Health Practitioner of the Year. Even after his retirement, he served as medical director of Prairie Maison in Prairie du Chien. He was so well respected that, at his retirement, he stood for almost seven hours at the head of a reception line of people wishing him well. (Courtesy the Smith family.)

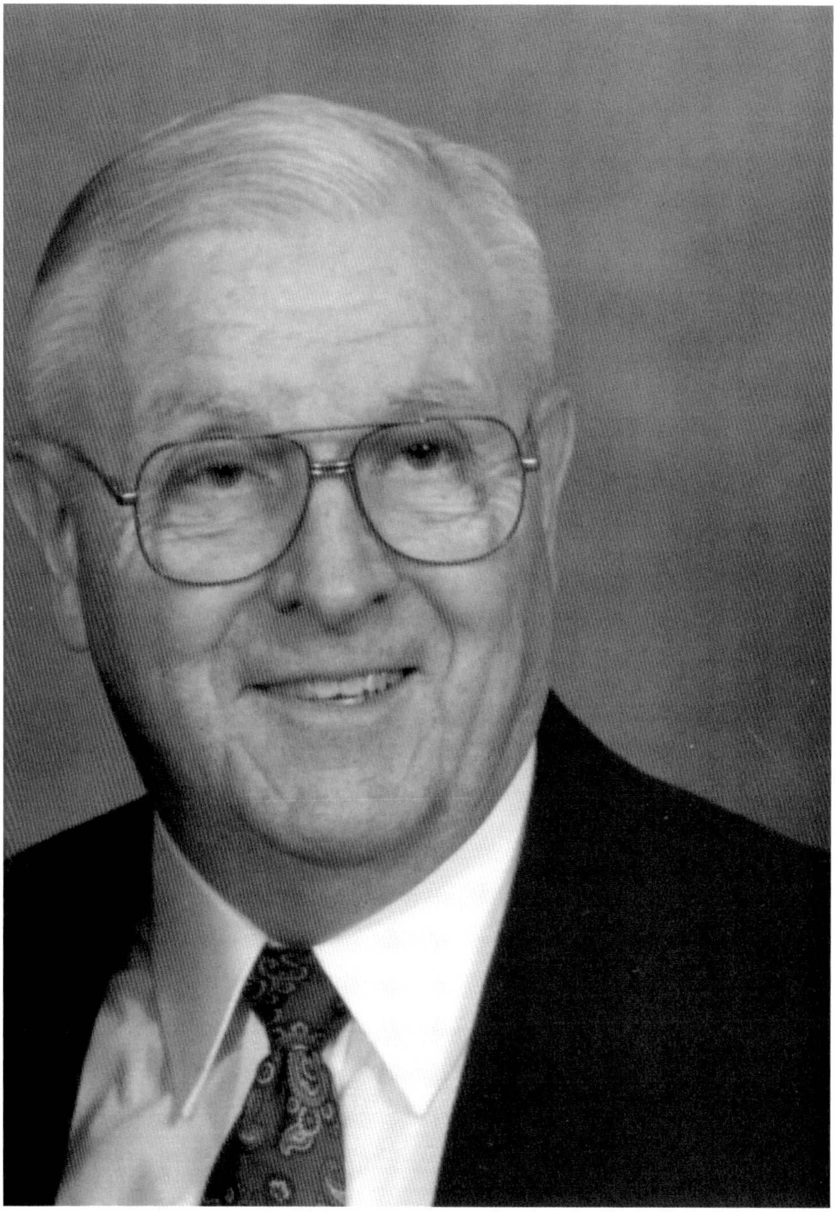

Morris McFarlane Jr.

"Mac" McFarlane put education at the center of his life, and one of his proudest achievements was Futures of Prairie du Chien Inc. Class president and a 1944 graduate of Prairie du Chien High School, after military service, Morris graduated from college, thinking only of teaching. He taught industrial arts for 35 years at Wauzeka, Portage, and, finally, at Mequon-Thiensville. Upon retirement, Morris and his wife, Maureen, returned to her family home in Prairie du Chien. Seeing the need for higher education, but realizing the costs of college, Morris began to develop plans for a scholarship fund. The idea moved to reality in 1992, when Morris gathered similar-minded Prairie du Chien graduates and friends. They established and incorporated Futures of Prairie du Chien. For the first three years, Mac and Maureen provided the money for the scholarships. Then, in 1996, funding was achieved to sustain the scholarships, and Futures has grown substantially. (Courtesy the McFarlane family.)

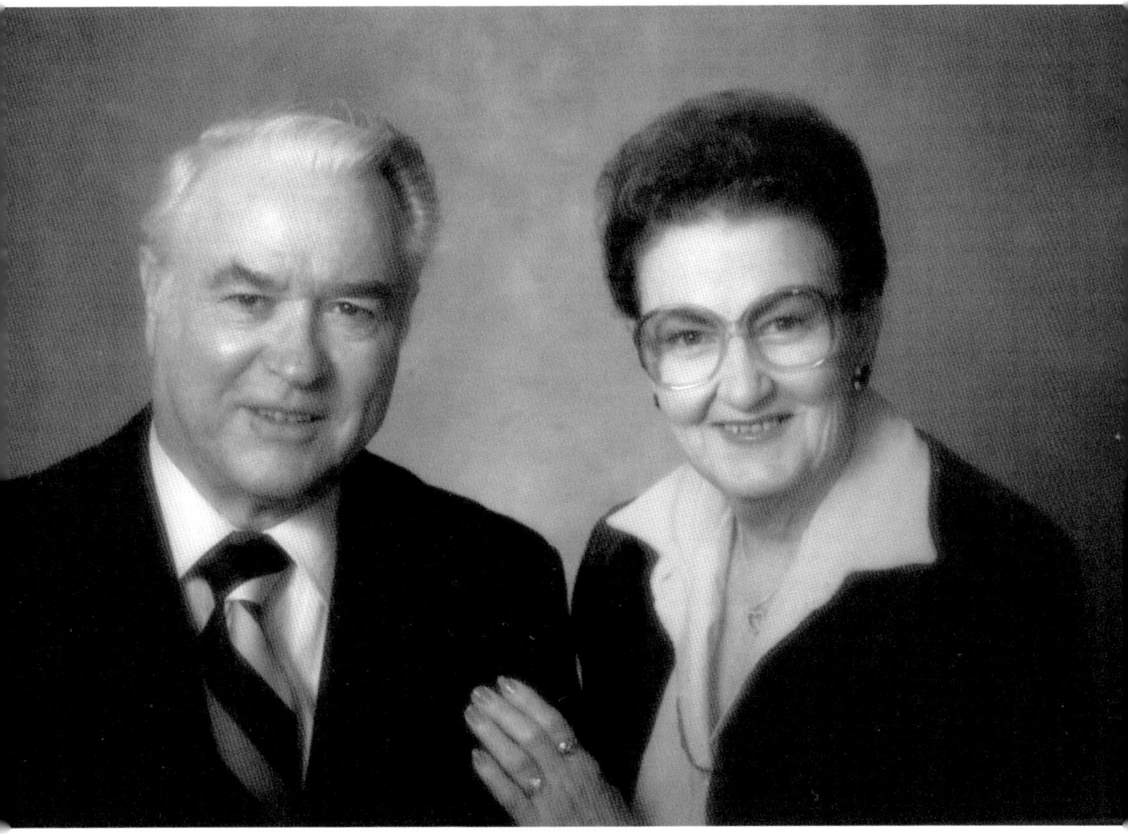

Roy L. and Geraldine E. George

Roy L. George's son said, "Mom was busy raising five children," so she did not have a lot of time to devote to the Piggly Wiggly store. She always supported Roy, and the family vacation often involved parents and children attending a Piggly Wiggly convention. Roy retired and sold the Piggly Wiggly to Mick Kneeland, a longtime employee, in 1987. Roy was always appreciative of the people of Prairie du Chien and the area who supported the grocery store. They kept coming, even after Roy had retired, so he wanted to give back to the community. Working with his son Roy C., Roy L. and Geraldine, known as Jerry, started the George Family Charitable Foundation in 1996. They felt the foundation would also be a means by which to keep the family together. The foundation assists programs and individuals with a vision and a plan to better the long-term quality of life in Crawford County, Wisconsin. (Courtesy the George family.)

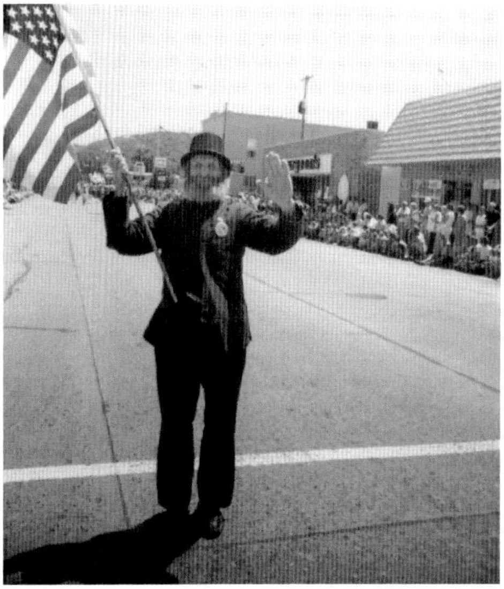

Julius Arthur Oswald
Known to all as "Judy," Julius Oswald was part of Prairie du Chien for over 50 years. He was a paperboy for the newspaper and custodian for many businesses. One day, before a parade was to begin, someone asked Judy if he wanted to carry the US flag. From then on, Judy led parades. When he lost part of his fingers and toes to frostbite, a special sling was made so he could continue to be the flag bearer, bringing smiles to all. (Courtesy Tom and Cathie Nelson.)

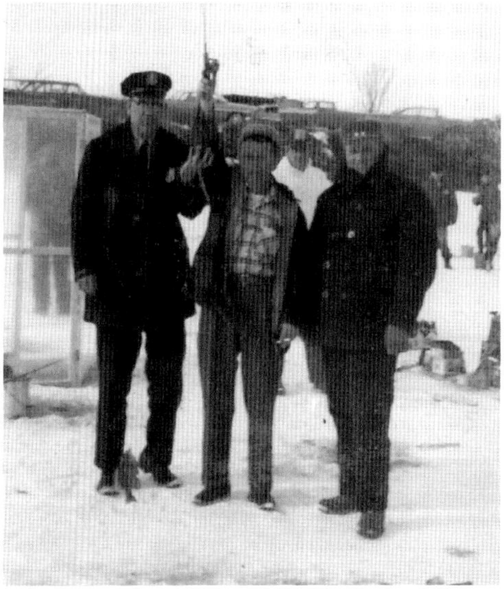

Donald Lyons
Since 1872, Prairie du Chien has had a chief of police. "Doc" Lyons (far left) served the community during the 1965 flood, made sure the kids behaved, watched over the ducks on the villa pond, and ran a tavern. (Courtesy Prairie du Chien Historical Society.)

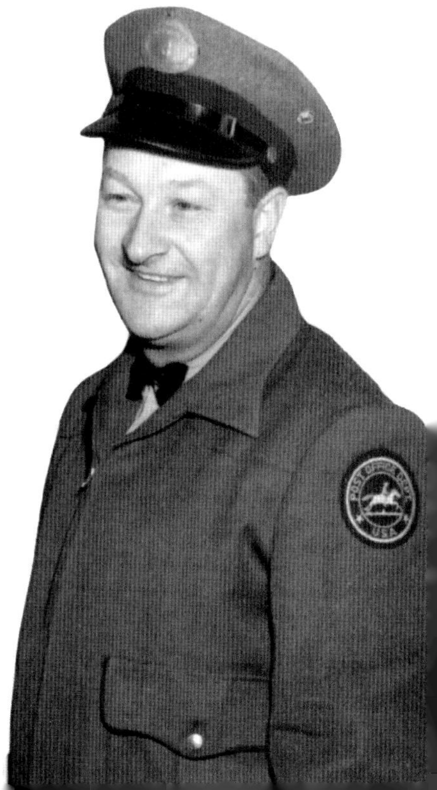

Lawrence Standorf
A dedicated mail carrier, Standorf made sure the residents received their mail for 33 years. (Courtesy Prairie du Chien Historical Society.)

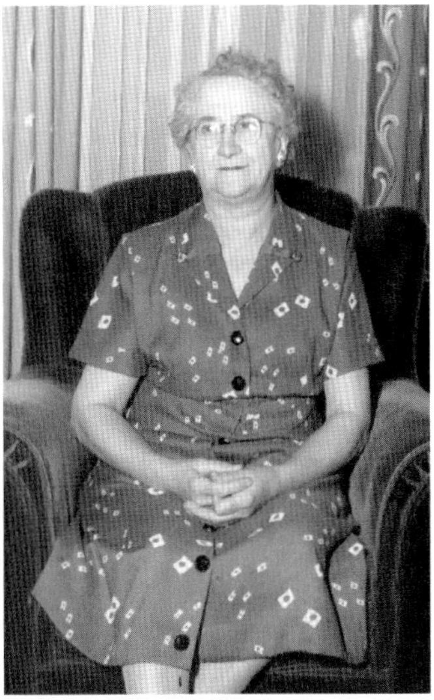

Sophie DeLorimer
Sophie DeLorimer represents the many women who gave of their time to cook and work to make sure church dinners were a tasty success. (Courtesy Prairie du Chien Historical Society.)

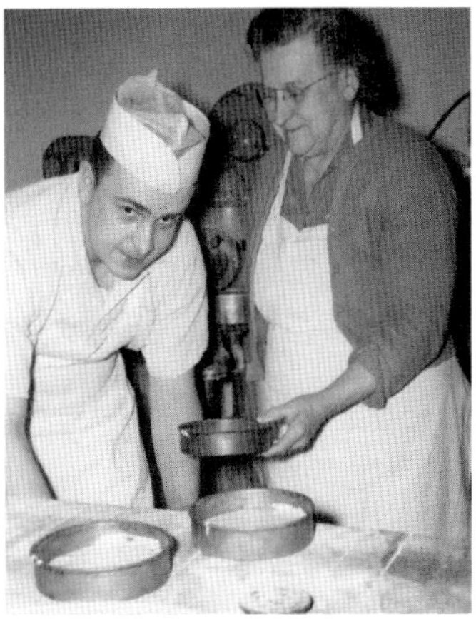

Robert and Gertrude Bohonek
For over 30 years, Gertrude (right) and sons Bob (left) and Felix Bohonek operated Bohonek's Quality Market and the Faultless Bakery in their building on Blackhawk Avenue. (Courtesy Prairie du Chien Historical Society.)

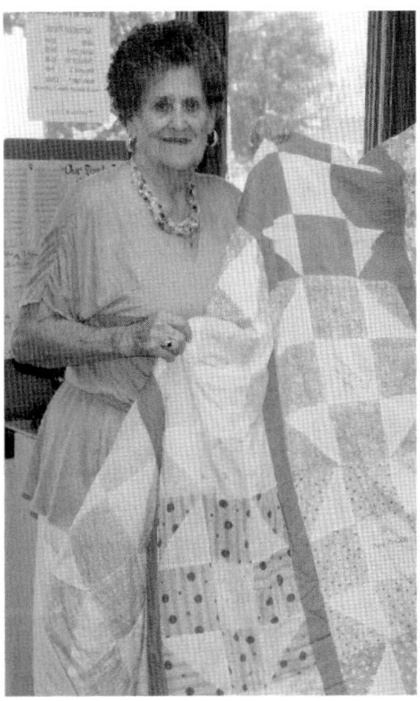

Dorothea M. Walker
Dorothea Walker was a mother and homemaker. For most of her married life, she was active in the Wisconsin Homemakers' Association. When she passed away in 2012 at age 92, the Crawford County chapter also died. (Courtesy Prairie du Chien Historical Society.)

INDEX

Abbelen, Rev. Peter Mathias, 48
Ahrens, Frank Sr., 111
Ahrens, Frederick Sr., 111
Ahrens, Frederick Jr., 111
Antoine, Francis John, MD, 22
Antoine, Francis John Jr., 118
Antoine, Matthew de Julio, 73
Asche, U. Stuart, 114
Aschom, Norbert J. Jr., 117
Beaumont, Dr. William, 56
Bebow, Paul Neil, 74
Beneker, Bette Valley, 90
Billings, Margaret Paris, 24
Bittner, Florence Craig, 84
Bittner, James Ralph, 101
Black Hawk, 17
Bloyer, Barbetta Cardin Koecke, 69
Bohonek, Gertrude, 125
Bohonek, Robert, 125
Boom, Daniel S., 107
Boom, Hazel, 107
Bowlen, Patrick Dennis, 67
Brisbois, Bernard Walter, 94
Brisbois, Michel, 11
Brown, Zernard Deyeorl, 81
Brunson, Rev. Alfred E., 92
Brunson, Ira Burr, 94
Cannon, Walter Bradford, MD, 56
Carriere, Julian, 76
Chenevert, Frederick, 2
Chenevert, William, 2
Clark, William, 13
Coryer, Albert, 76
Davis, Jefferson, 16
Day, Niles D., 96
de Ranitz, Sidney S., 54
Delagrave, Joe, 72
DeLorimer, Sophie, 125
Derleth, August, 84
Dessloch, Dr. Elias Max, 24
Dillman, Blair E., 46
Dillman, Bruce A., 45
Dillman, Robert G., 45
Dohse, Violet E., 52
Doll, Lucile McCloskey, 59
Dousman, Hercules L., 21
Dru'yor, James Alvin, 95
Dyrud, Martinus J., 97
Edwards, Dorothy Horsfall, 38
Edwards, Seymour J., 38
Farrell, Dr. Thomas Francis, 119
Fernette, John, 77
Frydenlund, Arthur J., 98
Galtier, Rev. Lucien, 20
Garnsworthy, Christopher, 30
Garnsworthy, Stanley, 30
Garrity, Margaret M., 51
Garrity, Michael S., MD, 120
Garrity, Peggy Ann, 61
Garrity, Robert P., 37
Geisler, Lauretta, 35
Geisler, Lawrence, 35
George, Geraldine E., 123
George, Roy L., 114, 123
Gokey, Peter E., 26
Grelle, Charles Jr., 27
Halpin, Marietta Jane, 41
Halpin, William T., 41
Hamann, Gertrude, 113
Hamann, Stanley, 113
Heal, Don, 69
Hoffman, William Stanislaus, 66
Horkheimer, Foley "Jack," 60
Howe, Henry E., 28
Howe, Lyman J. Sr., 28
Howe, William F., 87
Huebsch, Frederick G. Jr., 39
Jeffers, Dorothy, 36
Jeffers, George, 36
Jolliet, Louis, 10
Kaber, Clifford F., 31
Kaber, Henry J., 31
Kahler, George, 69
Kennedy, Bernard A., 50
Kieser, Russell, 31
Kluesner, Geraldine, 35
Kluesner, John, 35
Knapp, Lori Jane, 40
Kozelka, Albina, 32
Kozelka, Ralph, 32
Kramer, Elaine, 65
La Pointe, Charles Frederick, 100
Lawler, John, 49
Lessard, Jeff, 90
Lockwood, James H., 14
Lucey, Patrick Joseph, 58
Lyons, Donald, 124
MacGregor, Alexander, 93
Marquette, Rev. Jacques, 10
Mazzuchelli, Rev. Samuel, 19
McFarlane, Morris Jr., 122
Meyer, David, 99
Muir, John, 57
Mulrooney, Ann, 71
Mulrooney, John C., 70
Mulrooney, Mary Beth, 71
Mulrooney, Michael, 71
Mulrooney, Patrick, 71
Nelson, Catherine, 102
Nelson, Thomas, 102
Nichols, Mae, 106
Oehler, Maurice, 55
Oswald, Julius, 124
Panka, Peter, 29
Peacock, John H., 79
Peckham, Gordon L., 109
Pedretti, Bernard F., 42
Peters, Clarence N., 83
Pike, Zebulon M., 12
Polodna, Vincent, 121
Powers, Euphrosine, 19
Powers, Theresa, 108
Quimby, Mildred, 86
Ralph, Guy C., 52
Red Bird, 15
Reed, Alfred E., 89
Rickleff, Lloyd C., 44
Rogers, Marguerite A., 58
Rolette, Joseph, 11
Satter, Olaf Elmer, 120
Scanlan, Dr. Peter L., 82
Schlaugat, Walter P. Jr., 116
Scott, Rev. John M., 53
Sherry, Laura Case, 78
Shihata, Mahmoud M., 104
Shulka family, 115
Sims, Rev. E. Raymond, 110
Smith, Cecil F., 68

Smith, Charles, 69
Smith, Dr. Clifford C., 121
Standorf, Lawrence, 124
Stark, Frank C., 33
Steiner, Arthur B., 112
Steiner, Lavern, 81
Steiner, William C., 112
Street, Joseph Montfort, 18
Suhrada, Michael, 80
Sutton, George, 37
Swingle, Daniel, 64
Taylor, Zachary, 16
Thompson, Arthur W., 23
Tichenor, Donald, 35
Tichenor, Mary Jean, 35
Tiller, Franklin M., 41
Tiller, Patricia A., 41
Valley, Michael, 88
Valley, Reuben, 77
Walker, Dorothea M., 125
Weeks, Franklin A., 43
Wendt, George, 60
White, Jimmy J., 103
White, Thomas J., 42
Williams, Bradley G., 62
Williams, Eric, 62
Williams, Griffith H., 85
Yeomans family, 34